He

G

NATURAL ENVIRONMENT RESEARCH COUNCIL

INSTITUTE OF GEOLOGICAL SCIENCES

MEMOIRS OF THE GEOLOGICAL SURVEY OF GREAT BRITAIN
ENGLAND AND WALES

A short account of the

Geology of the

ISLE OF WIGHT

by H. J. OSBORNE WHITE, F.G.S.

LONDON
HER MAJESTY'S STATIONERY OFFICE
1921

The Institute of Geological Sciences
was formed by the
incorporation of the Geological Survey of Great Britain
and the Museum of Practical Geology
with Overseas Geological Surveys
and is a constituent body of the
Natural Environment Research Council

ISBN 0 11 880739 0

PREFACE

No DISTRICT of England of equal size is more interesting to the geologist than the Isle of Wight, alike from the variety of its formations, the excellence of the exposures and the abundance of fossils. In 1856 the Geological Survey published Professor Edward Forbes's memoir on the Tertiary Fluvio-marine formations of the Isle of Wight. The original survey was completed on the one-inch scale in 1856, and a memoir on the geology of the Island by H. W. Bristow was published in 1862. In 1886–7 the survey was revised on the six-inch scale by Mr. Clement Reid and Sir A. Strahan, who prepared a second edition of the memoir, published in 1889. This edition having sold out, it became necessary to consider the preparation of a handbook of the geology of the Island. Circumstances rendered it impossible to undertake a complete revision of the geological maps and still more of the palæontology which had filled so large a part of the second edition of the memoir. It was decided to entrust the work to Mr. H. J. Osborne White, to whom we are indebted for several valuable sheet memoirs dealing for the most part with rocks of the same age as those of the Isle of Wight. He has aimed at giving a condensed account of the vast mass of material available, and by his personal knowledge of the Island and his intimate familiarity with its rocks and fossils has enriched this memoir with many valuable observations.

The author desires to acknowledge his indebtedness to Mr. H. J. A. Mayo for help in the re-examination of many of the sections, as well as in the correction of the proofs of this memoir, and to Prof. H. L. Hawkins, Mr. R. W. Hooley, the Rev. J. C. Hughes, Mr. Ll. Treacher and Mr. S. Hazzledine Warren for assistance rendered.

JOHN S. FLETT,
Director

Geological Survey Office
28 Jermyn Street
London SW1

18*th October* 1920

CONTENTS

ILLUSTRATIONS

vii

Chapter I

INTRODUCTION

Definition and Area. In shape, the Isle of Wight approximates to the lozenge or conventional diamond, but with concave sides. Its longer axis, trending rather north of east, runs from the Needles to the Foreland, a distance of $23\frac{1}{2}$ miles; while Egypt Point and St. Catherine's Point, $13\frac{3}{4}$ miles apart, are the termini of the shorter axis, which is disposed nearly at right angles to the other.

The north-western and north-eastern sides of the Island, which meet in an obtuse angle at Cowes, opposite the mouth of Southampton Water, are each nearly parallel with the adjacent section of the Mainland shore, from which they are separated respectively by the Solent and by the waters about Spithead; though, in common parlance, the name Solent is extended to the entire strait. The nearest point to the mainland is Cliff End, by Yarmouth, barely a mile distant from the head of the shingle-spit that supports Hurst Castle, at the western end of the Solent. The opposite shores again approach to within a mile and a half of each other near Cowes, but between and east of these narrows the channel is generally from $2\frac{1}{2}$ to 4 miles in breadth.

The area of the Isle of Wight, as deduced from the Ordnance Survey, is 155 square miles 370·209 acres, in which are included 122·684 acres of water, 9 square miles 34·076 acres of foreshore, and 434·454 acres of tidal water.

Physical Features. The Island is fairly evenly divided into the two Hundreds or Liberties of East and West Medina by the Medina River, which traverses it almost completely from south to north, nearly along the line of its greatest breadth; but a more marked physical division is effected by a range of Chalk downs running lengthwise from the Needles to Culver Cliff, and forming what has been termed the "Backbone of the Island". For the greater part of its length this range consists of a steep-sided ridge, a quarter of a mile to half a mile in width, with an undulating crest which varies in altitude roughly from 300 to 650 feet, between the larger rivergaps. About midway, however, immediately to the west of the Medina, the ridge expands into a small upland 2 to 4 miles wide, which at Brixton Down attains an elevation of 700 feet, and affords the most comprehensive panoramic view of the Island.

The country lying to the north of the Chalk Ridge, or Central Downs, is occupied by Tertiary strata whose heavy soils support numerous copses and woods, of which Parkhurst is the most extensive. Between the principal streams the ground rises, as a rule, from an irregular belt of uneven lowland near the foot of the Downs, to a slightly-relieved range of gravelly plateaux, which follows the northern coast of the Island, and declines gently eastward, from about 180 feet near West Cowes to 120 feet near Bembridge. Two miles east of the Medina this range is connected with the Central Downs by a lateral ridge which has a nearly continuous northward slope between their respective summits; and supposed vestiges of a similar connection, west of that river, are discernible in the hills of Parkhurst Forest and Northwood.

1

The lateral ridge just noticed, which rises to about 300 ft near Downend; Parkhurst Signal Hill, 274 ft; and Headon Hill, nearly 400 ft, form the higher grounds of this relatively low-lying part of the Island.

The country south of the Central Downs is of more varied character, and presents in every respect a strong contrast to that on the north. The greater part of it is occupied by a spacious vale in which the fertile, red-brown soil mantles a surface whose normally flowing contours are interrupted here and there by the sudden lift of a sandy knoll, or the severe outline of some gravel-flat, long ago deserted by its parent stream. Outwards, on the broken borders of this tract, the ground rises sharply into hog-backed ridges, and into ledges of more angular profile: the woods which are few, mostly hang on their slopes. This is the "Bowl of the Island", the Vale of Sandown and Newchurch, and its narrowing westward extension by Kingston, Atherfield, and Brook.[1]

Farther south, in the seaward angle of the Island, rises the dominating range of the Southern Downs; scarped and deeply indented on its inland side; smoothly rounded in the crest, and breaking down to the English Channel in the flight of verdant terraces named the Undercliff. Here are the highest grounds in the Wight, St. Boniface above Ventnor reaching 787 ft; St. Catherine's, at the other end of the range, 781 ft; and Week Down, between them, falling not far short at 692 ft.

The two principal rivers of the Island, the Medina and Eastern Yar, have their origins in these Downs, and run, the one directly northward, the other north and north-eastward, through gaps in the Central Ridge. Excepting a few short brooks near the south coast, the Island streams all bear northward to the Solent and Spithead, their courses having been determined before the country assumed its present form. They include, besides those named, the Western Yar, which rises in a gap in the Central Downs at Freshwater Gate, a few yards from the sea; the Caul Bourne or Newtown River, with sources at the northern foot of the same ridge; and the Blackbridge and Small Brooks, whose headwaters are similarly located farther east. Excepting the last-named, each of the northern streams that have been mentioned opens on the coast in a well-marked estuary, that of the Medina being navigable by small vessels up to Newport, five miles above the mouth. The Eastern Yar was similarly navigable, for nearly two miles, up to Brading Wharf, until the winding channel was closed, about the year 1880, by the reclamation of the tidal flats in Brading Harbour.

The north-eastern or Spithead coast is shelving; land, at high-tide, ending in a low-wooded bank. Along the Solent the coast is bolder, especially towards the west, though here, too, there is much low-lying ground; but from Cliff End to the Needles, and thence nearly all the way round the south coast to the Foreland, the Isle is bounded by cliffs, through which the south-flowing rivulets make a hurried descent to the shore by ravines, such as the well-known chines of Shanklin and Blackgang. What with the jagged-crested Needles, the threatening overhang of the cornice above the Grand Arch, the sheer 400 ft of Main Bench, and (running through them all) the inspiring upward sweep of the serried lines of flint, the cliffs of Upper Chalk at the western end of

---

[1]Or Brooke. In the text of this Memoir the spelling of place-names adopted in the current edition of the Geological Survey Map on the 1-inch scale is followed. Brook, Carisbrook, and Merston have lately acquired, or resumed, a final "e," and Brixton has reverted to "Brighstone".

the Island are among the most impressive on the English coast. These cliffs change little in appearance from one decade to another, but the case is far otherwise with the cliffs of older Cretaceous sands and clays, forming most of the south coast of the Island. There, extensive falls and founders are frequent, and the wasting of the clays by flowage or guttering is in constant progress.

The sea surrounding the Isle of Wight is generally of slight depth. In the Solent-Spithead strait soundings exceeding 10 fathoms are almost confined to a chain of narrow basins or troughs which contour the southern shore, and quickly die out beneath the open water off the eastern and western ends of the Island. Within these hollows the deepest soundings range from about 12 fathoms north of Egypt Point, near Cowes, to 17 fathoms north-east of Ryde, and 31 fathoms (186 ft) between Cliff End and Hurst Castle. The exceptional depth of the last-named spot is attributable to the erosive action of the strong current that sets through the narrows during ebb-tide. Beyond both ends of the strait the bed of the sea shelves for a space above the 10-fathom line, before beginning its steady descent into the trough of the English Channel. South of the Island, the main 10-fathom line, while following the general contour of the shore-line, lies about two miles off-shore opposite the heads of Sandown and Compton Bays, but approaches to within half a mile where it skirts the intervening blunt promontory of the Southern Downs, between Dunnose and St. Catherine's; the distance apparently varying directly with the erodibility of the coast.

Geological Formations. In the following table the established formations and miscellaneous superficial accumulations described in this Memoir are named (as far as is practicable) in their descending order:

Landslips	
Blown Sand	RECENT
Rainwash	OR
Tufa	HOLOCENE
Alluvium and Peat	
Valley Gravel	PLEISTOCENE
Plateau Gravel	AND
Angular Flint-Gravel of the Chalk Downs	PLIOCENE
Hamstead Beds	
Bembridge Marls	
Bembridge Limestone	OLIGOCENE
Osborne Beds	
Headon Beds (Eocene?)	
Barton Sand ⎱ Barton Beds	
Barton Clay ⎰	
Bracklesham Beds	EOCENE
Bagshot Sands	
London Clay	
Reading Beds	
Chalk: Upper, Middle, and Lower	UPPER
Upper Greensand ⎱ Selbornian	CRETACEOUS
Gault ⎰	
Carstone (Upper Cretaceous?) ⎫	
Sandrock Series ⎪ Lower Greensand	LOWER
Ferruginous Sands ⎬	CRETACEOUS
Atherfield Clay ⎪	
Wealden Beds ⎭	

These formations will be described in ascending order, beginning with the Wealden Beds, the lowest and oldest strata exposed.

Underlying Rocks. There being no deep borings in or anywhere near the Island to show what lies beneath the Wealden Beds, we are left to infer that the descending sequence is conformably maintained in strata of Jurassic age, as on the coast of Dorset. From a remote epoch this region has been subject to repeated subsidence, with concomitant deposition of material wasted from surrounding landmasses, which have mostly disappeared; and, although the presence of an upwarped ridge of the Palaeozoic platform, at no great depth beneath the country a little north of the zone of intense plication that runs through Purbeck and the Isle of Wight, is well within the bounds of possibility, the data at present available lead rather to the inference that the Wealden Beds in and around the Island are underlain by many thousands of feet of earlier Mesozoic sediments; and hence, that coal, if present, is out of reach.

The remarkable tectonic structure of the Island, the nature of the earth-movements to which it is due, and its relation to the topography, are discussed in a late chapter; while the economic aspect of the local geology is presented in the concluding pages of this work.

Scope of this Memoir. Relating as it does to ground that has been diligently explored by at least four generations of geologists, among whom there have been many who have made some one or other part of it the subject of special study and minute description, the present Memoir is, to a great extent, and inevitably, a compilation of facts and inferences already familiar to the student of English geology. It is based on the second edition of the Geological Survey Memoir on the Isle of Wight, by Sir Aubrey Strahan and the late Clement Reid, which was published in 1889, and it contains numerous excerpts from that work. The smaller scale on which it has been planned, however, has entailed considerable textual reductions, irrespective of those needed to make room for fresh material. Much of the original subject-matter, therefore, reappears here in a condensed form, while more is omitted.

Lack of space forbids the inclusion of a list of the works comprised in the extensive geological literature of the Isle of Wight. References to the more important papers will be found in the text and footnotes: for the rest, the student must resort to the copious bibliographical appendix to the second edition of the Geological Survey Memoir on the Island, mentioned above.

Chapter II

THE WEALDEN BEDS

THESE BEDS appear at the surface in the south-western and south-eastern parts of the Island, where they are brought up along the axes of two anticlinal folds. The whole area occupied by them is rather less than five square miles, and the only good sections are on the coast. There, they are well displayed, for a distance of about six miles, in the cliff between Compton Bay and Atherfield Point, and in a less extensive section, about three-fourths of a mile in length, in Sandown Bay. Some 750 feet of them, representing roughly the upper third of the entire formation as developed at Swanage, is comprised in that part of the south-western coast-section which lies between Brook Bay and Atherfield Point: the thicknesses exposed elsewhere (in normal sequence) are less.

The Wealden of the Isle of Wight is divisible into two series of sharply contrasted lithological types; a lower series, known as the Wealden Marls or Variegated Clays, and an upper series, termed Wealden Shales. The former, by far the thicker of the two, may partly represent the Hastings Sands of the South-Eastern Counties.

The Marls consist of red, purple, green, and variegated clays and marls with numerous intercalated bands of sand, sandstone, and sandy limestone of variable thickness. Recognizable at a glance, the upper limit of this series seems to be the only horizon that can be positively identified in different exposures; for the limestones are of sporadic occurrence, and the sands and sandstones for the most part frankly lenticular, while the bedding of the marls and clays has a subtle irregularity that is hardly perceived till one attempts to correlate the bands on opposite sides of a landslip, or truncated fold.

Though the bulk of the Marls is poorly fossiliferous, drift-wood in great abundance, coniferous fruits, ferns, freshwater shells (notably *Viviparus fluviorum* (J. Sow.) (*Paludina*) and several species of *Unio*), remains of fish, and water-worn bones of aquatic and terrestrial reptiles of many orders, recur throughout the series, mostly in light greyish and greenish silty bands, one of which appears at, or a little below, the junction with the Shales.

The Wealden Marls of the Isle of Wight are purely freshwater deposits, accumulated far out in a wide lacustrine area of slow subsidence, bordered by low-lying country from which the inflowing rivers brought down, together with the detritus of sub-tropical forests, much calcareous silty mud, less sand, and but little gravel. The conglomeratic bands met with at intervals, and mentioned in the accounts of the sections given below, are made up of fragments of the harder bands of the Marls which had been undercut and broken up by the scour of currents. Sedimentation about keeping pace with subsidence, the lake remained shallow, and was subject to periods of desiccation, which allowed the ponderous reptiles of the time to explore and leave footprints in the sands and mud-flats on its bottom, but which were not of sufficient duration to permit of the establishment there of the more robust forms of vegetation, for no soils or root-beds are to be seen. All the plant-remains—tree-trunks, leaves, and fruits—have been drifted, and most of them, and of the associated

5

reptilian bones, were badly water-worn before they reached their resting places. Types of current-bedding suggestive of wind-action are met with in some of the thicker sandstones.

The Wealden Shales consist of evenly-stratified and laminated clays of dark-blue to black tint, with subordinate layers of clay-ironstone, sandstone, and shelly limestone. Their sombre colouring and perfectly regular bedding make them readily distinguishable from the brightly-tinted, massive, and obscurely-stratified Marls below. Fossils are abundant, though the number of species represented is comparatively small. The finer "paper" shales are crowded with valves of little ostracodous crustacea (*Cypris*, *Cypridea*, *Metacypris*). Of the mollusca, *Cyrena media* J. Sow. occurs in greatest profusion. Associated with it are *Viviparus elongata* J. Sow. and *Unio spp.*; *Ostrea distorta* J. de C. Sow. forms a few thin bands of limestone in the upper part of the Shales, and *Vicarya strombiformis* Schloth. (*Melania*, *Potamides*) abounds in the highest beds at Atherfield. Drift-wood occurs mostly in the lower beds, to which the reptilian remains (similar to, but less varied than, those in the Marls) appear to be restricted. Ferns are met with at intervals throughout the Shales, and bones and spines of fish are commonest in the upper part of this division.

The oncoming of the Shales marks a change from lacustrine to estuarine conditions, accompanied by an increase in the depth as well as in the salinity of the water. In the overlying Perna Bed of the Lower Greensand, the indicated conditions of deposition have become wholly marine, but there are signs of erosion at the junction, and the uncompromising character of the palaeontological break at this horizon suggests that the old Wealden basin may have suffered many unrecorded vicissitudes, ere it was finally submerged beneath the Aptian sea. The Wealden lake and its surroundings served as an asylum for many forms of life that had elsewhere become extinct; notably the flora and vertebrate fauna, which are more nearly allied to the life of the Jurassic period than to that of the Cretaceous.[1]

Description of Sections

In Brixton and Sandown Bays the Wealden Beds rise sharply from beneath the newer strata forming the Central Ridge of the Island, but on receding from the zone of maximum disturbance, with which that range coincides, their dip decreases, until they at length assume a horizontal position, as may be seen near Brook in Brixton Bay, and in Sandown Bay at a point about half-a-mile south-west of Yaverland. Farther south in each of these bays a gentle southward dip sets in which carries the Wealden Beds in succession below the beach.

Brook Bay: Sedmore Point to Hanover Point

We take this part of the coast-section first, for the reason that all authorities agree in regarding the group of beds there imperfectly exposed as the oldest to be seen on the Island; and we deal with it under a separate heading because the complete ascending sequence has not been determined, and a difference of opinion exists in regard to the identity of the oldest member of the group

---

[1]*Vide* A. C. Seward, 'Catal. Mesozoic Plants', *Brit. Mus.* (*Nat. Hist.*), 1895, p. 240, and A. S. Woodward, 'Note on the Affinities of the English Wealden Fish-Fauna', *Geol. Mag.*, 1896, pp. 69-71.

of beds referred to. The writer is disposed to claim this distinction for the mottled clays underlying the current-bedded sandstone at the foot of the cliff at Sedmore Point, but in the present state of the cliff between that spot and Brook Chine the question cannot be decided.

Above the Sedmore Point sandstone, which forms the base of the cliff for nearly a quarter of a mile, there come blue, purple, and dark-red marls,[1] succeeded by an impersistent bed of red-brown sandstone, with a calcareous conglomeratic band at the bottom, containing rolled bones. Blue and purple marls, with a light greyish band containing lignite, form the higher part of the cliff. Footprints, believed to be those of *Iguanodon*, have been observed in sandstone near Sedmore Point.[2]

"Between [Sedmore] Point and Brook Chine the strata have slipped, forming an undercliff, known as Roughland, along the whole length of which (some 500 yards) there is no clear exposure of rock in place, though the extent of the slip shows that the beds must be chiefly clays. As we approach Brook Chine the section becomes clear again. A greenish band may be seen to rise westwards from beneath the beach, and to run along the upper part of the cliff past Brook Chine to a small chine 180 yards south of Brook Chine, where it descends once more to the beach. This bed is easily traced by its colour, and by the fact that it is crowded with large flattened masses of lignite, especially to the south and west of Brook Chine."[3]

Where it declines to the beach, the green lignitic band is faulted down a few feet to the south, and about 20 yards south-westward it forms, with an underlying greyish sandstone, a marked reef on the shore. This band is most probably continuous with that seen above the "Pine Raft", presently to be described, for at times the immediately overlying mottled grey clay can be traced westward along the foreshore to Hanover (or Brook) Point, a little short of which it rises into the lower part of the cliff.

"The section at the Point shows upwards of 100 feet of red, purple, and blue clay with impersistent bands of sandstone, underlain by 13 feet of grey clay, the lower part of which contains numerous flattened masses of black shining lignite. This lignite band rests upon a bed of hard sandstone, to which the Point owes its existence. It is a whitish or pale-grey rock, about 6 feet thick, containing fragments of marl and clay, and with iron-pyrites abundantly disseminated through its upper part. It is irregularly stratified, and its surface is undulating and covered with fucoidal and hollow vertical markings.

"Below and partly imbedded in this rock lie the scattered trunks of coniferous trees, known as the 'Pine Raft'. They were first observed by Webster in 1811,[4] but were more fully described by Mantell in 1846.[5] The trunks lie prostrate in all directions, broken up into cylindrical fragments. They are covered by thin bark, now in the state of lignite, the wood having been converted into a black or greyish calcareous stone, with much iron pyrites. Many

---

[1] We here use the term "marls" in the loose sense of the older geologists. Much of the so-called "marl" of the Wealden Beds is silty clay of marly appearance.

[2] S. H. Beckles 'On . . . Reptilian Footprints in the Wealden Beds, &c.,' *Quart. Journ. Geol. Soc.*, vol. xviii., 1862, p. 443.

[3] A. Strahan in 'Geology of the Isle of Wight', *Mem. Geol. Surv.*, 2nd ed., 1889, p. 5.

[4] In Englefield's 'Isle of Wight', 1816.

[5] *Quart. Journ. Geol. Soc.*, vol. ii., 1846, p. 91.

of the trees still present traces of woody structure, and the annular rings of growth are clearly perceptible; but they are traversed also by numerous threads of pyrites. The trunks are generally of considerable magnitude, being from one to three feet in diameter; two, upwards of twenty feet in length, and of such size as to indicate a height of forty or fifty feet when entire, were noticed by Mantell."[1]

From the same bed there have been obtained remains of the "tree-fern" *Endogenites erosa* Mant., pine-cones, and teeth and scales of *Lepidotus mantelli* Agassiz.

"The 'Pine Raft' can be seen at low water only. During spring tides it may be observed to rest on variegated marls, but all attempts to trace it eastwards from [Hanover] Point have failed, probably on account of its being of local development only. The purple marls forming the cliff above it are apparently the same beds that have made the great slip of Roughland, and the Pine Raft, if it is continuous, should be found in the cliff near Sedmore Point; but though many large fragments of trunks are lying on the beach, there is no bed in the cliff exactly corresponding to that of [Hanover] Point.

"As suggested by Mantell, the trees were probably drifted from a distance, in the same manner as the trunks, brought down by the Mississippi at the present day, are deposited in large rafts in the delta of that river. It is not to be expected, therefore, that the 'Pine Raft' is of wider range, or that the horizon at which it occurs should be recognisable when the trees are not present."[2]

It was in the clay "immediately above the fossil forest" that Mantell first observed the freshwater shell which he named *Unio valdensis* (*op. cit.*, p. 94). The Wealden Beds of Brook Bay have yielded the remains of various large reptiles, including *Iguanodon bernissartensis* Boul., *Hoplosaurus hulkei* (Seeley), and *Heterosuchus valdensis* Seeley. The second of these, which, unlike *Iguanodon*, walked on all fours, is inferred to have attained a length of 70 to 80 feet.

HANOVER POINT AND COMPTON BAY

From Hanover Point north-westward we can trace an ascending sequence with comparatively little difficulty. The succession and the character of the beds is given, in descending order, in the following table.

"Descending Section of the Wealden Beds from Compton Bay to Hanover Point [Fig. 1 a, p. 11]

"Perna Bed (Compton Bay).

	ft	in.
Beds seen only in landslips, consisting of Cyprid Shales with a hard band, containing numerous fish-remains in the upper part, bands of limestone and ironstone; estimated at	65	0
Blue and grey clay and sand	2	0
Sand	1	0
Blue shale	3	0
White sand and grit	3	0
Ochry band (cinder-bed) passing into a solid ironstone where less weathered	0	6
Blue shale	17	0
Cinder-bed, as above	0	6
Grey clay, with large trunks of trees	9	0

The beds from "Blue and grey clay and sand" through "Cinder-bed, as above" are bracketed as "Wealden Shales".

[1]A. Strahan, *op. cit.*, p. 6.

[2]A. Strahan, *op. cit.*, pp. 6, 7.

	ft	in
Purple marls	41	0
White sandstone and clay with lignite	9	0
Purple marls with sand-beds, about	55	0
Fine white sand	3	0
Pale purple clay	12	0
White clay, crammed with great masses of lignite and trunks of trees ..	5	0
Yellow and white clay, passing down	6	0
Purple marls, about	35	0
White sandy clay, with bones	6	0
Deep red marls, about	12	0

[Here there is a fault, repeating the Wealden Shales].

Wealden Shales

	ft	in
Blue shales, not well seen, about	20	0
Shales, seen in the west bank of a small chine	21	0
Paper shale, with Cyprids	0	8
Cyrena limestone	0	2
Shales with lines of sand, Cyprids here and there	12	0
Paper shales with Cyprids	2	6
Cyrena limestone	0	1–2
Paper shales with Cyprids (in the east bank of the small chine mentioned above)	14	0
Shales, not well seen	25	0
Shale, with lines of sand and grit containing ferns (rises from below the beach on the east side of the small chine)	51	6
Yellow and white sand-rock, with large grains of pinkish quartz ..	5	0
Blue shale	3	0
Sand-rock, as above	12	6
Blue shale, with thin ironstone in the lower part	5	4
Coarse grit, with grains of pink quartz		
Shale parting	2	10
Sandstone		
Blue shale	0	7
Ironstone, with *Unio, Cyrena, Paludina,* Cyprids, and "Beef"	0	6
Blue shale	6	6
Fine ochry and dusky sand	1	0
Fine white sand-rock	2	6
Shales, with *Paludina* and Cyprids	5	6
Lenticular ironstone	0	0–4
Sandy shales, with ferns	5	0
Shale	6	0
Shales, full of *Cyrena* and *Paludina*	3	0
Sandstone, with lignite	0	6
White sandy clay	1	6
Blue marly clay, with large concretions and obscure fossils	3	6
White and blue marly clay	2	0
Pale variegated marl	5	6
White sandstone, with irregular top	3	0
Purple marls, estimated at	78	0
White sandstone, containing an abundance of grains of pink quartz (crops out west of Compton Grange Chine)	9	0
Red, purple, and green marls of Compton Grange Chine	78	0
White sandstone (east of Compton Grange Chine)	16	0
Variegated marl	30	0
Red sandstone	2 to 4	0
Greyish blue marl	10	0
White sandstone..	7	0
Purple marls	64	0
White band	1	0
Purple marls	40	0
Grey clay packed with lignite	2	0
White sandstone, thickening eastwards	0 to 5	0
Purple marls	36	0

	ft	in.
Red sandstone and marl, thinning out east at Hanover Point	6	0
Purple marls	41	0
Red marls	12	0
Grey sandstone	0 to 2	0
Grey sandy clay	7	0
Ditto with much lignite (seen in Hanover Point)	6	0
Current-bedded white sandstone, with much pyrites in the upper part (forms the foot of Hanover Point)	5	0+
The 'Pine-raft'; numerous trunks embedded in sandstone.		
Variegated marls, seen in the fore-shore.	"	1

"On rounding the Point we find the cliff composed principally of red and purple marls for a distance of about 700 yards, the thickness of strata amounting to 439 feet. In the marls there occur beds of sandstone often conspicuous from their whiteness, and a few green bands containing lignite. Passing over some thin and impersistent sandstones near the Point, we meet the first noteworthy bed 170 yards further west, where there is seen in the upper part of the cliff a grey clay packed with lignite, resting on a white sandstone 5 feet thick, but thinning away westwards. This is overlain by purple and variegated clays, and 100 yards westward a second bed of white sand-rock, 7 feet thick, succeeds. A third bed, 16 feet thick, is seen on the east side, and a fourth, 9 feet thick, on the west side of Shippard's[2] or Compton Grange Chine, the last-mentioned rock being of a pinkish hue from the abundance of grains of pink quartz in it."[3] At 190 yards distance from this chine, the purple marls, with a greyish to greenish silty band at their top,[4] are succeeded by characteristic blue Wealden Shales with *Cyrena*, *Viviparus*, and Cyprids. These blue shales, which are interstratified with sands in the lower part, are about 222 feet thick, and are well exposed up to and in a small chine 350 yards west of Compton Grange Chine, but beyond this they are disturbed by slipping.

About 60 yards west of the small chine just mentioned, the shales abruptly disappear from the section, the cliff and the slips below it showing only purple and red marls, similar to those which pass beneath the Shales about 300 yards to the south-east. The presence of a fault at this point was long suspected, but the actual fracture seems not to have been observed until about 1906, in which year it was described by Mr. R. W. Hooley.[5] The exposure, still in existence at the time of writing, some 13 years later, occurs in what seems to be a foundered mass of beds immediately above the beach (Fig. 2). The fault runs about E.N.E., and hades S.S.E., at a high angle. Along it the apparently down-thrown Shales and their included thin bands of clay-ironstone are crushed, and suffused with the red tint of the Marls; and in adjacent section, a few yards south-eastward, they are strongly contorted.[6]

---

[1]A. Strahan, *op. cit.*, pp. 9–11.

[2]Not to be confounded with Shepherd's Chine, near Atherfield.

[3]A. Strahan, *op. cit.*, pp. 7, 8.

[4]Apparently the band described as "White sandstone, with irregular top, 3 ft" in the above table.

[5]*Proc. Geol. Assoc.*, vol. xix, 1906, pp. 264, 265.

[6]The existing exposure of the fault-plane is too small, and too intimately associated with landslips, to allow one to judge of the real nature of the dislocation. In this part of the Island, any considerable fault of eastward trend is at least as likely to be of the reversed as of the normal type. It is noteworthy that the red colouration of the Marls extends for some distance south-eastward of the fault, and above the Shales, in the unrecognizable weathered and disintegrated material passing up into the Pleistocene deposits at the top of the cliff.

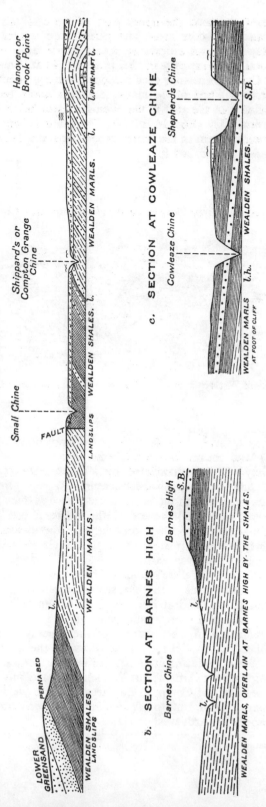

FIG. 1. *Sections in the Wealden Beds, in Compton Bay, at Barnes High, and at Cowleaze Chine*

Scales: Horizontal, 8 in. = 1 mile; Vertical, twice the horizontal

a. SECTION IN COMPTON BAY

b. SECTION AT BARNES HIGH

c. SECTION AT COWLEAZE CHINE

Alluvium.   Gravel.   *S.B.* Sandstone of Barnes High.   *h.* Hypsilophodon Bed.   *l.* Principal lignite and bone beds.

North-west of the fault the upper part of the cliff shows red and purple marls with bands of white sand, and three more regular beds of grey and white silty clay and sand containing much lignite and occasional large tree trunks; the total thickness of marls being about 193 ft. Blue shales with *Cypris* and bands of Cyrena-limestone then reappear, resting, as before, on a greenish-grey lignitiferous top-bed of the marls; but their lower beds only are seen *in situ*, the remainder of the cliff in the Wealden Beds being involved in a great slip of Atherfield Clay (Fig. 14, p. 59). Though it is impossible to obtain a satisfactory measurement of the Shales at this spot, it is fairly evident that their thickness cannot exceed 100 ft.

Fig. 2. *Fault and Contortions in the Wealden Beds, near Compton Grange Chine*

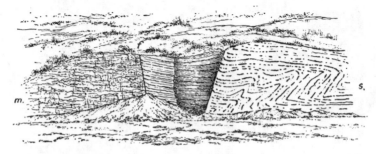

m. Red clay of Wealden Marls.   *s.* Wealden Shales, contorted.   *f.* Fault.

Prior to the exposure of the fault, it was a moot point whether the Wealden Beds of the Island contained two Shale Series or only one, and the reason of this uncertainty will be appreciated by all who examine the Compton Bay section. Not only are the Shales (incompletely represented) near Compton Grange Chine, south-east of the fault, at least twice as thick as those (apparently fully developed) to the north-west of the fracture, but they also display a lithological dissimilarity of which no adequate impression can be conveyed in writing, but which is mainly attributable to the relatively great development of white sandstones in the lower parts.

As the upper beds of the Wealden Shales show a similar association of cypridiferous paper-shales with thin shelly limestones in all four exposures of them in the Island, and at Punfield, near Swanage, as well, we may infer that it is the lower and more sandy beds which are mainly concerned in the remarkable reduction in the thickness of the series which takes place to the north-west of Compton Grange Chine. Possibly the Shales are thinning out westward or north-westward upon an inclined surface of the Marls; they are known to dwindle westwards, for at Punfield they are only $34\frac{1}{2}$ ft thick.

The Wealden Beds of Compton Bay seem to have yielded few determinable reptilian remains. Footprints of *Iguanodon* have been observed in sandstone on the foreshore 600 yards west of Hanover Point.[1]

---

[1]Beckles, *loc. cit.*

Brixton Bay: Sedmore Point to Atherfield Point

We now return to Sedmore Point, whence we started, and follow the coast eastward. In doing so we again traverse the Wealden Beds in an ascending succession which is broadly similar to that above described, though differing considerably in detail. The dip is gentle and nearly uniform; at first a little north of east, subsequently a little south of east. The section is given in the annexed table.

"*Descending Section of the Wealden Beds from Atherfield to near Brook*

"Perna Bed (Atherfield Point).

	ft	in.
Shales, with bands of *Vicarya*, 1 foot and 12 feet from the top, and Cyprids in the lower part	15	0
"Beef-bed"	0	2
Shales with Cyprids	8	10
Shales	6	0
Pale blue ironstone, with *Vicarya*, *Ostrea*, &c., abundant ..	0	2.3
Shales	4	3
Band with Cyprids and fish-remains..	0	0½
Shales, with impersistent ironstone	9	6
Lenticular sand with sandy shale .. .. .. 0 to 1		0
Shale, with fish remains at the base	1	6
Shale, with impersistent bands of ironstone, and bands of sand with ferns; Cyprids abundant in lower part	35	0
Shales	14	0
Dark limestone weathering red	0	0½
Shales, with *Candona mantelli* Jones..	9	0
Shales, with a band containing *Unio*, *Paludina*, and Cyprids near the middle, and sandy beds, containing ferns, in the lower part	40	0
Sandstone of Cowleaze Chine and Barnes High, massive, with bands of *Cyrena*	8	0
Sandstone of Cowleaze Chine and Barnes High, thin-bedded, with shale	13	0
Blue Shales,[1] with *Unio* and *Paludina* in the top, and *Cyrena* and *Paludina* near the bottom	19	0
White sand and clay[1]	2	6
White rock[1]	2	6
Red sand, with bones (*Hypsilophodon Bed*)[1]	3	0
Red and mottled marls, rocky and ripple-marked at the top ..	44	0
White and yellow sand, with fragments and large trunks of lignite passing westwards into sandstone, and splitting up and dying away before reaching the top of the cliff	9	0
Pale blue clay, becoming purple downwards	29	0
Hard green bed, containing lignite and bones (seen in the top of Barnes Chine)	2	0
Deep-red marls..	6	0
Purple and mottled marls	35	0
Sandstone, with clayey beds (crosses Barnes Chine)	13	0
Deep-red marls, purple below	28	6
Conglomeratic grit, with an occasional pebble of quartzite, or of sandstone	3	0
Pale mottled clay	14	6
Green and white clays, with lignite	3	0
Purple mottled marls	9	0
Deep-red marls	13	0
White sandy bed	3	0
Pale purple and mottled marls	21	6
Fine white sandstone (crosses the bottom of Ship Chine)	4	0

The first group of beds, from "Shales, with bands of *Vicarya*" to "Red sand, with bones", is bracketed as "Wealden Shales".

[1]These beds give a slightly different section in passing from Cowleaze Chine to Barnes High. Though included in the Shales in this table, the Hypsilophodon Bed is lithologically and stratigraphically more nearly allied to the Marls.

	ft	in.
Mottled marls	25	6
Black bed of Brixton Chine; lignite, bones, *Unio valdensis*	2	6
White sandy marl	3	0
Mottled red marls of Brixton Chine, with a lignite bed near the middle	94	0
Green sandy bed, with bones..	2	0
Red and white sandstone in beds of 1 to 3 feet, with partings of marl, and pockets containing shale and sandstone fragments; a band of of gravel of sandstone fragments, 3 inches thick, at the base, with fragments of bones	17	0
Mottled marls	49	0
Pebbly band, lignite and pebbles of sandstone (top of east bank of Chilton chine)	2	0
Red and mottled marls	23	0
Current bedded sandstone (near the bottom of Chilton Chine) about ..	12	0
Mottled marls	28	0
Purple marls, with white concretions	4	0
Red marls passing down into white sandstone, with partings of marl, current-bedded in large sweeping curves	9	0
Massive sandstone, bands of bone and sandstone breccia running irregularly through; 6 to 18 inches of gravel at base, with bones. This bed thins away westwards, and is last seen at Sedmore Point ..	18	0
Deep-red and purple marls (at Sedmore Point)	20	0
Current-bedded sandstone of Sedmore Point	8	0+"[1]

"The sandstone with 1¼ feet of conglomerate at its base, which first appears half way up the cliff at Sedmore Point (see pp. 7, 14), thickens eastwards and runs for a distance of nearly a mile, before it finally descends to the beach 500 yards west of Chilton Chine. There also it presents at its base 1½–2 feet of a gravel, composed of pebbles of sandstone with many small bones, though this conglomeratic band does not continue through the whole distance. Below this sandstone lie deep-red marls, and above it come red and green marls as at Sedmore Point. The latter may be well seen in Chilton Chine. They contain lenticular harder bands with potato-shaped calcareous concretions, and a little lignite. Another bed of sandstone comes in at the top of the cliff 250 yards east of the Chine, and descends to the beach about midway between Chilton and [Brixton] Grange Chines. This bed likewise has a gravelly conglomerate, about 6 inches thick, at its base. It contains quartz pebbles, small bones, and rounded pieces of wood similar to those composing the 'pine-raft'. It is much current-bedded, and of variable thickness, reaching sometimes as much as seven feet.

" . . . Grange Chine has been excavated in deep-red and green marls, the green beds containing much lignite. On the east side and near the top of the chine a conspicuous black band two feet thick contains abundance of lignite, many fragments of bones, and *Unio valdensis* in some brown irony concretions. The bed descends to the beach 200 yards west of Ship Ledge, and the cliffs above it consist of red and green marls with several bands of hard sandstone, liable to rapid variations in thickness."[2]

The cliffs between Chilton Chine and Barnes Chine have yielded determinable remains of several reptiles, including *Hoplosaurus* and *Vectisaurus valdensis* Hulke.

Barnes Chine presents a section of red and mottled blue marls, overlain by a hard, greenish, silty band (2 feet), containing much lignite, *Unio*, bones and teeth of dinosaurs (*Polacanthus foxi* Hulke, &c.) and the "Swanage" crocodile

[1] A. Strahan, *op. cit.*, pp. 14–16.   [2] A. Strahan, *op. cit.*, p. 11.

(*Goniopholis crassidens* Owen). This bed is about 80 feet below the base of the Shales, which comes down to the foot of the cliff 30 yards west of Cowleaze Chine.

The Hypsilophodon Bed, which crosses the bottom of Cowleaze Chine near its mouth, has yielded abundant remains of *Hypsilophodon foxi* Huxley, including, in a few instances, associated bones and teeth representing a considerable part of the skeleton of this relatively small bipedal dinosaur. Remains of the species have been found by Mr. R. W. Hooley in the Marls a little below the Hypsilophodon Bed in Brixton Bay, but not in the Shales above, and they have yet to be recorded from the Wealden Beds of Compton and Sandown Bays.

Near Cowleaze Chine the "white rock" mentioned in the foregoing table (p. 13) is a pale, calcareous, silty stone, indistinctly shaly in places, and having an uneven base. It contains *Unio* and water-worn bones. A few quartz-pebbles and subangular pieces of white siliceous rock (to $2\frac{1}{2}$ inches in diameter) occur at the bottom.

From the shales between the Hypsilophodon Bed and the massive sandstone which comes in at the top of the cliff at Barnes High, and runs through Cowleaze Chine, there have been obtained numerous vertebrate remains, such as spines and teeth of fish referable to *Caelodus* and *Hybodus*, and bones of *Iguanodon bernissartensis* Boul., *I. mantelli* Meyer, *Goniopholis crassidens* Owen, and of the flying reptile *Ornithodesmus latidens* Seeley, whose wingspread is estimated, in one instance, at about 16 feet.[1]

Ferns (*Lonchopteris mantelli* Brongn. (*Weichselia*), *Cladophlebis*, &c.) are common in the lower part of the shales which overlie the thick sandstone, and farther up there come the usual cypridiferous paper-shales, with thin layers of *Ostrea* and *Cyrena* limestone. The gasteropod *Vicarya strombiformis* Schloth., associated with *Cyrena* in the limestone bands, also occurs in great numbers at 30 feet, 12 feet, and 1 foot below the upper limit of the Shales. The highest band of *Vicarya*, just below the base of the Lower Greensand, contains *Cypris cornigera* Rup. Jones, together with the commoner *Metacypris fittoni* Mant., and fish-remains.

The total thickness of the Wealden Shales of Atherfield is 192 feet; that of the Marls, between Atherfield Point and Sedmore Point, about 550 to 560 feet.

SANDOWN BAY

Here the Wealden outcrop occupies about a mile and a half of the coast, and extends inland for rather more than a mile. The thickness of beds exposed is roughly 250 feet, of which approximately 170 feet belong to the Shales.

The axis of the anticline by which these beds are raised into view crosses the coast at Sandown ("Granite") Fort, three-quarters of a mile south-west of Yaverland Church, but, except for small exposures of blue shale, to be seen at times on the shore near Sandown Coast Guard Station, the strata on the low coast south-westward of the axial line are entirely hidden by the sea-wall and other buildings. North-east of that line a fairly complete sequence, detailed below, can be made out; partly in the cliffs (which are much slipped), partly on the foreshore (Fig. 3, p. 19).

---

[1]R. W. Hooley, *Quart. Journ. Geol. Soc.*, vol. lxix, 1913, pp. 372–421; also *Geol. Mag.*, 1911, p. 520; *ibid*, 1912, p. 444.

Section of Wealden Beds, Sandown Bay

		ft	in.
Lower Greensand: Perna Bed, green sandy clay		—	—
Shales; blue, top uneven and disturbed		12	0
"Beef-bed": Cyrena limestone with layers of cone-in-cone structure at top and bottom .. .. .. to		0	5
Shales with dwarf Cyprids, and thin layers of concretionary ironstone		22	0
Oyster-bed: limestone composed of black *Ostrea distorta* J. de C. Sow. with few *Cyrena* , *Viviparus*, **Ac.**, in reddish matrix. Lower half mostly loose shells to		0	5
Shales with Cyprids, seams of *Ostrea*, and bands of laminated sandstone		31	0
Cyrena limestone, reddish .. .. to		0	5
Paper shales with abundant large cyprids; also *Viviparus* and *Cyrena*..		18	6
Ironstone, dark-brown, laminated		0	5
Shales; coarse, mottled grey and bluish, with thin layers of iron-sandstone .. .. about		39	0
Sandstone; yellow and white, ironstained, with ripplemarks and worm tracks. Coarse at top .. about		8	0
Shales with layers of *Cyrena* and scattered *Viviparus* about		15	0
Clay-ironstone; sandy, dark brown; full of Cyprids and *Viviparus;* pyritic at base		0	4
Shales; dark grey, numerous seams of *Cyrena* and scattered Cyprids. (Even contact with Marls) about		19	0
Marl; grey, with coloured mottlings and irregular bands of large calcareous nodules in upper part (base obscured) .. .. about		10	0
Silt; pale greenish-grey; hard and vesicular in places, and with one or more bands of rolled concretions. Much pyritised lignite, *Uniones* (some phosphatised), reptilian bones, scales of *Lepidotus*, &c.		1	6
Clays; green, red, and variegated (mostly hidden by sea-wall) .. .. about		20	0
Silt, with lignite and bones; similar to that above ..		1	6
Clays and marls, variegated, with bands of current-bedded sand. Become sandy downwards, and near base of section, by Sandown Fort, contain three beds of brown calcareous sandstone, forming tabulur reefs on the shore .. .. .. seen for about		50	0

WEALDEN SHALES, about 170 ft

WEALDEN MARLS, about 80 ft

For a few yards beyond the eastern end of Sandown sea-wall, near Sandown Fort, the low cliff or bank of red sandy clay above the beach shows a band of rough, brown, black-spotted ferruginous limestone (3 inches to 1½ feet), mainly composed of drifted shells of *Viviparus fluviorum* (J. Sow.). The lower limit of the bed is notably uneven, the shells descending into hollows in the clay beneath. This limestone band dies out eastward before reaching the foreshore.

The coloured clays of the Marls Series, occupying the cliff-section between Sandown sea-wall and the short stone wall below Yaverland Fort, show nothing noteworthy besides some indications of contemporaneous erosion until one reaches the lower of the two greenish-grey silty beds (mentioned in the foregoing table), which comes down to the beach, in two slightly slipped masses of the cliff, between 10 and 50 yards west of the latter wall. The bed in question contains abundant pyritised drift-wood together with groups of *Uniones* of two or three species. Bones are to be found in it with a little searching, and

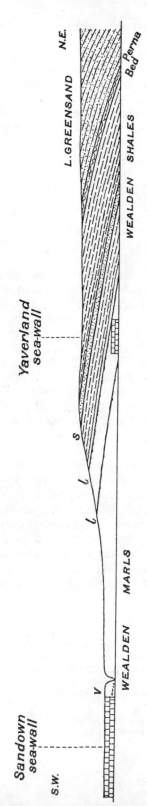

Fig. 3. *Section of Wealden Beds near Yaverland, Sandown Bay*

Distance, about ½ mile. Vertical scale and dips exaggerated

v. Viviparus limestone   *l.* Lignite and bone beds   *s.* Sandstone of Yaverland Fort
The upper part of the low cliff near Sandown sea-wall is in reconstructed material; a late Pleistocene or Recent land-wash

cones of *Zamia*-like plants are not uncommon. Teeth of *Iguanodon* and of carnivorous reptiles also occur. At times, a broad surface of the bed is laid bare on the foreshore off the eastern end of Yaverland wall, and of late years there has been a small exposure on the landward side of that end of the wall in which leaflets of *Weichselia* occur with abundant scales of *Lepidotus mantelli* Agassiz.

In an overlying green clay, which contains lenticular veins of "beefy" heavy spar (barium sulphate), the writer found a solitary pebble of dark blue-grey rock, of rounded wedge-like form, and measuring $2\frac{1}{2} \times 1\frac{3}{4} \times 1\frac{1}{4}$ inches. The pebble has a well-polished surface bearing minute scratches, and is probably a reptilian stomach-stone. Dr. H. H. Thomas describes it as "a highly tourmalinized quartzose breccia, composed of fragments of tourmaline-hornfels and tourmalinized fine-grained quartzite cemented with secondary quartz through which tourmaline needles run in all directions". He adds, that breccias of a similar nature occurring in superficial deposits are usually attributed to a "West of England" source. The stone, catalogued E.12008, is in the Geological Survey collection.

The higher silty lignitic bed, near the top of the Marls, is more conglomeratic than the lower, and contains pebbles of barium sulphate, presumably derived from veins of that mineral in the underlying clays. It is rich in remains of large reptiles (chiefly *Iguanodon*, including *I. mantelli* Meyer, together with less common *Goniopholis crassidens* Owen, and turtle (*Plesicochelys*?), and is the principal source of the wave-washed bones usually to be seen on the shore between Yaverland sea-wall and Redcliff.[1] The *Uniones* include *U. valdensis* Mant. (scarce), *U.* cf. *planus* F. A. Roëm., and *U.* cf. *subsinuatus* K. & Dunk.,[2] which are represented by shells in the silt and by casts in the conglomeratic seams. This bed comes down to the beach about 70 yards east of the sea-wall. It is often obscured by mud-flows. Near the same horizon a mass of light micaceous sandstone appears in the broken ground above the wall but does not extend to the shore.

The conspicuous yellow sandstone, about 35 feet above the base of the Shales, roughly corresponds in position to the thick sandstone of Cowleaze Chine and Barnes High. It has been impliedly identified with an ossiferous bed mentioned by Buckland,[3] but seems entirely devoid of bones.

The shales above the Cyrena limestone contain curvi-tabular concretions of grey limestone (showing distorted lamination), rich in bones and teeth of fish (*Lepidotus, Acrodus*), and yielding occasionally grouped spines of *Hybodus*, and radioles of regular echinids (*Cidaris* 2 *spp.*).

The Oyster and "Beef" beds, and the junction of the Shales with the Lower Greensand, are at present well displayed in a narrow cusp of the cliff (Fig. 4)

---

[1] The occurrence of reptilian remains in "sandstone" and on the beach hereabouts has been recorded by W. Buckland (*Proc. Geol. Soc.*, vol. i, 1825-33,p. 159); Mantell ('Geological Excursions round the Isle of Wight', 1st ed. 1847, pp. 137–8); T. F. Gibson (*Quart. Journ. Geol. Soc.*, vol. xiv., 1858, p. 175), and others. In recent years, a few pieces of *Endogenites erosa* Mant. have been found on the shore east of the sea-wall, by the Rev. J. C. Hughes, of Shanklin.

[2] The comparative determinations are by Dr. F. L. Kitchin. At least two other forms are common here, which he has been unable to identify.

[3] A. Strahan, *op. cit.*, p. 17.

between two bights of landslip; one in the Shales below, the other in the Atherfield Clay.

The few inland sections near Sandown are nearly all in the yellow sandstone about 35 feet above the base of the Shales. This bed rises to the cliff-top under Yaverland Fort, and is exposed in the cutting of the high road about 150 yards farther to the west. In Sandown Level it is hidden by alluvium, but it reappears

FIG. 4. *Section of the Upper Beds of the Wealden Shales, near Yaverland*

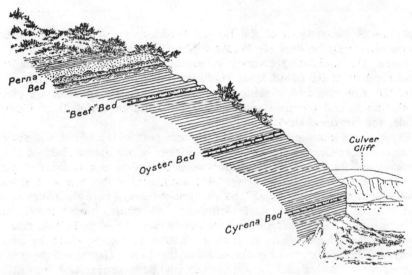

in a ridge on the southern side of the anticlinal axis above referred to, and is shown in a pit 300 yards south-west of Sandown Farm, and in the adjacent railway-cutting, where it has been utilized as supports for a footbridge. There its thickness has increased to nearly 20 feet. The overlying shales appear in slips in the same cutting, nearer Sandown Station.

Chapter III

LOWER GREENSAND

THE LOWER GREENSAND of the Isle of Wight comprises the thick series of arenaceous strata between the Wealden Shales and the blue clays of the Gault. It forms the undulating country of sandy soils which extends across the southern half of the Island from Sandown Bay westward, by Newchurch and Godshill, Kingston and Mottistone, to Compton Bay. Exposures are plentiful in this tract, and complete sections are presented in the cliffs of Compton, Chale, and Sandown Bays.

The Lower Greensand of the south-western part of the Island was subjected to minute investigation by Dr. W. H. Fitton in the earlier half of the last century, and the results of his studies were published in a number of papers, the most important of them being "A Stratigraphical Account of the Section from Atherfield to Rocken End", which appeared in full in 1847.[1] His researches, and those of E. Forbes, L. L. B. Ibbetson, and others, proved the formation to be not only thicker but much more fossiliferous about Atherfield than elsewhere in the Island, while the rich collection of fossils which he amassed confirmed the impression that the fauna of the Lower Greensand there is both distinct from that of the Upper Cretaceous Beds above, and has little or nothing in common with that of the Wealden Shales below.

It was early recognised that the great alteration in the fauna, observable on passing from the Wealden to the Lower Greensand, coincided with a change in the conditions of deposition, but the physical change was generally conceived as having occurred abruptly, owing to "sudden depression" and "influx of the sea"; whereas, later observations indicate a stratigraphical hiatus and disconformity between the Wealden and Lower Greensand, implying a lost time-interval of non-deposition, or of erosion, or both. The junction of the two formations is everywhere sharply defined, and although the discordance which is implied by the Lower Greensand overstep in Wiltshire and other parts of the Mainland is not apparent in the Isle of Wight, evidences of erosion at the contact are to be seen here in the puckering and brecciation of the top of the Wealden Shales, and in the presence of rolled fossils, derived from Wealden and older strata, in a seam of grit at the base of the Lower Greensand.

Dr. Fitton divided the Lower Greensand of Atherfield into 6 major and 16 minor groups. His classification, however, is only in part and with difficulty applicable to the other sections in the Island, and for purposes of mapping, the Geological Survey found a four-fold disposition more convenient. In the following table, Fitton's groups are compared with those adopted by the Geological Survey, for the Isle of Wight in 1887, and for the Weald of Kent and Sussex at an earlier date.

---

[1] *Quart. Journ. Geol. Soc.*, vol. iii., p. 289.

Fitton, 1845 (Atherfield)		Geological Survey, 1887 (Isle of Wight)	Geological Survey (S.E. of England)
XVI. Various sands and clays	F	Carstone.	Folkstone Beds.
XV. Upper clays and sandrock ..	E	Sandrock Series.	
XIV. Ferruginous bands of Blackgang Chine			
XIII. Sands of Walpen Undercliff ..			
XII. Foliated clay and sand			
XI. Cliff-end sands			Sandgate Beds.
X. Second Gryphaea bed			
IX. Walpen and Ladder sands ..	D	Ferruginous Sands.	
VIII. Upper Crioceras group ..			Hythe Beds.
VII. Walpen sands and clay ..			
VI. Lower Crioceras group ..			
V. Scaphites group			
IV. Lower Gryphaea bed			
III. The Crackers	C		
II. The Atherfield Clay	B	Atherfield Clay.	Atherfield Clay
I. Perna Mulleti bed	A		

It should be stated that the Atherfield Clay of the Geological Survey is not the exact equivalent of Fitton's Groups I and II, but includes also the lowest bed ("Lower Lobster Bed") of his Group III. Similarly, the Ferruginous Sands take in a thick bed of sandy clay forming the lowest member of Fitton's Group XV, the remainder of which, with the lower part of XVI, is included in the Survey's Sandrock Series; leaving the upper part of XVI to the Carstone.[1]

Despite the occurrence of pebbly bands with derived fossils, there is a complete passage from the Perna Bed to the top of the Sandrock. These and the intervening divisions are usually referred to the Aptian Stage (Zone of *Hoplites deshayesi*), though some recent writers, prefer to assign the Perna Bed and the Atherfield Clay to the Barremian. In the Lower Cretaceous of the North-Eastern Counties, the Perna Bed seems to be represented in the upper part of the Zone of *Belemnites jaculum*,[2] and the succeeding groups, as far up at least as the top of the Sandrock. in the Zone of *Belemnites brunsvicensis*.

The Carstone has a definite base, and there are signs that its deposition was preceded by a pause and some slight erosion of the Sandrock. Above, the Carstone everywhere passes into the Gault, of which it seems to be the locally-expanded basement-bed, or Zone of *Douvilléiceras mammillatum* (Albian). Following the plan adopted in the second edition of the Geological Survey Memoir on the Isle of Wight, we deal with this division separately, after we have described the other members of the Lower Greensand.

The thickness of the Lower Greensand is about 800 feet in the cliffs of Chale Bay, near Atherfield: thence it decreases eastward, to about 600 feet at Redcliff

---

[1] In 'Summary of Progress of the Geological Survey for 1900', p. 119, a rearrangement of the last column of the above table is proposed by G. W. Lamplugh, who would correlate the Carstone and upper half of the Sandrock with the Folkestone Beds; the lower half of the Sandrock and upper third of Ferruginous Sands with the Sandgate Beds, and the lower two-thirds of the Ferruginous Sands with the Hythe Beds.

[2] G. W. Lamplugh's beds "C 1 to 6" of the Speeton section, and the Tealby Clay of Donnington Station. *Cf.* that author's 'Speeton Series, &c.,' *Quart. Journ. Geol. Soc.*, vol. lii., 1896, table facing p. 184 and pp. 207, 208.

FIG. 5.   *Comparative Vertical Sections of the Cretaceous Rocks below the Chalk, in the Isle of Wight and on the Dorsetshire Coast*

Adapted from A. Strahan in "Geology of the Isle of Wight" (*Mem. Geol. Survey*), 2nd Ed., 1889, pl. III.

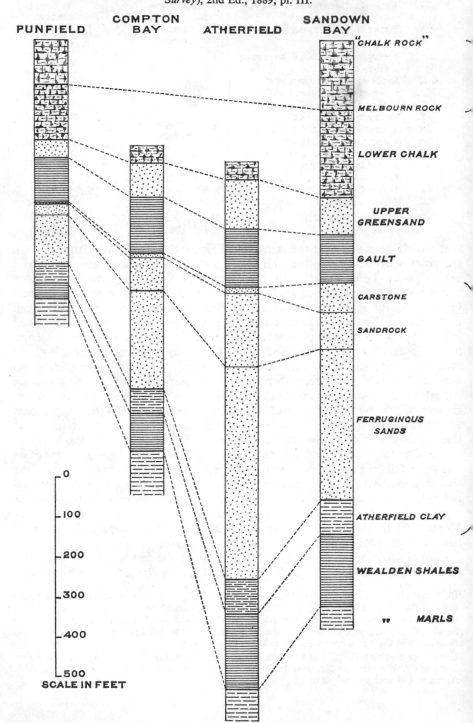

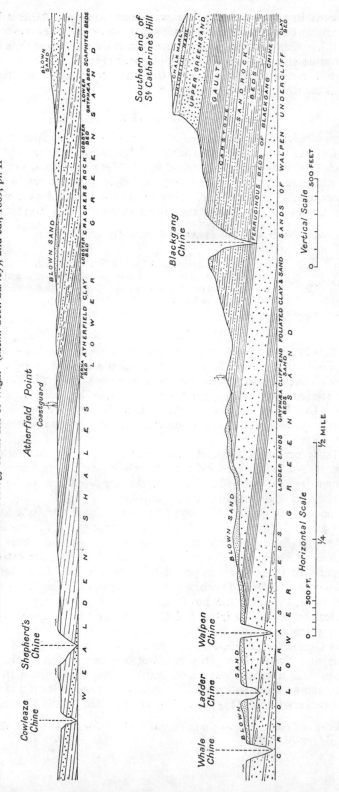

Fig. 6. *Section of Lower Greensand, from Atherfield Point to Blackgang Chine*

After A. Strahan in "Geology of the Isle of Wight" (*Mem. Geol. Survey*), 2nd ed., 1889, pl. II

in Sandown Bay, and more quickly westward, to about 400 feet in Compton Bay; while at Punfield on the Dorset coast, some 20 miles west of Compton Bay, it is less than 200 feet. From these data it would appear that the direction of most rapid thinning is rather west of north (Fig. 5).

We shall notice first the coast exposures, beginning with the Atherfield section as the most important (Fig. 6, p. 23).

ATHERFIELD POINT TO ROCKEN END

Atherfield Clay. The Perna Bed at the base of this division appears at the top of the cliff about 300 yards south of Shepherd's Chine, and descends to the beach 150 yards east of Atherfield Point. More often than not the section is greatly obscured by slips, but, failing satisfactory exposures in the cliff, one can resort to Shepherd's Chine, where the Perna Bed and its contact with the Wealden Shales are shown near the bridge on the Military Road.

Section of the Perna Bed near Atherfield Point

		ft	in.
Perna Bed	Ironstained calcareous sandstone, with many fossils	2	6
	Green-blue sandy clay; many fossils, including *Panopaea* in living attitude. A seam of coarse sand with phosphatic nodules and fish-remains at base	2	7
Wealden Shales (*see* pp. 13, 16).			
		5	1

The fossils include:—*Holocystis elegans* Lonsd., *Turbinoseris fromenteli* Dunc., *Terebratula sella* J. Sow., *Exogyra sinuata* J. Sow., *Perna mulleti* Desh. (*Pedalion*), *Arca raulini* Leym., *Corbis corrugata* J. Sow. (*Sphaera*), *Panopaea gurgitis* (Brongn.) (= *P. plicata* J. de C. Sow.), *Trigonia nodosa* J. Sow., *T. etheridgei* Lyc., *Aporrhais robinaldina* d'Orb. *Hoplites deshayesi* (Leym.), &c. The coarse monomyarian, *Perna mulleti*, after which Fitton named the bed, is confined to this horizon.

The fairly persistent seam of sand or grit at the bottom of the Perna Bed abounds in bones and teeth of fish (*Lepidotus*, &c.), with occasional saurian bones and freshwater shells, derived from the Wealden Shales, which here show little sign of disturbance at the junction.

The mass of the Atherfield Clay, also named by Fitton, is a light-blue silty clay, devoid of lamination, and containing numerous flat nodules of clay-ironstone. Its fauna is broadly similar to that of the Perna Bed: *Pinna robinaldina* d'Orb. and *Panopaea*, often in their burrows, are among the most prominent fossils, and fragmentary ammonoids (*Hoplites deshayesi*, *Douvilléiceras hambrovi* (Forbes)) not uncommon. This division is about 100 feet thick, including the Lower Lobster Bed, which is grouped with it on lithological grounds. The latter bed (25 to 30 feet) is an impure fuller's earth, containing the small lobster *Meyeria vectensis* (Bell), the crab *Mithracites vectensis* Gould,[1] the echinid *Echinospatagus renevieri* Wright, &c.

Ferruginous Sands. This series is about 500 to 510 feet thick. Many of its beds consist in a great measure of polished grains of brown iron-ore (often oolitic), such as occur so freely in the Sandgate beds of Kent and Surrey.

The Crackers Group (Fig. 7, p. 25), as restricted by the Geological Survey,

[1]New species of Crustacea (*Thenops*) from Atherfield are described by F. R. C. Reed in *Geol. Mag.*, 1911, pp. 115–120.

is about 60 feet thick. The lowest bed, distinguished as C. III No. 5 by Fitton, is that to which the name "Crackers" was originally applied, "from the resounding of the waves in the cavities below" it, in the little promontory where it comes down to the shore, 600 yards east of Atherfield Coastguard Station. This bed consists of coarse, compact, grey and brown sand (20 feet), containing two layers of large round and tabular calcareous concretions, exceptionally rich in fossils. Hard and often of unpromising appearance externally, these concretions have soft sandy cores, from which the fossils can be obtained in perfect condition. We can mention only a few prominent species, *e.g.*, *Gervillia* cf. *anceps* Desh., *G. sublanceolata* (d'Orb.), *Thetironia minor* (J. Sow.) (*Thetis*), *Panopaea gurgitis* (Brongn.) (= *P. plicata* J. de C. Sow.), *Trigonia nodosa* J. Sow., *Aporrhais fittoni* Forbes, *Actaeon albensis* d'Orb., *Natica rotundata* J. Sow., and *Hoplites deshayesi* (Leym.).

FIG. 7. *The Crackers Group, near Atherfield*

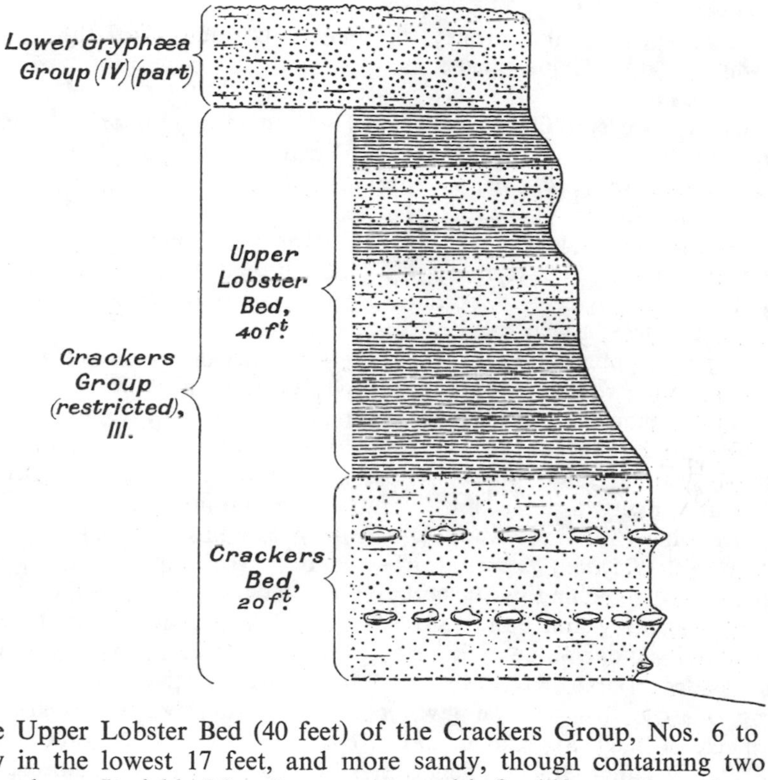

The Upper Lobster Bed (40 feet) of the Crackers Group, Nos. 6 to 10, is clayey in the lowest 17 feet, and more sandy, though containing two clay-bands, above. It yields *Meyeria vectensis*, and is fossiliferous throughout.

The succeeding Lower Gryphaea (= Exogyra) Group, IV (33 feet), comprises, in descending order:

	ft
Coarse brown and reddish sand with bands of *Exogyra sinuata* in upper part, and frequent *Pinna robinaldina* d'Orb. in lower part, (Forms a reef 350 yards west of Whale Chine)	10
Sand with *Terebratula sella* (here in maximum abundance), *Gervillia alaeformis* (J. Sow.) (*Perna*), *Rhynchonella gibbsiana* J. Sow., &c. .. .. .. to	2
Brown and rusty sands; nodules at base	21

c

Owing to its highly fossiliferous character, this group is easily identified. The Scaphites Group, V (50 feet), also is divisible into three beds:

	ft
Grey sandy clay with *Exogyra sinuata* in upper part, *Ostrea diluviana* Linn., &c.	27
Bands of nodules (to two feet diam.) with *Macroscaphites gigas* (d'Orb.), *M. hillsi* (J. Sow.) (*Scaphites*), &c.	3
Brown sands with clusters of *Exogyra sp.*, layers of *Serpulae*, brachiopods, &c.; near base	20

The Lower Crioceras Group, VI (16 feet), contains several bands of *Crioceras*? *bowerbanki* (d'Orb.), in sand. The lowest band (said to have yielded the best specimens to the early collectors) declines to the beach west of Whale Chine; the highest crosses the bottom of that chine.

The Walpen (and Ladder) Sands and Clay, VII (57 feet) comprise:

	ft
Clayey, passing down to sandy, beds: *Panopaea mandibula* (J. Sow.), *Pinna, Dentalium, &c.*	33
Dark-green clay with nodules containing *Exogyra sinuata* and *Douvilléiceras martini* (d'Orb.)	24

The clayey beds of this group, throwing out water, form the undercliff upon which Ladder Chine opens. They come to the beach about 200 yards east of that chine.

The Upper Crioceras Group, VIII (46 feet), contains four or more courses of *Crioceras*? *bowerbanki*, with *Douvilléiceras martini*, *Gervillia forbesiana* d'Orb., *Trigonia vectiana* Lyc., *Terebratulae, &c.* Its upper limit falls to the beach east of Walpen Chine.

The Walpen and Ladder Sand, IX (42 feet) is green and grey; more homogeneous than the sands next above and below it, and with a course of fossiliferous lenticular masses of dark olive-green stone at the base. About 6 feet above this course is a thin band of *Serpulae*.

The Upper Gryphaea Group, X (16 feet) consists of greensand with some clay. Bands of *Exogyra sinuata* and nodules containing *Enallaster fittoni* Forbes and ammonoids occur in the lower 12 feet. *Exogyra* occurs also in the upper part of this group, but is rare or wanting at higher horizons, in the Atherfield section. Small pieces of the fern *Weichselia mantelli* (Brongn.), which recur at many horizons, are common in this group.

The overlying Cliff End Sand, XI (28 feet), contains, in the lower part, a thin clay with *Trigonia nodosa* Forbes, and in the upper part, numerous cylindrical and branching pyritic concretions, in dark green and bluish sand.

The foliated Clay and Sand, XII (25 feet), is made up of interlaminated greenish sand and dark-blue pyritic clay, with some lenticular masses of coarse, current-bedded friable sandstone, similar to that of the Sandrock Series. Wasting quickly, this division gives rise to an extensive undercliff on the western side of Blackgang Chine, and its character is well seen in the southern side of Walpen Chine. Its weakness brings into relief the overlying beds, which form the well-marked scarp between Pyle Farm and Kingston, inland.

The Sands of Walpen Undercliff, Group XIII (about 100 feet), comprise, in descending order:

	ft	in.
Brown sands with bands of dark-green and black clay	about 19	0
Light-green and yellowish sand, giving bright green streak when scraped	25	9
Brown sand with *Astarte beaumonti* Leym, *Pinna, Pecten, Terebratula*	1	6
Green sand, moist	12	6
Sand, with gravelly seam of quartz and lydian-stone at base	29	8
White sand and sandstone	about 10	0

Beds of this group are the highest seen in the cliff (below the blown sand) between 200 yards and half-a-mile east of Walpen Chine.

The Ferruginous Bands of Blackgang Chine, XIV (20 feet), are made up as follows:

	ft	in.
Ferruginous concretions, immediately above the cascade	1	0—6
Brown and yellow sand	5	0
Ferruginous concretions, with many vacant moulds of fossils, most abundant near Walpen High-Cliff	1	0
Sand, with fossils	7	0
Ferruginous sandrock, with fossils	5	0

Owing to its comparative hardness, this group is responsible for the cascade in the lower part of Blackgang Chine, and for the verticality of the foot of the cliff south-eastwards. Its upper limit falls to the beach about 600 yards north-west of Rocken End.

The fossil-species in this group can be identified in several cases with those of the Perna Bed, about 600 feet below, e.g., Panopaea plicata J. de C. Sow. (P. gurgitis Brongn.), Corbula striatula J. de C. Sow., Thetis minor J. Sow. (Thetironia), Trigonia caudata Agas., Pinna robinaldina d'Orbigny.

We have now reached the highest bed of the Ferruginous Sands; the dark-grey sandy clay, 35 to 40 feet thick, which Fitton regarded as the lowest member of his Group XV, or "Upper clays and sandrock". At Blackgang Chine it forms an undercliff, which narrows south-eastward into a sloping shelf in the cliff as the bed gradually declines to the spot where it passes out of sight, about 200 yards short of Rocken End.

Sandrock Series. This series is thickest in the southern part of the Island, and there presents in their typical form the beds of slightly coherent white and yellow quartz-sand, which are so conspicuous in the upper part of Black-gang Chine, and to which the name 'sandrock' is singularly applicable.

The following complete section of this division was made out near the chalybeate spring 200 yards north-west of South View House, south-east of Blackgang Chine.

"Section of the Sandrock Series near the Chalybeate Spring

	ft
"Carstone (for details, see p. 48).	
Grey sand with wood, large concretions and seams of clay; a line of quartz pebbles at the base	20
Grey and yellow sand interlaminated with clay	7
Current-bedded yellow sandrock, with wood; thins away southwards (4th sandrock of Fitton)	14
Laminated sand and clay, with wood; throws out the chalybeate spring ..	22
A variable bed; contains clay with partings of sand, sometimes nearly all sand, and passes down into	16
White sandrock (3rd sandrock of Fitton) .. .. about	25
Variable sand and clay, with a line of nodules about the middle	60
White sandrock (2nd sandrock of Fitton)	20
	184"[1]

[1]'Geology of the Isle of Wight,' *Mem. Geol. Surv.*, 2nd ed., 1889, p. 31.

Shells are rarely preserved in the Sandrock. In the slopes south-east of Blackgang Chine, Mr. G. W. Lamplugh found casts of marine pelecypods and plant-remains. They occurred in a band of ferruginous concretions 10 feet below the base of the Carstone.[1]

The middle and upper beds of the Sandrock Series appear at intervals, from beneath the landslips, between Rocken End and Binnel Bay.

COMPTON BAY

The base of the Lower Greensand in Compton Bay is seldom to be seen *in situ*, owing to the big slip of Atherfield Clay, already mentioned, but it is not difficult to find fallen masses which show the junction with the Wealden Shales as clearly as if it were in place. The Perna Bed, with its dark-green to bluish colouring, gritty texture, and rusty cap, is readily recognised. Beneath it, the Wealden Shales are seen to be disturbed and broken up to a depth of one or two feet, and the junction is slightly uneven.

The Atherfield Clay is hidden by sludge-streams, but appears to be much thinner than at Atherfield; and the diminished thickness of the remainder of the Lower Greensand is evident. The descending succession is as follows:

Compton Bay[2]

		ft	in.
Carstone, 6 ft	Brown Sand, with 3-inch pebble-band at the base, containing rounded quartzite pebbles up to ¾ inch in diameter, some phosphatic pebbles, and many pieces of wood. Cylindrical phosphatic nodules also occur	6	0
	Blue clay..	2	6
Sandrock Series, 81 ft 6 ins.	Pebble-band with quartzites, &c., 0–3 inch .. .. Grey and greenish sand, with a layer of pyritised wood 8½ feet from the top, and scattered fragments near the top, about 12½ feet .. .. Pebble-band, as above, 6 inches	13	0
	Bright-yellow sand, with an irony seam at the base ..	10	0
	Clean white sand and blue clay, interbedded in wavy laminæ, and giving out copious chalybeate springs ("foliated series")	56	0
Ferruginous Sands, 251 ft 6½ ins.	Clayey grit, weathering green, with a band of quartzite pebbles, five inches thick, at the base	26	0
	White sand like gannister	2	0
	Dark sand and clay intermixed, with much vegetable matter in the upper part, and looking like a rootlet bed ..	3	0
	Band of small quartzite pebbles	0	3
	Sand like gannister	5	0
	Very black and sooty-looking sand or silt	7	8
	Lighter do striped	10	0
	Band of soft yellow rolled phosphatic nodules, with some quartzites	0	1½
	Lighter coloured and striped "sooty" sand, with many small soft yellow phosphate pebbles near the base ..	4	0
	'Foliated' sand and clay as above, passing down into paper-shale	5	8

[1] '*Summary of Progress of the Geol. Survey for* 1900,' p. 118.

[2] This table is taken from 'Geology of the Isle of Wight', *Mem. Geol. Surv.*, 2nd ed., 1889, pp. 21–23, with slight alterations.

		ft	in.
	Very green gritty sand, with hard pale-yellow phosphates, some cylindrical, some rounded	3	6
	Brown sandstone	1	2
	Green grit as above	1	6
	Brown sandstone	1	2
	Green and grey silty sand, with fucoidal markings ..	1	0
	Brown sandstone	1	0
	Green and grey silty sand, with fucoidal markings ..	2	0
Ferruginous Sands, 251 ft 6½ ins.	Brown sandstone, with small pebbles and pieces of lignite scattered throughout; an impersistent band of silty sand in the middle	42	0
	Green silty sand, passing down	11	6
	Clay	3	0
	Brown and red grit, made up largely of rounded grains coated by iron oxide; forms the cliff east of Compton Chine	54	0
	Yellow sand, much fretted by the weather in the upper part	20	0
	Pale green sandy clay, with light-grey nodules containing fossils, and passing down into	10	0
	Yellow sand, clayey in parts	15	0
	Grey silty sand, with bands of soft yellow sandstone below ..	21	0
Atherfield Clay, 60 ft	Pale blue clay, mottled red and grey (much obscured) with clay ironstone and phosphatic concretions		
	Perna Bed: Calcareous and ferruginous grit with *Modiola*, &c. (1 foot) passing down to green sandy clay with *Exogyra sinuata*, &c. (9 inches)	60	0?
Wealden Shales: paper shales, disturbed		—	
	About ..	399	

The precise correlation of the beds of the above section with those near Atherfield appears to be impossible. They are not only much thinner as a whole, but have also changed in character, and, above the Perna Bed, fossils are comparatively scarce. Dr. Fitton identified a "mass of brownish clay and sand" lying next above the Atherfield Clay (and not apparent in the above section) as the Lower Lobster Bed, and a prominent portion in the lower part of the brown and red grit ("54 feet") as the Lower Gryphaea bed of Atherfield. The higher beds are rather similar to those seen in the upper part of Blackgang Chine, but are thinner, and contain no bands of sandrock. The annexed figure (8) shows the arrangement of these upper beds in the cliff.

Redcliff

The last of the three complete sections of the Lower Greensand is presented in the nothern part of Sandown Bay. There as elsewhere on the coast, the unstable Atherfield Clay is masked by slips. The Perna Bed, which has been visible for some years in the sides of a narrow projection of the cliff (Fig. 4, p. 19), just south of the red-brown mud-flows, has much the same character as at Atherfield, but is a little thicker. The top of the Wealden Shales is disturbed, as at Compton Bay.

In the cliff, the Perna Bed is much weathered, and the fossils are carious or represented by hollow moulds. It is seen to better advantage, at low tide, in the narrow reef that runs straight out to sea, in a direction rather south of east, below Redcliff, and is there rich in well-preserved shells of the species noticed at Atherfield. The sub-spherical coral *Holocystis elegans*, and *Perna mulleti*, are common. The smaller curved reef of the same bed, to the west, is part of an old landslip.

Fragmentary casts of *Hoplites deshayesi* are not uncommon in the Atherfield Clay. The small clay-ironstone concretions in this division frequently contain lustrous crystals of sphalerite (zinc sulphide) in the crevices.

FIG. 8. *The Sandrock Series, Compton Bay*
From "Geology of the Isle of Wight", (*Mem. Geol. Surv.*), 2nd ed., Fig. 7, p. 23.

a. Soil and gravel.   *b*. Gault.   *c*. Carstone, with *d*. pebble-band at base.
e—m. Sandrock, comprising:
    e. Blue clay and sand, with small pebbles and lignite.
    f. g. Bright yellow sand with irony seam at base.
    h, i, k, l. Interlaminated blue clay and white sand.
    m. Chiefly sand, throwing out much chalybeate water.
n. Ferruginous Sands; green and gritty clay.

"Southwards from the slip caused by the Atherfield Clay, the cliff consists of ferruginous sands and becomes mural, continuing so until the softer beds of the Sandrock series are reached. On the yellow and white sands and blue clays of this series there rests a great thickness of Carstone, which passes up into the Gault. A small fault crosses the cliff at an oblique angle at this point, running W. 30° N., and throwing the beds down to the north. It is best seen in the base of the Carstone, which it crosses about half way up the cliff.

"The Gault forms a small gully descending the cliff obliquely, and occupied by a footpath. This formed a convenient starting point for the following section:

"*Section of the Lower Greensand at Redcliff*

		ft	in.
"Gault, blue micaceous clay passing down into			
	Brown clayey grit, becoming more sandy below; small scattered pebbles, and a line of pale phosphatic concretions made up of grit and grains of iron oxide 9 feet from the top	10	3
"Carstone,	Pebbly band, with small quartzites	0	6
72 ft 9 ins.	Brown sand with many scattered quartzite pebbles, and phosphatic concretions as above at several horizons. Wavy lines of iron oxide, and some beds with many grains of oxide	60	0
	Loose brown sand and grit	2	0

		ft	in.
"Sand-rock Seriès, base uncertain, about 93 ft 6 ins.	White sand and blue clay interlaminated	12	0
	Do. with occasional lines of blue clay	32	0
	Striped sand and clay	9	0
	Do. chiefly clay and very sulphury ..	4	0
	Seam of iron oxide	0	6
	Bright-yellow and white sand, with ferruginous band at base	31	0
	Grey striped sand and clay	2	0
	White sand	3	0
"Ferruginous Sands, about 367 ft 6 ins.	Blue and striped sandy clay (? = 40 feet clay of Blackgang)	21	0
	Hard brown sandstone	3	6
	Grey sand, 'soot-coloured'	6	0
	Pebbly bands, containing small quartzites, phosphates, and iron oxide	2	0
	Dark-green or bluish clay and sand	1	0
	Ferruginous pebbly band with small phosphates and pebbles of iron oxide	1	6
	Soft yellow sand	6	6
	Dark clayey sand	6	0
	Pebbly band, containing many rolled phosphatic casts of ammonites and bivalves	0	4
	Pale-brown ferruginous sand	3	0
	Pebbly band, with small quartzites and numerous flakes of iron oxide	0	2
	Pale-brown sand with flakes of iron oxide	11	0
	Brown pebbly grit with small quartzites and grains and flakes of iron oxide	4	0
	Loose pale-green sand	17	0
	Greenish grit with many wavy seams of iron oxide ..	3	0
	Brown and green gritty sand	3	0
	Dark-green or nearly black clayey sand	6	0
	Brown sand with flakes and grains of iron oxide ..	68	0
	Greensand, with a vivid green streak; lines of clay occasionally; a layer of broken oysters nine feet from the base. Forms a smooth vertical wall	60	0
	Brown and reddish brown sandstone with grains of iron oxide very abundant about 20 feet from the top; forms the cliff on which [the remnant of] Redcliff Fort stands ..	114	0
"Ferruginous Sands, about 367 ft 6 ins.	Green sandy clay with wood and a line of large nodules	2	0
	Fine and very clayey sand with wood; lines of nodules in the upper part, and veins of iron oxide	14	0
	Seam of brown iron oxide	0	5
	Fine grey clayey sand	2	0
	Band of blood-red iron oxide	0	1
	Fine grey clayey sand	10	0
	Fine white clayey sand	2	0
"Atherfield Clay, 83 ft 4 ins.	Pale-blue clay with pale-blue nodules, weathering brown	77	0
	(Perna Beds, 6 ft 4 ins.) Calcareous and ferruginous grit with many fossils, 1 ft 6 in. to	2	0
	Passing down into pale-blue sandy clay with fossils	3	6
	Impersistent grit, with scales and bones of fish, and phosphatic pebbles, some of which are rolled ammonites and bivalves; about ..	0	3
	Pale-blue sandy clay with fossils	0	6
	Grit, as above	0	0½—1
		617	1"[1]

[1]'Geology of the Isle of Wight,' *Mem. Geol. Surv.*, 2nd ed., 1889, pp. 35, 36.

Vacant moulds of *Exogyra sinuata* occur in bands about 55 and 80 feet above the Atherfield Clay.

"The occurrence of a band of rolled phosphatic nodules in the upper part of the Ferruginous Sands has attracted the attention of several observers. The nodules seem to be on the same horizon as those noted at Compton Bay, but in the 'coprolite bed' 4 inches thick at Redcliff, are larger, harder, and better preserved. Among the specimens Mr. Keeping identified *Ammonites biplex* Sow., *A. cordatus* Sow., *Pleurotomaria sp.*, *Cardium striatulum?*, *Lucina sp.*, *Myacites sp.*, *Cytherea rugosa?*, *Arca contracta* Phill., all being fragmentary and much rolled."[1]

Pieces of vertebral and other bones of reptiles also occur, together with reptilian teeth, and less frequent palatals of fish. About 18 per cent of the nodules are obvious casts of molluscs. Small pebbles of quartz, and a few quartzite and other pebbles up to three inches in diameter, occur in the same bed. Derived fossils are present also in the other pebbly bands, 12 to 14½ feet higher.

These phosphatic bands, which are not seen in the Shanklin and Blackgang sections, are unaccompanied by other phenomena suggestive of a break in the stratigraphical sequence. Remains of their indigenous fauna seem to have been entirely destroyed by the deep weathering to which the Ferruginous sands of Redcliff owe their ruddy tint.

SANDOWN TO BONCHURCH

At Sandown the Atherfield clay and its slips are hidden by the buildings near and north-east of the Pier. Rolled pieces of the Perna Bed, which was formerly exposed on the foreshore, are to be seen occasionally in the patches of shingle.

The Ferruginous Sands displayed in the cliff between Sandown and Shanklin probably represent Fitton's Groups IV to XIV, but most of the lower beds are devoid of distinctive organic remains, and, so far, only a few of the horizons recognized in the Atherfield-Blackgang section have been identified.

Near the southern end of Sandown Esplanade, the lower half of the cliff is in greenish-grey loamy sand (1, Fig. 9), with two conspicuous and a few other courses of ferruginous concretions. The upper limit of this division, defined by a discontinuous layer of concretions, and by a belt of vegetation on the cliff-face, dips to the shore, at 5°, about 250 yards south of the foot of Lake Stairs. Lignite and ill-preserved casts of shells (*Exogyra*, *Trigonia*) occur, but there seem to be no definite fossil-bands.

Next comes some 50 feet of more plainly stratified sands (2), clayey at the top, and including current-bedded bands near the middle. Where they form the upper part of the cliff, these sands are light brown and greyish, but gradually become dark-green as they descend below the zone of weathering. Much of the dark leaden-grey argillaceous matter present in the upper beds, occurs in the forms of irregular lenticles and solid and tubular moulds of borings. Bored and pyritised logs of driftwood are not uncommon. The upper limit of (2), slanting down the cliff southwards, with a decreasing dip, meets the beach 200 yards north of Little Stairs. About 10 feet below that limit, and visible only on the foreshore at low tide, there occurs a band of discoidal concretions,

---

[1]*Ibid.*, p. 37.

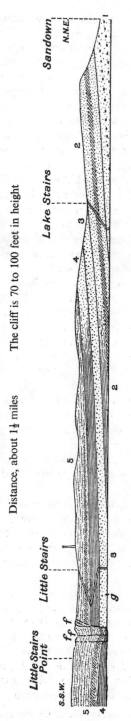

FIG. 9. *Section of the Ferruginous Sands between Little Stairs Point and Sandown*

Distance, about 1½ miles   The cliff is 70 to 100 feet in height

1—5.   Divisions of the Ferruginous Sands described in the text.   *fff*.   Faults.   *g*.   Wooden groyne.

N.B.—Division 3 has been drawn too thin, and division 5 extended too far to the right.

a few of which bear impressions of parts of large ammonoids. The concretions resemble those of the "Upper Crioceras Beds" of Atherfield (Group VIII), to which horizon the writer is disposed to refer them.[1]

The succeeding 30 feet of coarse, compact greensand (3) exhibits the same change in tint as it descends the cliff. Chalybeate water is thrown out at its base, cementing the shore-cobbles into hard ferruginous pudding-stone. About 10 feet above that limit a band of ironstone is developed at the foot of the cliff. This division not improbably corresponds to groups IX and X, for an abundance of vacant moulds of *Exogyra sinuata*, in the highest 10 feet, strongly suggests the correlation of that portion with the "Upper Gryphaea Bed" (X).

The overlying dark loamy greensand (4), about 25 feet thick, is a marked feature near middle of cliff-section at Little Stairs. Small pebbles of quartz and siliceous rocks are plentiful in the upper half, while irregular inclusions of dark clay, like those in (2), are thickly distributed below. Lenses of divergent current-bedding occur close to the base.

The highest beds seen near Little Stairs are brown loamy sands (5), with bands of current-bedding, the most conspicuous and persistent of which lies 10 to 15 feet above the junction with division (4).

At the new wooden groyne near the foot of Little Stairs, the general strati-fication of the Ferruginous Sands is sensibly horizontal. About 150 yards southwards one comes to a zone of dislocation, the details of which are usually much obscured by deep weathering, talus, and rain-wash. Under favourable conditions, however, one can distinguish three upwardly-branching faults, striking about E. 20° S. The first or northernmost fault has a downthrow of roughly 50 feet to the south, which brings the upper limit of division (4) to the foot of the cliff. At times, its course is clearly seen on the foreshore, the surface of which rises in a low step on the downthrow side of the fracture. The second and third faults, within 20 yards of the first, are smaller, their aggregate downthrow being only $8\frac{1}{2}$ feet, to the north. The south-south-westward dip reappears at the first fault, but at the second it is reversed, the beds rising thence gently southward, through the third fault and Little Stairs Point, to Small Hope Chine, at the northern end of Shanklin Esplanade, where they again become horizontal.

At Little Stairs Point the pebbly and clayey greensand (4), at the base of the cliff, contains small drift-wood and scattered pieces of dark shale. Here Mr. G. W. Lamplugh found a slab of bored fossiliferous Kimmeridge Shale, measuring $8 \times 6 \times 1\frac{1}{2}$ inches, which is of interest as showing that erosion of Upper Jurassic rocks was in progress at no great distance during the deposition of this sand.[2]

Off and to the south of Little Stairs Point, a coarse current-bedded greensand, rather lower in division (4), rises in a low reef of curiously imbricate form on the foreshore. Farther south, opposite Small Hope Chine, there is occasionally to be seen a yet lower greensand—presumably the upper part of (3)—con-taining clusters of *Exogyra sinuata*, with *Ostrea diluviana* Linn., &c. Fitton identified this bed with part of his Second or Upper Gryphaea Group, X, and recognised Group XII ("No. 40"), in "the next stratum above" it, in a "narrow undercliff" which has since disappeared; omitting mention of the

---

[1]Fitton (*op. cit.*, p. 317) mentions the occurrence of *Crioceras* in a quarry "not far from the shore" between Sandown and Shanklin. The working is not now identifiable.

[2]'*Summary of Progress of the Geol. Survey for* 1900,' p. 118.

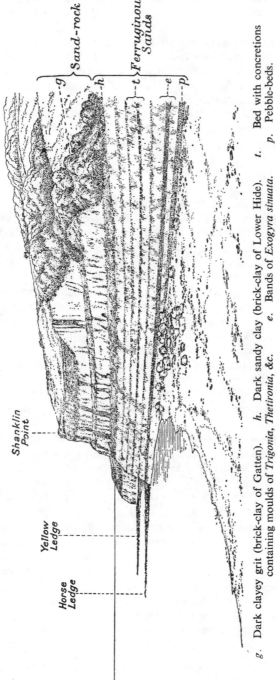

FIG. 10. *Section in Knock Cliff, Shanklin*

g. Dark clayey grit (brick-clay of Gatten). *h.* Dark sandy clay (brick-clay of Lower Hide). *t.* Bed with concretions containing moulds of *Trigonia, Thetironia,* &c. *e.* Bands of *Exogyra sinuata.* *p.* Pebble-beds.

The last three divisions are recognisable in the weathered surfaces at Appley Steps, to the right of that portion of Knock Cliff represented in the figure.

intermediate Group XI, which is 28 feet thick near Blackgang Chine, and may be represented, together with Group XII, in division (4) of the present description.

On the shore in the immediate vicinity of Little Stairs Point lie some blocks of orange-coloured fossiliferous ironsand which have fallen from a lenticular mass in division (5). They consist largely of massed *Exogyrae* (a small, undescribed species, cf. *E. harpa* Goldf.), with *Ostreae* (*O. diluviana, O. spp.*), *Multocrescis* cf. *laxata* d'Orb., *Pseudodiadema fittoni* Wright, &c., and probably belong to Fitton's Group XIII.[1] The blocks become less fossiliferous as they are followed from the neighbourhood of the faults to the south side of the Point, where they disappear. The fallen blocks of dark greensand with abundant *Exogyra sinuata*, noticeable at the foot of the cliff hereabouts, most probably come from the Exogyra Beds described below in the account of the Knock Cliff section (Fig. 10, *e.*).

In the cliff above Shanklin Esplanade the bedding is approximately horizontal as far southward as the Lift, beyond which point the south-south-west dip is resumed, and continues to the end of the Sandown Bay section at Dunnose. The division numbered (4), reddened by iron-water at the top,[2] is easily followed, but does not become conveniently accessible till Shanklin Chine is reached. At the mouth of the Chine, where it occupies the lowest 12 feet of the cliff (Fig. 10), it is found to have become more coarsely pebbly in the upper part, while a persistent reddish band of ironsand, 8 to 10 feet above it, also has assumed a pebbly facies, and contains scattered *Exogyra sinuata*.

Where their outcrop passes from the cliff to the shore, the pebble beds are usually covered by talus. Their character, however, is well shown in the blocks of them which (with masses fallen from higher beds) strew the shore between 400 and 500 yards south of Shanklin Chine. Here the pebbles are at their coarsest, those of green-stained quartz ranging up to 1½ inches, and those of sandstone and other darker siliceous rocks up to three or four inches in diameter; the sandstones often being subangular.[3] With the pebbles are many pieces of wood, but most of the fossil-wood on the beach is derived from a nodular bed in the Sandrock, described below.

In darker greensand, 10 to 25 feet above the pebble-beds, there are two layers and some impersistent seams of well-preserved *Exogyra sinuata*, whose stout, flesh-coloured shells, and the "knolls" of pearly *Rhynchonella parvirostris* (J. Sow.) associated with them, stand out with exceptional distinctness on the face of the cliff; also inclusions of light speckled greensand with large, white, ramose bryozoa (*Siphodictyum gracile* Lonsd., *Chisma furcillata* Lonsd., *Choristopetalum impar* Lonsd., &c.), and nests of *Serpulae*, more clearly seen in the wave-washed detritus on the beach. These Exogyra Beds, forming the foot of Shanklin Point and the southern part of the adjacent Horse Ledge, are at higher horizons than any of the similar beds noticed in the Atherfield section. Fitton refers them (together, apparently, with all the underlying fossiliferous beds exposed in Knock Cliff) to his Group XIII, which is comparatively barren

---

[1]T. Leighton describes a fall of similar rock at this spot, and doubtfully refers it to Group XII. *Proc. Geol. Assoc.*, vol. xiii., 1894, pp. 188–190.

[2]Shanklin Chalybeate Spa is supplied from these beds:

[3]These pebble-beds are not mentioned by Fitton. G. W. Lamplugh appears to have been the first to describe them, in '*Summary of Progress of the Geol. Survey for* 1900', p. 119...

in Walpen undercliff. Mr. G. W. Lamplugh has noted the occurrence of *Acanthoplites cornuelianum* (d'Orb.) in Horse Ledge.

The Exogyra Beds pass up into a more argillaceous and pyritous greensand, about 20 feet thick, and containing fossiliferous concretionary ironstone, which makes little show in the cliff, but appears in the shore-ledges and among the beach-material in the form of tough, dark-grey to brown, cinder-like, subspherical masses, each a little compendium of Lower Greensand mollusca. Among the species abundantly represented in the clustered moulds, and casts are, *Thetironia minor, Trigonia alaeformis, Gervillia sublanceolata, Panopaea gurgitis*, with *Aporrhais robinaldina?* and other gasteropods, and *Terebratula sella*. These concretions and their contents resemble those in Group XIV at Blackgang, and can be matched in the Sandgate Beds of Sussex. The clayey greensand containing them runs out to sea in Yellow Ledge,[1] 350 yards south of Horse Ledge.

The next 20 feet of greyish greensand is poor in fossils. Above it lies a conspicuous bed, 8 feet thick, of grey sandy clay, which descends to the beach 300 yards short of Luccomb Chine. It corresponds to the similar but thicker clay-bed which forms the highest member of the Ferruginous Sands at Blackgang. In Knock Cliff its position is marked by the ledge or shelf (*h*, Fig. 10) which runs out at the clifftop 300 yds south of Shanklin Chine. The bed has been traced inland through brick-pits at Lower Hide and Sandford.

The *Sandrock Series* is clearly exposed on the coast from Knock Cliff to Bonchurch. Its base is marked by the ledge or undercliff formed by the clay last described. A descending section is as follows:

"Sandrock Series at Luccomb and Knock Cliff

		ft
"Carstone (p. 44)		
"Sandrock Series	⌈ Bright yellow and white sand with laminæ of blue clay in planes of current-bedding. A few bands of very green sand throwing out chalybeate water	35
	White and grey sand	50
	Very green clayey grit, forming a ledge in the cliff, and throwing out water	8
	⌊ White and ashy grey sand and sandrock	20
"Ferruginous Sands [dark sandy clay].		

113"[2]

The "green clayey grit", responsible for the higher and smaller ledge in Knock Cliff (Fig. 10, *g*), is about 10 feet above the beach at the mouth of Luccomb Chine. It is rich in plant-remains and especially noteworthy as the probable source of the rare and interesting cycadophyte, *Bennettites gibsonianus* Carr., recorded from this locality. The bed contains phosphatic and pyritic concretions, which, with mineralised wood, occur most abundantly in a pebbly band at the base, where they are often cemented into cakes of tough nodular stone. Much of the wood is in shapely pieces, like billets cut from sapling firs. Tapered cones resembling those of the spruce also occur.

The upper beds of the Sandrock are accessible in the cliff about Dunnose and in Monk's Bay (p. 44).

[1]The "Horse Ledge" of Fitton, *op. cit.*, p. 319.

[2]'Geology of the Isle of Wight,' *Mem. Geol. Surv.*, 2nd ed., 1889, p. 34.

INLAND SECTIONS

ALONG THE CENTRAL DOWNS

Little is to be seen of the *Atherfield Clay* inland, and such small exposures as occur are devoid of interest. Parts of the overlying sandy divisions, on the other hand, are displayed in a large number of pits and road-cuttings, only a selection of which can be noticed in the present work. Fossils are rarely encountered.

The *Ferruginous Sands* and *Sandrock Series* will be taken together.

"Commencing our description on the west, we find the Ferruginous Sands rising into a characteristic escarpment, slightly lower than the Chalk Downs, which runs eastward from Compton Bay on the north side of Brook, Mottistone, and Brixton. The higher part of the ridge is formed by the iron-sand which comes down to the beach on the west side of Compton Chine. The more massive ironsand which forms the cliff on the east side of Compton Chine crops out in the southern slope of the hill, and gives rise to the terrace of deep-red sand on which Brook Church stands. The position of the Sandrock Series is marked by the abundance of white sand in the soil.

"At Mottistone a ravine has been cut through the Ferruginous Sands. The top of the Atherfield Clay seems to occur at the Church. The clay is overlain by a great thickness of ferruginous clayey sands with a marked bed of brown iron-sand, which seems to be the same as that on the east side of Compton Chine."[1]

Blocks of dark iron-sandstone, of the same kind as that composing the Longstone menhir and its recumbent neighbour, abound in the soil on Castle Hill. Many include portions of a pebble-bed in which rounded pieces of silicified, chert-bearing, fossiliferous limestone, of Portlandian aspect, are mingled with more numerous pebbles of quartz.

The passage into the Sandrock is seen at the upper end of the ravine near the Longstone, and the same beds are less clearly exposed in the lane to Calbourne, by Black Barrow Hill, which is composed of white and grey sandrock. The current-bedded sands of this series by the roadside at Rock are remarkable for their varied and harmonious colouring. Above them is seen the pebbly ironstone base of the Carstone.

Good sections in the Ferruginous Sands occur in the lanes on the ridge eastward of Rock, near Yafford Mill, at Wolverton, and in the Shorwell-Atherfield road-cutting near the latter place; also, farther east, in the road-cuttings at Kingston.

"The sections in the Sandrock Series are more numerous. The beds of rock, which become a noticeable feature above Brixton, increase in number and thickness eastwards, and form small features along the strike near West Court and Presford. They are generally white, though tinged here and there with red or yellow. So abundant is the white sand soil on these strata that some of the fields on the east side of Bucks had the appearance of being partly covered with snow in the dry summer of 1887."[2]

Near Cridmore, the upper beds of the Ferruginous Sands acquire a Sandrock facies, making it difficult to separate the two series. After passing the Medina,

---

[1] *Ibid.*, p. 40.

[2] *Ibid.*, p. 41.

however, the base of the Sandrock is marked by a bed of coarse white quartz-grit, which can be seen about Upper Yard, and is of almost gravelly coarseness in a pit 300 yards north-west of Birchmore.

The top of the Sandrock is exceptionally well displayed in the long face of the Marvel Wood sand-pit, which forms so conspicuous a feature from the railway between Shide and Blackwater.

Marvel Wood Sand-pit

		ft
Carstone	Ferruginous grit, irregularly cemented in bands of iron oxide; small pebbles in the lower part .. .. .. seen for	12
	Grey sand with fragments of clay, having the appearance of a reconstructed bed (*see also* p. 42), resting on the edges of the current-bedding below	3
Sandrock	White sands with current-bedding and fine seams of grey clay ..	30+

The grey sand, which contains scattered quartz-pebbles and ironstone concretions, has been grouped with the Sandrock Series, but as it passes into the Carstone it is more consistently referable to that division. About 30 feet lower than the floor of the pit near its northern end, a dark blue-grey clay (probably the upper clay of Knock Cliff, *g*, Fig. 10) was shown in an adjacent well, dug in 1919.

A similar clay is seen near the middle of the section in Standen sand-pit, which shows upwards of 70 feet of the Sandrock Series. The Ferruginous Sands are exposed in cuttings or pits near Stone; south of Garrett's; about Arreton and Merston (or Merstone); at Horringford Station and Newchurch, and west of Adgestone; while the Sandrock appears in several places about Knighton and Kern.

AROUND THE SOUTHERN DOWNS

In describing the Atherfield section mention was made of an escarpment, formed by the firm sands of Groups XIII and XIV, which run through Pyle, Corve, and Kingston. "There are many sections in the roads descending the hills at these places. On the top and extending nearly to the brow of the terrace, soft, brown, buff, and white sand appears, similar to the sand noted at Cridmore, and approaching the type of the Sandrock Series. Lower in the hill-side, greyish-green sand follows, weathering brown, and of considerable thickness. On descending to the foot of the escarpment, we find a line of springs and a belt of peaty ground marking the outcrop of a soft and clayey bed, doubtless the 'foliated sand and clay' of Walpen Chine (Group XII of Fitton). The escarpment spoken of runs through Kingston, and, sweeping thence to the south-west round Gun Hill, points for Haslett and Wolverton, but becomes obscure in that neighbourhood.

"A second terrace is formed locally by a thick bed of red and brown sand with numerous grains of iron-oxide. This feature includes the bold brow known as Warren Hill, three-quarters of a mile west of Corve, and stretches thence by Dungewood towards Small Moor. There, like the other terrace, it also becomes obscure, so that whether it is a continuation of the bed which we traced by Brook Church must be left in doubt."[1] The source of the Medina

---

[1] *Ibid.*, p. 44.

at Chale Green is situated on the upper of these two terraces. Blake Down is a spur of the uppermost beds of the Ferruginous Sands, capped with flint gravel. "As the river is about 100 feet below the highest strata of this spur, the 'foliated sand and clay' might be expected to be reached. There can be little doubt that this is the case, for a terrace, closely resembling that of Pyle, Corve, and Kingston, runs through Godshill, north of Sandford, towards Lessland, and perhaps to Branstone. From the foot of the bold brow which terminates this terrace at Godshill, springs wander through wide peaty marshes, as at Corve, while the brow itself is composed of a ferruginous sand and greyish-green sand, exposed to considerable depth in the road-cuttings.

"The lower beds of the Sandrock Series are seen in a pit near Sibbecks, which gives the following section:

	ft
"Soft sands with seams of clay	20
Soft yellow and white sandrock (perhaps the third sandrock of Fitton).. ..	18
Thin bedded yellow and white sand with brown loamy partings..	6+

"Similar beds are seen in the grounds of Wydcombe, Redhill, Fairfields, and under the gravel at Ford Farm. Near Itchall a pit exposes the top of the series, namely, white sandstone, more than 15 feet thick, overlain by eight feet of Carstone. The base of the series is difficult to fix throughout the neighbourhood of Chale Green, but a blue clay seen in the brook south of Roud, in the lane at Russell's Farm, and in the high road north-east of this farm, is presumably the same bed which we have already noticed at the top of the Ferruginous Sands at Shanklin [h, Fig. 10, p. 35.].

"The characteristic scenery produced by the Sandrock Series and the overlying Carstone is admirably shown around Sainham and Godshill Park. The base line of the Carstone, the beds being nearly horizontal, meanders round a number of short but deep valleys, the sides of which are composed of bright-white sand and sandrock.

"A remarkably coarse grit has been already described as occurring at the base of this series near Blackwater; a somewhat similar bed may be noticed in a lane south of Sandford, but not elsewhere. The clay-bed of Roud, however, referred to above, seems to have been well developed at Sandford, where it was formerly worked for bricks, and where it is still exposed to a depth of 8 feet. An outlier of the Sandrock Series occurs here, its top capped with gravel, its sides showing the usual white sand soil, while a line of springs around its base marks the position of the clay-bed.

"Crossing the Wroxall stream, we find a sand-pit near Winstone, showing 10 feet of white sand, and another by the side of the railway half a mile east of Winstone, presenting more than 18 feet of white sand with thin lines of clay."[1]

The clay-bed at the top of the Ferruginous Sands has been worked for bricks by the side of the railway at Lower Hide. The higher clay, about 20 feet above it in the Sandrock Series in Knock Cliff (Fig. 10), is seen to the west of Lower Hide in the railway cuttings, one of which shows:

---

[1]Ibid., pp. 44–46.

"Railway Cutting three-quarters of a mile west of Shanklin

	ft
Dark clayey sand	4
Dark-green sandy clay with scattered grit and pyritised wood	15
Brown pebbly and ferruginous grit with wood, about	½
White sand with black grains	2
Hard brown pebbly rock	2
Coarse brown grit with numerous concretions	5
Grey sand or white sand with black grains	5
White sandrock with bright-yellow and brown staining	14
Dark sands	3+
	50½

"The strata dip gently (at about 2° to 3°) a little to the south of west, and the green clay slopes down to the level of the rails in the next cutting. The sands lying upon this clay are dark and ferruginous, but are not well seen.

"The upper clay-bed, seen near Upper Hide, runs along the valley in Apsecastle Wood, where it has caused a good deal of slipping; the lower clay-bed occurs at Apse Farm, but elsewhere is overspread by a downwash of sand.

"The Ferruginous Sands between these localities and the River Yar form an undulating tract, in part overspread with river-gravel, but in part rising into flat-topped hills capped with gravel. The dip, if any exists, is too gentle to be detected in the small sections that occur, except on Blackpan Common.

"The features of this tract suggest that the same beds which form the escarpments of Pyle and Kingston, and of Godshill, extend here across the valley of the Yar in a neck of about a mile in breadth. The base line of the beds on the east side of the neck seems to run from the cliff near Little Stairs Point, by the west of Lake, past Borthwood, across the river near Alverstone, and thence eastwards. The western boundary, which we have already traced through Godshill to near Branstone, seems to be continued in the hill on which Newchurch stands, and to trend thence eastwards, but all evidence of its position is lost in the valley."[1]

THE CARSTONE

The name Carstone was first applied to the highly ferruginous coarse sand or grit, forming the upper part of Dr. Fitton's Group XVI, by Sir Aubrey Strahan in 1889, on account of its resemblance to the Carstone of Lincolnshire and Norfolk, "of which", he remarks, "there is reason to suppose it to be the stratigraphical equivalent."[2]

The Carstone of the above-named counties passes up into strata of Lower Selbornian age which, in the South of England, have a thin, sandy, phosphate-bearing basement-bed, referable to the Albian Zone of *Douvilléiceras mammillatum*, a zone now generally regarded as the lowest member of the Selbornian, and of the British Upper Cretaceous system. Of that basement-bed, the Carstone of the Isle of Wight is probably a development, for although it greatly exceeds in thickness the lithologically similar Mammillatum Zone of

[1]*Ibid.*, pp. 46, 47.

[2]'Geology of the Isle of Wight,' *Mem. Geol. Surv.*, 2nd ed., p. 52.

D

Surrey, Hants, and Dorset, and has so far yielded no example of the characteristic ammonoid, its scanty and ill-preserved fossils include the Selbornian species, *Exogyra conica* (J. de C. Sow.), *Lima (Mantellum) gaultina* Woods (*L. parallela* Newt. & Jukes-Browne), *Syncyclonema orbicularis* (J. Sow.), *Neithea quinquecostata* (J. Sow.), and *Cleoniceras beudanti* (Brug.), the last named being a species commonly associated with *Douvilléiceras mammillatum* (Schloth.), and ranging above it. A few specifically determinable Lower Greensand (Aptian) fossils also occur, such as *Plicatula carteroniana* d'Orb., and *Leda scapha* (d'Orb.) (*Nuculana*). It is the Upper Cretaceous species, however, that date the Carstone; and the occurrence in it (albeit infrequent) of remanié Lower Greensand fossils, is but one of a number of slight indications of a break between the Carstone and the beds upon which it rests.

In its more familiar aspect, the Carstone is a coarse sand and friable sandstone, of warm brown to light gingerbread tint, laced with seams and veins of iron oxide. An argillaceous element is scarcely indicated, and there is little or nothing to suggest an affinity with the Selbornian Beds; but where unweathered it is a dark olive-green, glauconitic, loamy sand with irregular laminae of blue clay, and closely resembles the basal beds of the Gault as seen in deep brick-pits on the Mainland.

While the other divisions of the Lower Greensand thicken southward, the Carstone thickens to the north-east, from a few inches at Punfield on the Dorset coast, to 6 feet at Compton Bay, 12 feet near Blackgang, 30 feet near Bonchurch, and 72 feet at Redcliff (Fig. 5, p. 22).

We notice first the principal exposures along the Central Downs between Compton Bay and Redcliff, and subsequently those around the Southern Downs.

COMPTON BAY TO REDCLIFF

At Compton Bay the Carstone is a brown sandstone having at its base a three-inch band of small quartzite pebbles, subcylindrical phosphatic concretions evidently formed *in situ*, rolled phosphatic nodules, and bits of wood. The Carstone passes up into the dark blue sandy clay of the Gault, and rests, with a slight unevenness, on a bluish sandy clay, which seems to belong to the Sandrock Series. In the indigenous phosphatic concretions Mr. Lamplugh observed casts of marine shells (cf. *Nuculana, Turbo, Trochus, &c.*).[1]

The base of the Carstone is exposed at Rock (p. 38). Farther east, near Coombe Tower, this division begins to form a distinct feature in the landscape, and eventually gives rise to the most pronounced of the Lower Greensand ridges.

The junction with the Sandrock can be seen in a pit by the high road from Chale to Chillerton, near Billingham Cottage; in the Rookley-Blackwater road-cutting south-west of Birchmore; and in the cutting at Sandway, 300 yards east of Whitecroft.

At Marvel Wood, north-west of Blackwater, the Carstone rises into a strongly-marked ridge, crowned with pines, about 190 feet above the Medina. The section there is noticed above (p. 39). As pointed out in the last edition of the Geological Survey Memoir on the Island, the bottom-bed of the Carstone at this spot looks as if it were a reconstruction of the clays and white sand of the Sandrock Series, upon which it rests with an appearance of unconformity.

---

[1] MS. note, 1900.

Beyond Marvel Wood the topographic influence of the high dips more than counterbalances that of the increasing thickness of the Carstone, which thenceforward makes only a slight and impersistent feature. There are exposures east of Standen; in the lane at Great East Standen; and 300 yards south-east of Heasley Lodge, near Arreton.

At Knighton the Carstone-ridge is more marked, and the rock is exposed in the wooded bank east of the brook; also in the valley a quarter of a mile west of Kern, and in the copse a quarter of a mile south-east of Yarbridge.

The coast-section at Redcliff has already been described (p. 30). The Carstone here attains its greatest thickness in the Island, namely 72¾ feet. Whitish and pale-brown phosphatic concretions are thinly distributed throughout, and are most noticeable near the passage into the Gault. They consist of cemented masses of grit, often with indefinite boundaries, and evidently formed *in situ*. A few contain clusters of *Exogyra conica* (J. de C. Sow.). In one of them, near the middle of the Carstone, Mr. Lamplugh found a fragmentary cast of an ammonoid, cf. *Cleoniceras beudanti* (Brongn.).[1]

FROM NITON TO GODSHILL PARK AND BONCHURCH

In the Undercliff below Niton and about Blackgang Chine there are several good exposures, of which that described below will serve as the type:

Section above Chalybeate Spring, near South View House

		ft	in.
"Gault; blue clay passing down.			
	Brown grit, interbedded with grey clay, and containing phosphatic nodules in the upper part	8	0
"Carstone	Blue clay	3	0
	Reddish-brown grit, very red in parts	1	0
	Line of small quartz pebbles with rolled phosphatic nodules up to 2 inches in diameter	0	2
"Sandrock Series (for details, *see* p. 27).			

	12 2"[2]

As in the Compton Bay section, some of the phosphatic nodules appear to be derivative.

In Blackgang Chine, and on both sides of it, the Carstone and part of the overlying Gault are repeatedly exposed. North of the chine the Carstone strikes inland, and can be seen in small openings along the western side and at the northern end of St. Catherine's Down. North-east of the Down it forms the upper part of the three hills near Sibbecks. Its base can be seen in sandpits 300 yards west, and the same distance north, of Itchall; also at Sheepwash, where the Carstone forms a feature corresponding to that at Marvel Wood. The strata being nearly horizontal, the Carstone runs along the tops of steep spurs of white sand and sandrock that jut out from the hill-side. South of Godshill Park, as in many other places on the slopes of the Southern Downs, the Carstone is covered by masses of clay that have flowed down from the Gault.

In Appuldurcombe Park there are other extensive Gault slips. The Carstone is seen by the road-side north of Wroxall, and its base is well exposed at Yard Farm, where it rests on white sand.

---

[1]MS. note, 1900.

[2]'Geology of the Isle of Wight,' *Mem. Geol. Surv.*, 1889, p. 57.

In the lower part of Luccomb Chine, and in the cliffs thence south and south-westward to Bonchurch, the Carstone is finely displayed. The section in Monk's Bay is as follows:

Section in Monk's Bay

		ft	in.
"Gault. Blue micaceous clay passing down.			
	Blue micaceous clay with lines of grit	3	0
	Brown ferruginous rock with derived phosphatic concretions containing oolitic grains of iron oxide	1	0
"Carstone	Sandy and gritty blue clay, passing down	1	0
	Clayey brown grit with nodules as above	3	0
	Brown grit	6	0
	Brown grit with many small pebbles	20	0
	Pebbly band, with quartzites up to half-an-inch in length ..	0	3–6
"Sandrock Series. Bright-yellow and white sand [with seams of laminated grey clay].			
		34	6"[1]

FIG. 11.   *Junction of Carstone and Sandrock, Monk's Bay*
Scale: 1 inch = 4 feet

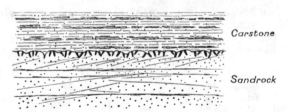

Showing the change in the character of the stratification at the junction, and the slightly eroded and bored top of the Sandrock.

The base of the Carstone is uneven, the pebbles descending into little pockets in the Sandrock, the top of which is riddled with clayfilled borings (Fig. 11). The current-bedding planes in the Sandrock are truncated by the Carstone. A derived and water-worn specimen of *Enallaster fittoni* Forbes was found in the "clayey brown grit, 3 feet". The species is recorded from the Atherfield Clay and Ferruginous Sands. In the "pebbly band", at the bottom of the Carstone, *Exogyra sinuata* occurs as an indigenous fossil, but it is rare.

---

[1]*Ibid.*, p. 59.

Chapter IV

SELBORNIAN BEDS:
GAULT AND UPPER GREENSAND

THE GAULT and Upper Greensand are different lithological facies of a single sedimentary series, for which the name Selbornian, proposed in 1900 by the late A. J. Jukes-Browne, has been generally adopted. The broad division of this series, into blue clays and marls below and green sands above, holds good in the Isle of Wight as in the South-Eastern Counties, though the two divisions are so closely connected by a thick group of passage-beds that difficulty has been experienced in deciding where to draw the line between them. We here follow Jukes-Browne in including the passage-beds in the Upper Greensand on palæontological grounds.[1] The Upper Greensand and Passage Beds of the Isle of Wight appear to be the equivalent of the Upper Gault of Folkestone. Owing, however, to the local scarcity of Lower Selbornian fossils, a close comparison of the Gault Beds of the Island with those of the standard section in Folkestone cliffs is impracticable.

Should further research prove the Carstone to belong to the *Douvilléiceras mammillatum* Zone, the Selbornian of the Isle of Wight will require to be extended downward to the top of the Sandrock. The probability of this correlation has already been pointed out. It was chiefly the exceptional thickness attained by the Carstone in the eastern part of the Island that deterred Jukes-Browne from including it in the Selbornian Series. At present, that series comprises:

Upper Greensand	{ Glauconitic Sands and Sandstones, 82 to 86 feet	{	Zones of *Cardiaster fossarius* and
Passage Beds	Sandy Clays and Marls, 15 to 44 feet		*Mortoniceras rostratum.*
Gault	Clays and Marls, 95 to 103 feet ..	{	Zones of *Hoplites denarius* and *H. interruptus*

As the Passage Beds belong to the Zone of *Mortoniceras rostratum*, which includes most of the overlying beds, they are described below under the heading Upper Greensand.

The Selbornian Beds are wholly marine, and are inferred to have accumulated at depths increasing from 50 to 100 fathoms, near the beginning of the period of deposition, to 200 fathoms or more at the end of that period, by which time the world-wide overflowing of the continental border-lands, known as the Cenomanian transgression had fairly set in.

GAULT

The Carstone passes into the Gault by an accession of silty micaceous mud and a concomitant failure of the coarse pebbly sand or grit: the transition being accompanied by a change of colour, from the ferruginous-brown (where

---

[1] 'Gault and Upper Greensand of England,' *Mem. Geol. Survey*, 1900, p. 126.

unweathered, dark-green) of the typical Carstone to the dark-blue tint characteristic of the Gault. The mass of the Gault is an indistinctly-bedded silty clay, with scattered, white-coated phosphatic concretions, and acicular selenite, which doubtless, replaces much of the calcium carbonate originally disseminated through the clay in the forms of calcareous mud and hard parts of various organisms.

The few fossils of zonal value so far recorded were found near the upper and lower limits of the formation. Probably the greater part of the blue clay belongs to the Zone of *Hoplites interruptus*, which species has been obtained low down in it at Redcliff and Compton Bay. At Bonchurch, *Cleoniceras beudanti* (Brongn.)—another Lower Selbornian ammonoid—was met with 28 feet above the Carstone; and *Hoplites denarius* (J. Sow.) occurs near the Passage Beds at Compton Bay. The section in the last-named locality is the best in the Island.

Section at Compton Bay

		ft
Passage Beds:	Dark bluish sandy clays.	
	Mortoniceras rostratum (J. Sow.)	
	Greenish clay	2
	Dark blue clay	20
	Hoplites denarius (J. Sow.), *Lima parallela* d'Orb.	
Gault	*Panopaea plicata* J. Sow. (*Pleuromya*.)	
(lower.)	*Syncyclonema orbicularis* (J. Sow.)	
	Vermicularia concava (J. Sow.), Fish-scales, &c.	
	Blue Clay	73
	Hoplites interruptus (Brongn.) *Gyrodes genti* (J. Sow.)	
	(*Natica*), *Inoceramus sulcatus* Park, &c. in lower part.	
Carstone:	Brown sand.	

At Blackgang the whole of the Gault is exposed, but is not easily accessible. A few Lower Gault fossils have been found about Southlands House, and in the ravine west of the hotel.

The lowest beds of the Gault, much obscured by wash and slips, are seen in the cliffs between Bonchurch and Knock Cliff, the passage into the Carstone being conveniently situated for examination in the brow of the low cliff at Monk's Bay. Fish-remains, *Cleoniceras beudanti* (Brongn.), *Syncyclonema orbicularis* (J. Sow.), and a few other fossils have been noticed at about 28 feet above the base of the formation in this neighbourhood. Bits of lignite are not uncommon. Phosphate casts of *Hoplites interruptus* occur on the beach at Dunnose.

In Sandown Bay the Gault crops out in the hollow between Redcliff and Culver Cliff. The lowest beds, containing casts of *Hoplites interruptus* and *Inoceramus concentricus* Park., are at present clearly exposed on the verge of the cliff south of the pathway to the shore, but the rest are obscured by overgrown slips. Fossils, however, have been observed at horizons about 5, 40, and 50 feet from the top of the Gault: they include *Schloenbachia bouchardianus* d'Orb. (at 50 feet), and 17 other forms of little or no value for purposes of correlation within the limits of the Selbornian Series.

Inland, the Gault occupies narrow belts of ground overspread by wash and rubble from the Upper Greensand and Chalk, and sections are rare. Weathered Gault clays are worked in brick-pits west of Rookley, and at Bierley near

Niton. The brick-pits by the side of the railway between Cliff Farm near Shanklin and Wroxall are dug in Gault that has flowed down the hill-side.

The landslips associated with the Gault are noticed in a later chapter (p. 177).

UPPER GREENSAND

This division gives rise to some conspicuous features in the landscapes of the southern part of the Island, such as the cliff which dominates the Undercliff from Bonchurch to Blackgang, and the inland bluffs of St. Catherine's Down, Gatcliff, and Cook's Castle (Fig. 12). In the central range it forms the scarp of Rams Down, and the hog-backed ridges south of the Chalk near Brading.

The *Passage Beds* consist of blue to blue-grey silty to sandy micaceous clays and clayey sands, partly calcareous and nodular; the argillaceous element predominating below, the arenaceous above. Their thickness decreases from about 40 or 50 feet in the western and southern parts of the Island to about 15 feet in the Culver section in the east. Of the fossils, which are not plentiful, the most noteworthy are *Vermicularia concava* (J. Sow.) and *Mortoniceras rostratum* (J. Sow.), the latter making its first appearance in the lowest part of these beds.

The *Upper Greensand* proper is mainly composed of speckled, light-greenish to bluish-grey sandstones, in which fine quartz-sand and silt, with a variable proportion of glauconite granules and flakes of white mica, are more or less firmly bound together by white amorphous alumina silicate, or by calcite. Small chocolate-coloured phosphatic concretions, often of angular outline, occur in most of the beds, and especially in the more glauconitic sandstones. Cylindrical and tubular aggregations of the lighter and of the darker mineral particles, observable almost throughout the formation, bear witness to the activities of boring and burrowing animals, when the sands were in course of deposition.

Many of the beds abound in hard, calcareo-siliceous nodules, known as "cornstones",[1] which give a rugged character to weathered surfaces; others contain larger calcareous concretions or "doggers". Brown, bluish, and black chert, of which there is, in places, a great development in the higher beds, occurs in scattered concretions, and in definite courses of the same; also diffusedly, forming ill-defined masses of cherty sandstone. Spicules of siliceous sponges, or their moulds (either vacant or filled with glauconite), are a notable feature of the cherty sandstones.

The stratification is regular, and, in conjunction with vertical jointing, gives the sides of the quarries the appearance of masonry. While the beds individually vary much in width, their aggregate thickness remains about the same (namely, 80 to 90 feet) throughout the visible extent of the Upper Greensand.

Messrs. Jukes-Browne and W. Hill[2] divide the Upper Greensand and Passage Beds of the Undercliff into two zones and six lithological stages, as shown in the subjoined table:

---

[1] "Other local names, of less common occurrence, are 'hassock' for the sands, 'whills 'for sandstone, 'shotter-wick' for chert, 'firestone' for a stone formerly employed for lining hearths, and 'rubstone' for a stone once used for whitening hearths or doorsteps." 'Geology of the Isle of Wight,' *Mem. Geol. Surv.*, 2nd ed., 1889, p. 66.

[2] Jukes-Browne, *op. cit.*, p. 137.

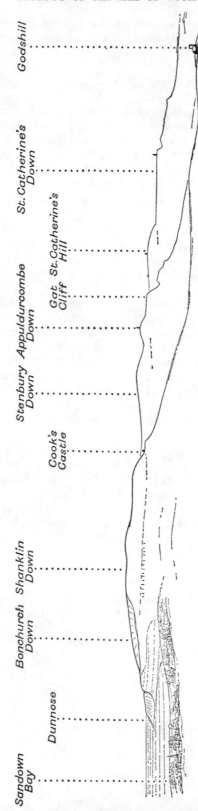

FIG. 12.   Outlines of the Southern Downs, from the north-east

Note the angular feature marking the outcrop of the Upper Greensand at Cook's Castle, Gat Cliff, and St. Catherine's Down

Upper Greensand in the Undercliff

			ft
Zone of *Cardiaster fossarius*	F.	Sands with layers of calciferous concretions, often partly phosphatised	about 6
	E.	Chert Beds	22 to 24
Zone of *Mortoniceras rostratum*	D.	Firestones and Freestones [8–18 feet]	30 to 40
	C.	Sandstoes with phosphatic nodules and courses of large calcareous doggers	
	B.	Rough sandstones with irregular concretions	30 to 40
	A.	Bluish sandy clay or micaceous silt [Passage Beds]	43 to 50
		Total about	130 to 160

The sands and sandstones of divisions (B) and (C), which lie between the the Passage Beds and the Freestones, have yielded the greater number of the fossils, including a turtle (*Hylaeochelys lata* Owen), fish-teeth (*Lamna*), *Mortoniceras rostratum* (J. Sow.), *Hoplites splendens* (J. Sow.), *Schloenbachia varicosa* (J. de C. Sow.), *Nautilus spp.*, *Gyrodes genti* (J. Sow.), *Neithea quadricostata* (J. Sow.), *Plicatula gurgitis* Pict. & Roux, *Trigonia aliformis* Park., *Echinospatagus murchisonianus* Mant., and sponges, including *Siphonia tulipa* Zittel.

From the Freestones (D), which contain a similar assemblage, two examples of the cycad *Clathraria lyelli* Mant. have been obtained. The same species has been seen in the Chert Beds (E), which yield *Aequipecten asper* (Lam.), *Arca mailleana* d'Orb., *Lima semiornata* d'Orb., &c.

The highest division (F) also contains *Aequipecten asper*, with *Plagiostoma globosa* (J. de C. Sow.), *Discoidea subucula* Klein, and *Cardiaster fossarius* Ben., all four species, and many associated forms, ranging into the Chalk.

With one exception, the six lithological divisions (A to F) are recognisable in all the coast sections, as Jukes-Browne has shown. The exception is the Freestone division (D), which is limited in its occurrences to the Southern Downs and adjacent parts of the Central Downs near Gatcombe. The bands of chert especially characteristic of division (E)– the "Chert Beds"—have their greatest development in the same area as the Freestones, and are but feebly represented near the eastern and western ends of the Island.

DESCRIPTION OF SECTIONS

Having regard to the limited space available in this Memoir, and to the rather monotonous character of the Upper Greensand, we include a detailed description of only one of the coast-sections (Gore Cliff), and merely draw attention to noteworthy peculiarities of the others.

We begin with the *Undercliff*, where the Upper Greensand is seen in a form typical of the southern and central parts of the Island. Here the Chert Beds present vertical faces in which the regular bands of chert stand out in ledges between the grooves worn in the intervening soft sands by wind and rain (Fig. 13). Beneath the Chert Beds, the main band of freestone, 5 feet thick, runs along the cliffs for some miles, and is usually recognisable at a glance. The so-called "malm-rock" (which only superficially resembles the true malm-rock of Surrey and Hants) forms a steep slope below the cliffs.

The general succession is well shown near Blackgang in the

Section at Gore Cliff

ft

"Chloritic Marl.

[F] Greenish grey glauconitic sands with two layers of calciferous concretions having brown phosphatised rinds .. ..   [5]

[E] Soft grey glauconitic sandstone with conspicuous layers of black or grey chert   10

Similar sandstone with layers of calcareo-siliceous concretions which here and there pass into chalcedonic chert   12

[D] Grey glauconitic sandstone with a layer of calcareous lumps or cornstones at base   2

'Bastard freestone,' a smooth fine-grained glauconitic sandstone weathering to a yellowish-grey or buff colour   1

'Freestone,' a massive fine-grained sandstone weathering a yellowish grey   5

[C] Grey sandstone, weathering buff, and containing small brown phosphatic nodules, and small ragstone lumps which weather out as rough projections 3½

Smooth grey sandstones with small brown phosphatic nodules ..   5

A series of large doggers or masses of calcareous sandstone in grey sand   4

Firm grey sandstone, weathering as usual, with some phosphatic nodules and a layer of calcareous concretions in the lower part ..   7½

Course of large calcareous doggers, which are grey inside and often enclose pieces of brown phosphate 1½

[B] Firm grey sandstone weathering irregularly into harder and softer portions; a few phosphates   13

Similar sandstone, but without phosphates   16

Course of hard and heavy doggers of compact bluish-grey siliceous limestone from 9 inches to   1

[A] Firm yellowish sand mottled with bluish grey   3

Bluish-grey marly micaceous sand, mottled with buff 10½

Similar sand with less of the buff mottling   6

Bluish grey fine micaceous sand or silt with a layer of smooth rounded doggers of grey siliceous limestone at the base   9

―――

115"

―――

A more convenient spot for examining the sandstones is the Cripple's Path, which ascends the cliff obliquely south-east of Niton. There, and in the cliff to the east, 12 feet of Chert Beds and about 80 feet of the underlying strata are exposed (Fig. 13). A similar section is to be seen at St. Lawrence Shute, where, however, the main freestone contains hard lumps which lessen its value as a building stone.

Cliffs and quarries about Ventor afford many good sections, and it is from them that most of the Upper Greensand fossils recorded from the Island have been obtained. The highest beds and their junction with the Chloritic Marl at the base of the Chalk, are displayed in a small quarry under St. Boniface Down, north-east of Trinity Church; in the yard of Ventor Station; and in the quarry west of Zigzag Road: the first and last of these sections taking in the Chert Beds, and the second showing the Freestones, in which the entrance to the tunnel, and several caves or adits used as storehouses, have been excavated. Dr. G. J. Hinde observed that the Chert Beds of the Station section

―――――――――――――――――

[1]Jukes-Browne, *op. cit.*, pp. 131, 132.

"so abound with [sponge] spicules that they may be considered as a continuous sponge-bed."[1]

FIG. 13.   *Sketch of the Upper Greensand escarpment in the Undercliff near Niton*

e. Chert Beds.   *d.* Freestones.   *c.* Sandstones with concretions.

Lower Chalk appears in the slope above the cliff. The road below is on slipped and fallen rock. Cripple's Path, mentioned in the text, is a short distance to the left (west).

The Southern Downs. Following the outcrop round the eastern and northern sides of these Downs from Ventor, we find a succession of quarries at or near the sides of the high road to Shanklin. The largest of them, in Greatwood Copse, half a mile south-west of Shanklin Church (St. John's), gives a clear section of the Freestone and Chert Beds, the former being moderately fossiliferous.

---

[1]'On Beds of Sponge Remains,' *Phil. Trans. Roy. Soc.*, vol. 176, 1886, p. 417.

Quarry on the north Side of Greatwood Copse

		ft	in.
"[E]	Chert, rag, and sand (top not seen)	15	0
	Rag	0	0–6
	Firestone	2	0
	Rag	0	0–8
	Firestone	2	0
	Rag	0	0–12
"[D]	Rubstone	0	8
	Freestone	4	0
	Rag	1	0
	Inferior stone or malm	5	0
	Rag	1	0
	Inferior stone	2	0"[1]

Many other exposures of these beds are to be seen in the inland cliff which contours the northern slope of the Downs, e.g,, in Cliff Copse, near Shanklin, in the pits south-east of Wroxall, at Gat Cliff, and farther west (Fig. 12, p. 48). Chert bands of exceptional thickness occur in St. Martin's Down. The railway tunnel between Wroxall and Ventor traverses the lower and middle beds of the Upper Greensand.[2]

"On the west side of St. Catherine's Down several small pits occur along the scarped brow formed by the chert and freestone, the former material being used for road-metal. The outcrop of the Upper Greensand is narrow, but steep, and on the broader slope of Gault lie many huge masses of Greensand that have slipped bodily down. The long flat-topped spur of St. Catherine's Down which juts out to the north, and marks the line of strike, is capped with a strip of Chert Beds, about 1,300 yards in length, but only from 50 to 80 yards in breadth, and terminates northwards in a remarkable semicircular hollow, which seems to have been formed by a landslip."[3]

Passing now to the *Central Downs*, we follow the Upper Greensand from Compton Bay to Culver Cliff.

In the cliff-section at Compton Bay the Upper Greensand is 130½ feet thick, including the Passage Beds (44 feet), which present the same features as in the Undercliff. The Freestone is wanting, however, while the Chert Beds are only one-third as thick as in the latter locality, and the chert is largely replaced by siliceo-calcareous concretions. The fossils include *Mortoniceras rostratum* which seems not to have been observed above the bed regarded as the highest of division (C).[4]

The most complete of the inland sections is that in the cutting of the Shalcombe road, north of Brook; all but the Passage Beds and a little of the overlying sands being shown. The Chert Beds, or what corresponds to them, contain little or no clear chert. As at Compton Bay, the Freestones are absent. Other exposures of the upper beds occur north of Mottistone and of Rock.

---

[1]'Geology of the Isle of Wight,' *Mem. Geol. Surv.*, 2nd ed., 1889, p. 70.

[2]'The cutting by which the tunnel is approached has been made in the Malm Rock, the Gault, so far as can be seen, lying about the level of the rails. At the south end of the tunnel the rails are about eight feet below the freestone; the tunnel descends southwards at the rate of 1 in 173, and is about 1,300 yards in length. From these data it may be calculated that the dip of the strata to the south amounts to 1 in 38 or an angle of rather less than 2°.' *Ibid.*, p. 72.

[3]*Ibid. loc. cit.*

[4]For detailed section, see Jukes-Browne, *op. cit.*, p. 140.

"Proceeding eastwards we find the Chert Beds at Coombe Tower beginning to form the feature, which becomes so conspicuous in the central and southern parts of the Island. In this neighbourhood the chert, white in colour and accompanied with much chalcedony, is exposed repeatedly all along the crest of the escarpment to Shorwell, where it is quarried, or rather dug, for building.

"East of Shorwell the escarpment becomes steadily bolder, and we find blue chert associated with the white along the crest of the hill. At the east end of this hill, over the Chillerton road, freestone is worked in a quarry below the Chert Beds, this being the most westerly appearance of the bed so prominent about Ventor."[1]

The Chert Beds, dipping southward, cap the small outlier which forms the ridge of Sibdown or Gossard Hill, west of Rookley. Numerous old quarries in them and the underlying Freestones indent the brow of the scarp above Gatcombe and Whitcombe, and some of the highest beds, with cornstones, appear in the shallow road-cutting south-east of Carisbrook Castle.

East of Carisbrook the bands of chert quickly decrease in number, but the Upper Greensand still forms a strong topographic feature in places where its dip is comparatively low, as about Knighton and Yaverland. Small sections are to be seen north-west of Kern, at Yarbridge, and north of Yaverland. About Yaverland, chert occurs only in isolated concretions, with a few feet of the junction with the Lower Chalk. Fossils noted in the highest beds hereabouts included a nautilus of the *N. elegans* J. Sow. type and ? *Mortoniceras rostratum* (J. Sow.), both ill-preserved.

At Culver Cliff the Upper Greensand is 98 feet thick, including 15 feet of Passage Beds which are here seen at their thinnest. The beds corresponding in position to the Freestones are so loaded with phosphatic and calcareous concretions as to be useless for building purposes, while the Chert Beds are reduced to less than 10 feet, and contain only a few lenticular masses of chert. On the other hand, the highest beds (F) are thicker than elsewhere (10 feet), and possibly in part replace the Chert Beds: they are made up as follows:

		ft
Chloritic Marl.		
[F]	Grey glauconitic sand, piped by overlying marl; layer of hard siliceo-calcareous concretions at top	1
	Ostrea vesiculosa J. Sow., *Exogyra conica* J. de C. Sow., &c.	
	Grey glauconitic marly sand with layers of calcareo-siliceous concretions	9
	Ostrea vesiculosa, *Exogyra conica*, *Plicatula gurgitis* Pict. & Roux, *Grammatodon carinatus*, (J. Sow.), &c.	
		10[2]

[1]'Geology of the Isle of Wight'; *Mem. Geol. Surv.*, 2nd ed., 1889, p. 71.

[2]For details (mostly lithological) of rest of section, see Jukes-Browne, *op. cit.*, p. 138.

Chapter V

THE CHALK

The main outcrop of this division of the Upper Cretaceous rocks runs the length of the Island, from the Needles to Culver Cliff. In the area of low-dipping to horizontal strata between Mottistone and Carisbrook, the outcrop surface is a combe-indented upland, which attains a width of over three miles, whereas in the rest of the range, where the dips are high, it is a sinuous ridge usually less than half-a-mile across. A large outlier of slightly-inclined Chalk, about 6½ miles in length by 2¼ in breadth, forms the higher parts of the Southern Downs.

Since the publication of the last edition of the Geological Survey Memoir on the Isle of Wight, in 1889, the Chalk has received more attention than any other formation in the Island. Among those whose researches have contributed most largely to the great advance in our knowledge of the stratigraphy of the lower beds of the Chalk, are the late William Hill (long known as an earnest student of the Upper Cretaceous rocks) and Mr. J. B. Hue, of Ventnor, whose notes were incorporated by the late A. J. Jukes-Browne in his memoir on the Lower and Middle Chalk of England.[1] For much of the information concerning the local features of the higher parts of this formation, which is given in his subsequent memoir on the Upper Chalk, Jukes-Browne was indebted to Hill, to Mr. R. M. Brydone, and to the late Charles Griffith, of Winchester College. The latter work, which formed the third volume of the "Cretaceous Rocks of Britain", published by the Geological Survey, was issued in 1904. Four years later there appeared the concluding part of Dr. A. W. Rowe's remarkable study of the White Chalk of the English Coast,[2] in which the zonal divisions of the Middle and Upper Chalk of the Isle of Wight were for the first time clearly defined, and their boundaries traced and mapped throughout the Central Downs. More recently, Mr. Brydone has published short papers relating chiefly to the delimitation of certain sub-divisions of the Upper Chalk of the Island and other parts of the South Coast. His repeated and ultimately successful efforts to partition the old unwieldy zone of *Actinocamax quadratus* meet with due recognition in the following pages. Mention should be made of Dr. W. Fraser Hume's work, "Chemical and Micromineralogical Researches on the Upper Cretaceous Zones, &c." (London, 1893), much of which relates to the Chalk of Culver Cliff.

In the Isle of Wight the Chalk attains its maximum known thickness for the British Isles, namely, about 1,630 feet. Here, as on the Mainland, it was formerly crudely divided into two parts, respectively characterised by the presence and the absence of flints, but for many years past three stages have been recognised, which roughly correspond to the Cenomanian, Turonian, and Senonian of Continental geologists. These three stages, distinguished in the later editions of the Geological Survey Map, are in turn divisible into a number

---

[1] *Mem. Geol. Survey*, 1903, pp. 79, 408.
[2] *Proc. Geol. Assoc.*, vol. xx., 1908, pp. 209–251, with plates and maps.

of zones and sub-zones, the classification adopted in the present memoir
being as follows:

Stages	Zones		Sub-Zones
	⌈ Belemnitella mucronata		
	Actinocamax quadratus		
	Offaster pilula		⌠ Offaster pilula
Upper			⌡ Echinocorys depressus
Chalk	⟨ Marsupites testudinarius		⌠ Marsupites
			⌡ Uintacrinus
	Micraster coranguinum		
	Micraster cortestudinarium		
	⌊ Holaster planus		
Middle	⌠ Terebratulina lata		
Chalk	⌡ Inoceramus labiatus		
Lower	⌠ Holaster subglobosus		Actinocamax plenus (at top)
Chalk	⌡ Schloenbachia varians		Stauronema carteri (at base)

The Chalk preserves the records of the deepest and most widespread submergence that has affected the British region since the Carboniferous period.
The depth of water in which it accumulated is inferred to have ranged from
about 200 to 600 fathoms or more. Increasing depth and distance from land is
indicated both by the change in the fauna and the decrease in the amount of
terrigenous sediment which are observed as one passes upward from the sandy
base of the Lower Chalk to the almost purely calcareous beds near the middle
of the Upper stage. The seams of laminated grey marl which recur throughout
the formation, and are often accompanied by signs of slight erosion, point to
variations in the trend and speed of currents, while periods of slow deposition
are marked by the development of nodular structure, increase in the per-
centages of calcium phosphate and fluoride, concentration of organic remains
(notably of sponges), and, in the case of the Upper Chalk, by a diminution in the
number of flints.

LOWER CHALK

This division, which includes the beds known as Grey Chalk and Chalk
Marl, shows a decrease in thickness westward, from about 210 feet at Culver
Cliff to 160 feet at Compton Bay, which is due to the thinning of some of the
beds in the Zone of Schloenbachia varians.

The Chloritic Marl of the Isle of Wight, as defined by Jukes-Browne, comprises a small group of beds, ranging from 4 to 12 feet in aggregate thickness,
and varying in character from dark-green, highly glauconitic, marly sand and
sandstone to light grey sandy marl. It affords a complete passage from the
Upper Selbornian to the Lower Chalk, though the transference, by boring and
burrowing organisms, of portions of the dark glauconitic sand into a multitude
of tubes and pockets in the underlying, lighter-coloured Selbornian sand,
gives an irregularlity to the contact which has been interpreted as an indication
of a stratigraphic break, with interformational erosion. The Marl, and especially
the dark-green part of it, contains a host of rough brown phosphatic concretions. There are also numerous larger nodules of hard concretionary limestone, similar to the cornstones and ragstones in the sands below, and, like
them, formed in situ.

Fossils abound in places, many species being represented both in the phosphatised and in the normal condition. Particularly noteworthy is the development of cephalopods (ammonoids) and sponges. Of the latter, *Stauronema carteri* Sollas, though occurring both above and below the Chloritic Marl, is sufficiently abundant in that division to form a fairly satisfactory subzonal index. There is no palæontological break at this horizon, but a great change takes place in the relative proportions of the species, many forms that are scarce in the Upper Selbornian becoming abruptly abundant in, or immediately above, the highest of the beds which Jukes-Browne includes in the Chloritic Marl.

On the whole, the Chloritic Marl presents a good example of a fairly deep-water marine deposit, slowly accumulated under tranquil conditions.

The beds forming the mass of the *S. varians* Zone are soft, laminated grey marls alternating with firmer homogeneous marly chalk of bluish tint and conchoidal fracture. The stratification is even and strongly marked. The lowest 10 to 20 feet of these beds is characterised by an abundance of *Plocoscyphia labrosa* (T. Smith) (= *maeandrina* Goldf.), which stands out in white convolute knobs on weathered and wave-worn surfaces. Pebbles of chalk enclosing this sponge are common on the southern shores of the Island. Farther up, cephalopods (*Scaphites, Baculites, Turrilites*) are plentiful in some localities; *Schloenbachia varians* (J. Sow.) occurs throughout the zone, and usually in profusion in the lowest beds.

At a distance of about 110 feet above the Chloritic Marl in the east of the Island, and of about 50 feet in the west, there occurs a lithological change, which roughly coincides with the lower limit of the *Holaster subglobosus* Zone. The chalk assumes a lighter tint (almost white when dry), loses its laminate structure, and forms massive beds with curved jointing. Tubules and elongate nodules of decomposed marcasite are distinctive features of this massive chalk. Fossils are infrequent: *Holaster subglobosus* (Leske), which appears before the lithological change just noted, occurs sparingly in the lower half of its zone, and is largely replaced by *Holaster trecensis* Leym. in the upper half.

The grey laminated ("Belemnite") marls of the *Actinocamax plenus* Subzone, 5 to 9 feet thick, at the upper limit of the Lower Chalk, contain impersistent bands of firm light-grey chalk. The characteristic belemnoid is seldom forthcoming. As at Winchester, it makes its first appearance a little below the Marls.

DESCRIPTION OF SECTIONS

We notice first the coast-sections, beginning on the east.

Section at Culver Cliff

		ft
Zone of *Holaster subglobosus*	*Act. plenus* subzone: grey marl with bands of lighter chalk ..	6
	Actinocamax plenus (de Blainv.)	
	Firm pale grey to white chalk in massive beds	85
	Holaster trecensis Leym., *H. subglobosus* (Leske), *Discoidea cylindrica* (Lam.), &c.	

			ft
	Grey chalk in regular courses .. .. about		45
	Aequipecten beaveri (J. Sow.)		
	Schloenbachia varians (J. Sow.)		
	Turrilites tuberculatus Bosc., &c.		
	Bluish-grey marly chalk with harder courses of grey chalk about		40
	S. varians, Terebratula biplicata J. Sow.		
	Soft bluish-grey marl, passing down into firmer sandy marl		
	with *Plocoscyphia labrosa* T. Smith .. .. .. about		15

Zone of Schloenbachia varians

Harder bluish sandy marl, with masses of *Plocoscyphia labrosa*
and some brown phosphatic concretions .. .. about   12
Schloenbachia varians (J. Sow.), *Serpula umbonata* J. de
C. Sow, &c.

Chloritic Marl
- c, Bluish-grey glauconitic marl with brown phosphatic concretions and bands of calcareous concretions .. .. 7½ ft
- *Stauronema carteri* Sol. .. ..
- *Card. fossarius* Bennett, *Aequipecten asper* (Lam.), *Lamna* (teeth)
- a, Layer of calcareous doggers .. .. 1 ft

8½

———
211½

THE UNDERCLIFF

The cliffs between Bonchurch and St. Catherine's Point afford many good sections in the Varians Zone. Most of them occur in the great slices of Upper Cretaceous strata that have slipped from the southern slope of the Downs some 300 to 400 feet above. A large number of fossils have been obtained here from beds in the lower two-thirds of the Varians Zone. Those from the Chloritic Marl include *Aequipecten asper* Lam., *Ae. puzosianus* d'Orb., *Plicatula gurgitis* Pict. & Roux, *Cardiaster fossarius* Ben., *Holaster laevis* de Luc, together with more characteristically Lower Chalk species, such as *Schloenbachia varians* (J. Sow.), *S. coupei* Brongn., *Turrilites tuberculatus* Bosc., *Nautilus deslongchampsianus* d'Orb., *Inoceramus latus* d'Orb., *Rhynchonella grasiana* d'Orb., *R. martini* Mant., *Micrabacia coronula* Goldf., *Plocoscyphia labrosa* (T. Smith), and *Stauronema carteri* Sollas.

Of the fossils observed in the rest of the Zone we need mention only *Metacantholites rotomagensis* (Brongn.), *Scaphites aequalis* J. Sow., *Kingena lima* (Defr.), and *Serpula umbonata* J. de C. Sowerby.

Above Ventor clear sections of the Chloritic Marl are to be seen in the yard of the Railway Station, and in a quarry under St. Boniface Down, north-east of Trinity Church. The succession in the latter is given below.

Section in St. Boniface Down

			ft	in.
	Chalk marl		15	0
	Two beds of hard grey chalk separated by 6 inches of marl		2	6
	Soft grey marl, slightly glauconitic		0	6

Zone of Schloenbachia varians

Chloritic Marl, 7 ft
- c, Firm greenish glauconitic sandy marl, full of phosphatic nodules and casts of fossils   3   0
  Schloenb. varians (J. Sow.), *S. coupei* Brongn., &c.
- b, Firm greenish sandy marl with hard concretions and a few phosphates, passing   1   3
  down into dark glauconitic sandy marl   2   0
- a, Layer of hard concretions with brown phosphatic crusts .. 6 inches to   0   9

E

		ft	in.
Selbornian (Upper Greensand)	Firm yellowish-green glauconitic sand, piped with the overlying marl	1	6
	Sand with calcareous brown-coated concretions and an irregular layer of grey chert	2	9
	Chert Beds		

The bed (*b*), absent at Culver Cliff, is seen again at St. Lawrence Shute, west of Ventor, where it has thinned to 6 inches, and the Chloritic Marl is only 4½ feet thick in all. In another exposure, in a slipped mass at Binnel Point, west of St. Lawrence Shute, bed (*b*) is missing, and the Marl is yet thinner. Further sections are to be seen in foundered blocks at Rocken End, and along the top of Gore Cliff at the southern end of St. Catherine's Hill. Phosphatic nodules (highly fossiliferous) abound at Gore Cliff, and were formerly dug for conversion into phosphate manure. Wind-erosion is active there, and fossils can be collected with exceptional facility. Upwards of 50 feet of Varians Chalk is exposed at St. Lawrence Shute, and about 40 feet in Gore Cliff, above South View House.

Near the western end of the Island the following succession appears in the cliff at Compton Bay.

Section at Compton Bay

Middle Chalk: nodular chalk — ft

Zone of Holaster subglobosus	*Actinocamax plenus* Subzone: firm grey marl, laminated, .. *Act. plenus* (de Blainv.)	9
	Greyish-white chalk in definite courses, divided by seams of marl	90
Zone of Schloenb. varians	*Holaster trecensis* Leym., *H. subglobosus* (Leske), *Teredo amphisbaena* J. Sow., &c.	
	Grey chalk in alternating soft and harder courses .. .. *Schl. varians* (J. Sow.), &c.	40
	Grey chalk with small brown phosphatic nodules	1½
	Bluish-grey chalk, slightly glauconitic	10
	Plocoscyphia labrosa T. Smith, *P. reticulata* Hinde *Schl. varians*, *Mantelliceras mantelli* (J. Sow.), *Turrilites wiesti* Sharpe	
	Chloritic Marl — *c*, Glauconitic marl with many phosphates and cephalopods	6
	b, Sandy marl without phosphates .. .. *Stauronema carteri* Sol., &c.	3½
	a, Nodule bed, with phosphatised concretions..	1

Selbornian; greenish-grey sand, piped with marl

161½[1]

Inland Sections

The space available in this Memoir allows of but little more than a bare enumeration of the Inland exposures of Lower Chalk.

CENTRAL DOWNS: COMPTON BAY TO CULVER CLIFF

The road-cutting at Brook Shute shows the Chloritic Marl and about 100 feet of overlying beds in the Varians and Subglobosus Zones. The section is similar, in most respects, to that in Compton Bay.

[1]Compiled from 'Lower and Middle Chalk of England', *Mem. Geol. Surv.*, 1903, pp. 86, 89–92.

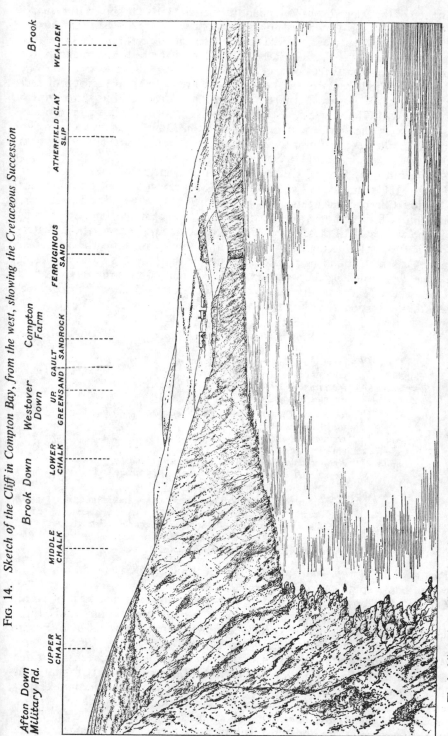

FIG. 14. Sketch of the Cliff in Compton Bay, from the west, showing the Cretaceous Succession

The bedding-planes dip to the left, at an increasing angle, as indicated by the faintly-dotted lines. Under the word 'Greensand', the upper part of the cliff intersects an apron of Pleistocene chalky rubble, on the lower slope of Afton Down.

The top of the Subglobosus Zone and the Plenus Marls are shown in a quarry in the salient of the Downs north of Mottistone. Farther east, the Varians and Subglobosus Beds are worked in a series of excavations north-east of Black Barrow, and the Plenus Marls, with some of the beds above and below them, appear in a small pit north of Bottlehole Spring, above Rock.

Portions of both zones of the Lower Chalk are exposed in a group of four pits near Coombe Tower, and in the eastern part of the Dell at the northern end of Shorwell. The Subglobosus Beds are well shown at the last-named place; in a quarry on the southern point of Chillerton Down; and in two smaller workings north-west and north of Chillerton Street. Other pits have been opened in the same zone above Gatcombe and Garstons.

A large but dirty face of Varians Chalk is seen in the disused quarry east of Upper Mill, near Shide. The Plenus Marls appear in a small pit north-east of Arreton Church, and again, 300 yards north-west of Heasley Lodge, and at the lime-kilns north-east of Mersley Farm; some of the underlying beds being shown in each of these places, and in a pit north of Kern. At the Water-works north-east of Knighton Farm, an example of *Actinocamax plenus* (Blainv.) has been found in a poor exposure of the Marls. Two examples of the same were noted by the writer in a fallen block of the firm greyish chalk just below the Marls, in the quarry north of Morton Manor at Yarbridge, where the succession is as follows:

Section north of Morton Manor

		ft
Zone of *Inoceramus labiatus*	{ Firm white lumpy chalk, becoming hard, nodular, and greyish below .. .. about *Inoceramus labiatus* Schlot., *Rhynchonella cuvieri* d'Orb., &c. (*see* p. 65)	30
Zone of *Holaster subglobosus*	{ Greenish-grey marls of *Act. plenus* Subzone, with bands of greyish chalk .. .. *Ostrea vesicularis* (Lam.) Light-grey massive chalk .. .. *Actionocamax plenus* (Blainv.) at top, *Holaster trecensis* Leym., *H. subglobosus* (Leske), *Aequipecten beaveri* (J. Sow.)	5 90
Zone of *Schloenbachia varians*	{ Alternations of firm to hard grey marly chalk and laminated grey marl .. .. seen *Schloenbachia varians* (J. Sow.), *S. coupei* (Brongn.) *Calycoceras naviculare* (Mant.), *Metacanthoplites roto-magensis* (Brongn.), *Scaphites aequalis* J. Sow.	95

Part of the Chloritic Marl and the top of the Upper Greensand appear in the road-banks south-east of this quarry.

On the southern salient of Brading Down, about half-a-mile east of Kern, an overgrown marl-pit shows in places a little hard, grey, lumpy chalk (probably near the middle of the Varians Zone) containing clusters of *Scaphites aequalis* J. Sow., and *Baculites baculoides* Mantell.

Along the northern boundary of the copses on the Upper Greensand ridge which runs from the Yar Valley to Culver Cliff, lumps of richly fossiliferous chalk, belonging to the highest bed (*c*) of the Chloritic Marl, and the immediately overlying Chalk Marl, are turned up by the plough. Ammonoids (*S. varians*, *S. coupei*, *Mantelliceras mantelli*) and sponges (*Plocoscyphia*, *Jerea*, *Doryderma*, *Stauronema*) are the most conspicuous forms. The ammonoids are more abundant here than in the corresponding beds in the adjacent section at Culver Cliff.

THE SOUTHERN DOWNS

The principal sections on the south side of this range were noticed above. Several old pits in a partly degraded condition exist on the slopes of Shanklin and St. Martin's Downs. The majority are in the Varians Zone, and in one of them, west of Greatwood Copse on Shanklin Down, the marly beds at the top of the talus are fairly fossiliferous. The sides of the lane following the Shanklin-Bonchurch parish boundary, north-west of Luccomb, give a good idea of the succession in the Lower Chalk.

There are many more old workings, again mostly in the Varians Beds, on Wroxall, Week, Stenbury, and Appuldurcombe Downs, but they present no features of special interest.

The Chalk in St. Catherine's Hill is about 180 feet thick and therefore probably belongs entirely to the Lower division of the formation. Some of the Varians Beds, traversed by a small fault, are poorly exposed in the quarry at the northern end of the hill, and in other workings on the western and southern slopes.

MIDDLE CHALK

This stage also thins westward, from about 194 to about 148 feet. As far as can be judged, the Zones of *Inoceramus labiatus* and *Terebratulina lata* are both concerned in this thinning, but the Culver section is too obscured by faults and dust to allow of their separate measurement at the eastern end of the Island.

The Zone of *Inoceramus labiatus* (to revert to a former and better title for the beds for some time known as the Zone of *Rhynchonella cuvieri*) is mainly composed of hard, gritty, faintly-yellow lumps and nodules in a base of pale greenish-grey waved and streaky marl. The nodular structure, most pronounced at the base, gradually dies out towards the top of the zone, where the chalk is normally white, firm, and homogeneous. Besides the streaky marl around the nodules, there are definite seams of coarsely laminated grey marl, with included chalky lenticles, which divide the zone into regular beds. Lenticles of small pebbles of hard white chalk in a coarse gritty base of comminuted shell abound in the nodular beds. In the one-inch Geological Map, and in the second edition of the Geological Survey Memoir on the Isle of Wight, the lowest 6 to 8 feet of this zone is referred to as "Melbourn Rock", but the chalk in this position differs from the massive, outstanding, knotty rock which occurs at the same horizon at Melbourn, near Cambridge and in the Chiltern Hills.

The zonal index-fossil, *Inoceramus labiatus* Schlot., occurs throughout the zone; becoming abundant about 10 feet above the slightly uneven junction with the Plenus Marl; forming, with its comminuted shell, no small proportion of the chalk of the middle beds, and dying out gradually towards the ill-defined lower limit of the overlying zone.

The Zone of *Terebratulina lata*, from its base to within 25 feet of its summit, consists of firm, blocky, white chalk, finely veined with grey marl, and sharply divided into beds from one or two to six or more feet in thickness by seams of the same material.

The highest 20 to 25 feet is mostly nodular chalk, which, with three associated marl-seams, forms an interesting group of beds, easily to be recognised. The group comprises:

		ft	in.
e. Grey marl-seam (upper limit of zone)	.. ..	0	1
d. Hard nodular chalk ("Vectensis Bed")	.. ..	8 to 10	0
c. Black marl-seam	.. ..	0	1
b. Hard nodular chalk, with one or more layers of green-coated nodules 6 to 10 feet down, and passing into smooth white chalk at the base	.. ..	10 to 15	0
a. Marl-seam	.. ..	0	1

See Fig. 15.

FIG. 15. *Group of Beds including the Junction of the Zones of* Holaster planus *and* Terebratulina lata, *in a quarry west of Yarbridge*

Scale: about 1 inch = 10 feet

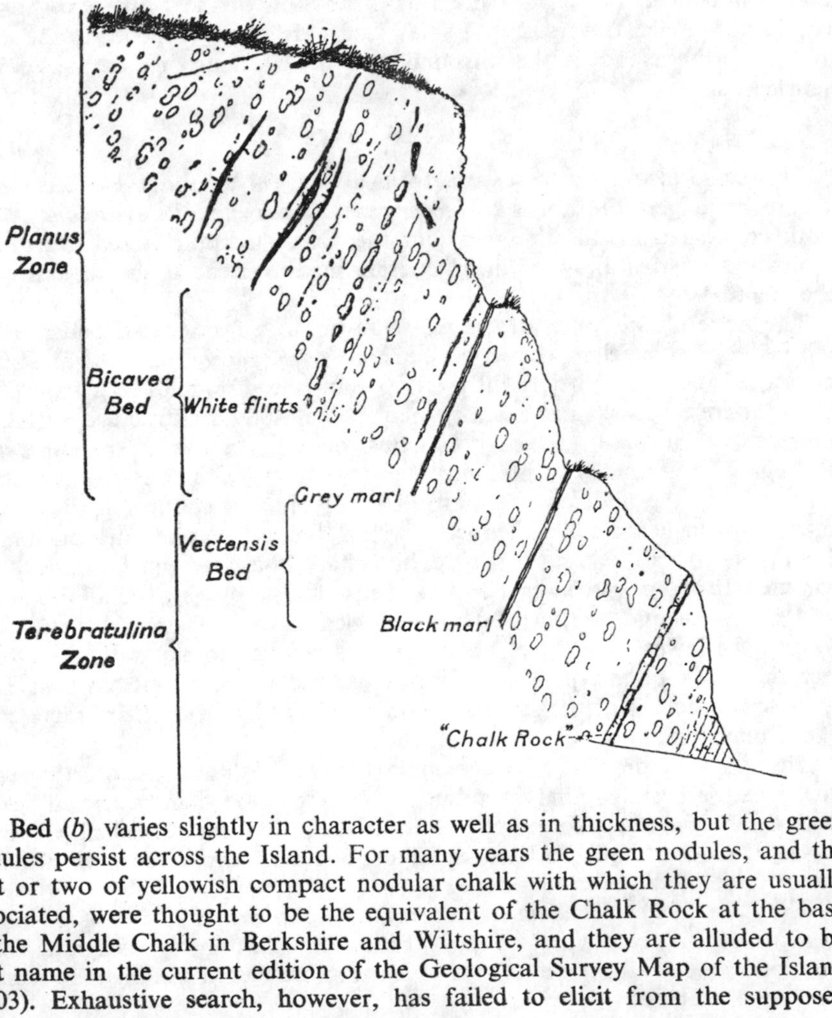

Bed (*b*) varies slightly in character as well as in thickness, but the green nodules persist across the Island. For many years the green nodules, and the foot or two of yellowish compact nodular chalk with which they are usually associated, were thought to be the equivalent of the Chalk Rock at the base of the Middle Chalk in Berkshire and Wiltshire, and they are alluded to by that name in the current edition of the Geological Survey Map of the Island (1903). Exhaustive search, however, has failed to elicit from the supposed

Chalk Rock of the Isle of Wight any representative of the highly characteristic faunule of the *Heteroceras reussianum* Subzone, in which the true Chalk Rock of the Mainland is developed; and it has been recognized for some time past that the green nodule-band is merely an exaggerated phase of the nodular condition normally obtaining in the highest beds of the *Terebratulina lata* Zone.

The black and grey marl-seams (*c* and *e*) also are persistent, though the exceptionally dark tint of the former is lost on the coast. Mr. R. M. Brydone has lately observed that the intervening nodular bed (*d*) is characterised by the presence of a bryozoon which he has named *Membranipora vectensis*.[1]

The little brachiopod *Terebratulina lata* Eth. occurs sporadically throughout its zone, and is abundant in the nodular beds at the top. Small, brittle, siliceous nodules, having the outward semblance of flints but white and chalk-like within, are sparsely distributed in the upper half of the zone, occurring both in the chalk and in at least two of the intercalated marl-seams; while in the highest nodular bed (*d* of the above table) a few true flints are met with.

DESCRIPTION OF SECTIONS

From the thickness of the Chalk in the Southern Downs, it is to be inferred that the greater part, if not the whole, of the Middle Stage of the formation is represented beneath the higher summits near Ventor. Firm to hard chalk with nodular bands and few *Inoceramus labiatus* shows at St. Boniface's Well. It forms part of a large and slightly-outstanding mass which looks as if it had slipped a little on the steep slope of the down. The whole thickness of the Labiatus Zone seems accounted for in small fossiliferous exposures along the path above and north-east of Ventor Waterworks. There appears to be ample room for the Terebratulina Zone farther up, but the only direct evidences of its presence are furnished by rabbit-burrows, considerably below the top of St. Boniface Down.

The exposures in the Central Downs will be noticed in their geographical order, from Compton Bay to Culver Cliff.

Section at Compton Bay

		ft	in.
Zone of *Hol. planus:* Nodular chalk with flints			
	Grey marl	0	1
	Hard nodular chalk, *Terebratulina lata*, &c.	7	7
Zone of	Grey marl (= the "Black marl" mentioned above, p. 62)	0	1
Terebratulina	Hard nodular chalk, containing yellowish band with		
lata,	green nodules at top (so-called "Chalk Rock") and		
64 ft 9 in.	passing into firm white chalk below: fossils abundant ...	12	10
	Marl-seam		
	Firm white chalk with frequent marl-seams, two of which,		
	15 to 18 feet apart, contain siliceous concretions (p.		
	62), *Terebratulina lata*, &c.	44	1

[1]'The Base of the Zone of *Holaster planus* in the Isle of Wight,' *Geol. Mag.*, 1917, pp. 245–249. The author also points out that some significant faunal elements of the Zone of *Holaster planus* occur at the same horizon, and advocates the inclusion of this "Vectensis Bed", and even of the "Chalk Rock" bed (*b*), in that subdivision of the Upper Chalk; a course not lightly to be adopted, since it would entail a considerable modification of prevalent conceptions of the constitution of the *Hol. planus* Zone, and, incidentally, the relegation of such important forms as *Echinocorys scutatus* Leske and *Micraster praecursor* Rowe to the class of accessory "guide fossils".

		ft	in.
Zone of	Firm white chalk with yellow nodules at base: *Inoceramus labiatus* scarce in upper part	48	7
Inoceramus labiatus,	Hard white lumpy chalk with abundant *I. labiatus*, &c...	26	0
84 ft 7 in.	Hard rough nodular chalk with seams of grey marl ("Melbourn Rock")	10	0
Sub-zone of *Act. plenus:* grey marls.			

149   4

The zonal thicknesses are those given by Dr. A. W. Rowe.[1] The fossils recorded from the lower zone include *Cardiaster pygmaeus* Forbes, *Salenia granulosa* Forbes, and *Serpula avita* J. de C. Sow.; those from the upper part of the Terebratulina Zone, *Scalpellum maximum* J. de C. Sow., *Leptomaria perspectiva* (Mant.), *Plagiostoma hoperi* (J. de C. Sow.), *Holaster planus* (Mant.), *Micraster corbovis* Forbes, and *Onchotrochus serpentinus* Duncan.

The junction of the two Middle Chalk zones here rises from the shore below the iron fence which runs from the top of the cliff to the reservoir, and it crosses the Military Road beween the telegraph poles numbered 25 and 26.

South east of Five Barrows the upper beds of the Labiatus Zone, the Terebratulina Zone, and part of the zone above, are well displayed in a quarry close to the high road from Shalcombe to Brook, the details being similar to those at Compton Bay. The junction with the Lower Chalk is seen in a pit north of Mottistone.

North of Rock, the lowest of a series of three pits on the north side of the Calbourne road shows the lower and middle beds of the Terebratulina Zone, and the two other pits the junction with the *Holaster planus* Zone. The highest pit affords one of the best inland sections of the group of beds which include the so-called "Chalk Rock". The base of the Labiatus Zone appears in a small pit farther down the road; also at the top of the Dell quarry above Shorwell. Other exposures of chalk in the same zone occur in the farmyard at Cheverton; on the southern end of Chillerton Down; and half-a-mile west of Gatcombe.

A good section of the Terebratulina Zone, with parts of the zones above and below it, is exhibited in a large quarry, with a working kiln, near the Convent east of Carisbrook Castle.[2] Noteworthy fossils recorded[3] from this quarry are *Pachydiscus peramplus* (Mant.), found in both zones of the Middle Chalk, and *Radiolites mortoni* Mant., *Nautilus* cf. *atlas* Whiteaves, and *Conulus subrotundus* Mantell, from the Terebratulina Zone.

We must pass over the numerous exposures of Middle Chalk beds between Carisbrook and Yarbridge, pausing only to note the occurrence of *Bicavea rotaformis* Greg., near the top of the Terebratulina Zone ("Vectensis Bed") in a small pit at Arreton, and of a band with numerous radioles of *Cidaris hirudo* Sorig., between 3 and 4 feet above the base of the "Melbourn Rock", at Mersley Limekilns.

---

[1] 'Zones of the White Chalk, &c.,' *Proc. Geol. Assoc.*, vol. xx, 1908, p. 219.

[2] The 2nd Ed. of the Geological Survey Memoir of the Isle of Wight, 1889, gives (p. 86) a description of a strike-fault 4 feet below the "Chalk Rock" bed here, running "W. 15° S . . . , its effect being to depress out of sight an unknown thickness of the upper beds of the Middle Chalk". The chalk is much shattered and cleaved in places, but, in the present writer's opinion, the sequence of beds in the Terebratulina Zone is complete.

[3] By A. W. Rowe, *op. cit.*, pp. 280, 281, 297.

West of Yarbridge, on the north side of the upper road to Adgestone, a quarry shows at its south-western end a few feet of *Holaster subglobosus* Chalk; in a small dell in the quarry-floor, a little of the *Inoceramus labiatus* Beds; and in the main face, a good exposure of the junction of the *Terebratulina lata* and *Holaster planus* Zones (Fig. 15). The succession in the upper part of the Terebratulina Zone is similar to that at Compton Bay and intermediate localities, but we note the occurrence here of white siliceous nodules (like those at lower horizons to the west) just below the "grey marl" (*e* of table, p. 62) and below the "Chalk Rock" bed (*b*); also of flints, grey throughout, in the "Vectensis Bed". In the last-named bed, *Holaster planus* (Mant.) and *Bourgueticrinus ellipticus* (Miller) are common, and associated with numerous bryozoa, and the large *Terebratula semiglobosa* J. Sow. usually present at this horizon.

In the section north of Morton Manor, described above (p. 60), the Labiatus Beds have yielded *Roveacrinus sp.*, *Discoidea dixoni* Forbes, *Serpula avita* J. de C. Sow., &c. Terebratulina Beds with siliceous nodules were exposed in a trench north of the quarry.

About 250 yards east of the river at Yarbridge a small degraded pit shows a little firm chalk which apparently includes the junction of the Labiatus and Terebratulina Zones, both of the zonal index-fossils, and *Rhynchonella cuvieri* d'Orb., occurring there sparingly.[1]

At Culver Cliff, the Middle Chalk section, though rather spoiled by heavy falls and dust, is clear enough to show that the ascending succession is much the same as in other parts of the Island. The nodular "Melbourn Rock" beds with *Inoceramus labiatus*, forming a marked contrast to the underlying Plenus Marls, pass up into the homogeneous white chalk which includes the passage into the succeeding marl-seamed chalk constituting the main mass of the Terebratulina Zone. Follows the group of nodular beds with the "spurious Chalk Rock" and the "grey marl" at the contact with the *Holaster planus* Zone; the total thickness being 194 feet. Of the fossils observed here, we shall mention only *Cardiaster cretaceus* Sorig., *Hemiaster minimus* (Agas.) and *Pachydiscus peramplus* from the Labiatus Zone, and *Craticularia fittoni* Mant., *Onchotrochus serpentinus* Duncan, and *Radiolites mortoni* Mantell from the zone above. The "Chalk Rock" and "Vectensis" Beds can be studied in the numerous fallen blocks.

UPPER CHALK

This is much the thickest of the three stages of the Chalk, the total of the zonal measurements made by Dr. A. W. Rowe at the western end of the Island amounting to 1,326½ feet, and at the eastern end to about 1,019 feet.[2] It will be seen later that the decrease in the thickness eastward, that is to say, in the opposite direction to the thinning observable in the Middle and Lower Chalk, is due to post-Cretaceous erosion.

In this great body of Chalk, eight zones are represented, of which three much exceed, and two nearly approach, the Middle Chalk in thickness; hence

---

[1]This section is not mentioned by Rowe. According to the map illustrating his paper (*op. cit.* plate F), it is in the *Micraster cortestudinarium* Zone, which, as entrenchments have shown, crops out 60 or 70 yards to the north.

[2]*I.e.* Rowe's total (*op. cit.*, p. 285) of 1,213 feet for the "White Chalk", less 194 feet for the Middle Chalk, at the eastern end of the Island.

it is seldom that portions of more than two zones appear in a single section, away from the coast; and we cannot conveniently follow the Upper Chalk in its entirety across the Island as we did the Lower and Middle stages of the formation. We shall therefore deal with each zone in its turn, prefacing the description of its chief exposures by a short review of its lithological and faunal characters. The zones will be taken in ascending order, and their exposures from west to east.

ZONE OF HOLASTER PLANUS

This is a rough, nodular chalk (59 feet 9 inches thick, in the west) with a faint greyish tinge due to the marly nature of the material by which the hard, white to yellowish chalk-nodules are thinly invested. The presence of a few definite marl-seams serves to heighten the resemblance to the lower beds of the *Inoceramus labiatus* Zone, which in the past were occasionally mistaken for it, in limited exposures. Flints make their first appearance (in the Upper Chalk) five to eight feet above the "grey marl" mentioned above as marking the upper limit of the Terebratulina Zone. At this horizon they are white throughout, or nearly so, an area of clouded grey usually appearing near the centre. In the succeeding layers the flint nodules quickly assume the normal aspect; dark grey to black inside and with a white cortex of variable thickness.

Fossils are abundant, especially in the lowest or "Bicavea" bed, 6 to 8 feet thick, which includes the white flints. In dry situations, weathering produces a remarkable crop of small organic remains, prominent among them being the lotus-like bryozoon, *Bicavea rotaformis* Gregory, after which the bed has been named, with several other bryozoa and ossicles of asteroids and crinoids. There is, however, a scarcity of the larger zonally-important forms *Echinocorys scutatus* Leske, *Micraster praecursor* Rowe, and *M. leskei* Desmoulins. A single specimen of the first is recorded from this horizon by Dr. Rowe; an example of the second has been observed by the writer, and the third species seems unknown here. This is approximately the horizon at which the true Chalk Rock and *Heteroceras reussianum* Sub-zone fauna occur on the Mainland. In the Island, the Rock is wanting, and as far as is known at present, its peculiar fauna is represented by only two species, an *Aporrhais* and *Inoceramus costellatus* Woods. Of the Planus Zone fossils, *Holaster planus* (Mant.) is common throughout the zone; *Cyphosoma radiatum* Sorig. hardly less so in the lower beds; *Micraster leskei* Desm. occurs sparingly just above the Bicavea Bed, and *Micraster praecursor* Rowe is well represented thence up to and above the junction with the Zone of *Micraster cortestudinarium*.

Notes of Exposures

This zone first appears in the cliff under Main Bench, but does not become easily accessible until the outcrop reaches the eastern horn of Freshwater Bay, where it forms the southern face of the Arched Rock (Fig. 40, p. 167). Eastward, the junction with the Terebratulina Zone rises from the shore of Compton Bay under the low memorial stone on the top of the cliff, the Bicavea Bed being well represented in the fallen blocks. The occurrence here of *Echinocorys scutatus*, *Aporrhais sp.*, and "*Inoceramus sp.*" (= *I. costellatus* Woods)—the latter two suggestive of the Reussianum Sub-zone—is recorded by Rowe,[1] who fixes the upper limit of the Planus Zone at the higher of two marl-seams (one foot eight inches apart) 59 feet 9 inches above the basal "grey marl".

The zonal outcrop crosses the cutting of the Military Road between telegraph-posts Nos. 23 and 25, and, running inland, passes through the northern part of the quarry west of the Brook—Shalcombe road near Five Barrows, where the Bicavea Bed and about 10 feet of the overlying chalk are clearly shown.

The next sections are in the pits north of Rock (see p. 64), in which the surfaces of the lower beds are in exceptionally good condition for collecting. Beyond Rock there are no clear exposures till one comes to the quarry east of Carisbrook Castle (p. 64). Here again, the lower beds only are seen, in a much cleaved and slickensided condition, in the northern face of the working. This quarry is in constant use, and is at present the only one in the Island in which the quarry-men keep the larger fossils for sale.

The disused pit in a plantation on the western side of the high road a quarter of a mile south of Downend shows the Bicavea Bed in a small shaded surface which bristles with fossils, including the characteristic bryozoon in abundance. The overlying beds, seen in the north-eastern part of the pit, also show on their surfaces many larger fossils—*Holaster planus*, *Micraster praecursor*, *Terebratulae*, *Spondylus spinosus* (J. Sow.), &c.

Another excellent and more extensive section of the Bicavea Bed and of the chalk above and below it, is to be seen to the west of Yarbridge (Fig. 15). Here, too, much of the surface is dry-weathered, and the faunas of the beds above and below the "grey marl" can be readily compared. *Holaster planus*, *Spondylus spinosus*, and *Terebratula semiglobosa* (J. Sow.) are conspicuous in the nodular beds below and above the "black marl"; ossicles of *Pentacrinus* abound for six inches above the "grey marl" where fish-teeth (*Lamna*, *Oxyrhina crassidens* Dixon) also occur; *Micraster praecursor* Rowe ("sutured") has been found a foot higher, and the same species is common above the first course of (white) flints.

The section at Culver Cliff is unsatisfactory owing to the falls. Parts of the zone *in situ* can be examined above the talus, and to the east of the electric cables. Among the less common fossils noted here are *Aequipecten pexatus* Woods, and *Scalpellum maximum* J. de C. Sowerby.

ZONE OF MICRASTER CORTESTUDINARIUM

This sub-division also consists mainly of hard, nodular chalk, but with some beds of smoother and softer character in the upper parts. Its thickness (52 feet 9 inches in the west) is but little less than that of the zone below, from which it is broadly distinguishable, in the coast sections, by its faint red flush, due to iron oxide. The flints are mostly black and solid, and disposed in close-set irregular courses: tabular seams are of frequent occurrence.

The characteristic group-forms of *Micraster*—*M. cortestudinarium* (Goldf.) and the narrower *M. praecursor* Rowe—are well represented; so, too, are the usually-associated species of *Cidaris*, *Serpula*, and bryozoa; but the ordinarily common gibbous, small-based *Echinocorys*, and *Holaster placenta* Agas., are comparatively scarce. The occurrence of the gasteropods *Solariella gemmata* (J. de C. Sow.) and *Leptomaria perspectiva* (Mant.) at the base of this

---

[1]*Op. cit.* pp. 221, 300.

zone is noteworthy. On the Mainland these two species are constant associates of the Reussianum Subzonal fauna, and not infrequently recur together about the junction of the Planus and Cortestudinarium Zones, where there is apt to be a repetition of the special lithological conditions of the Chalk Rock.

Notes of Exposures

This zone first becomes accessible in Watcomb Bay. The higher of the two marl-seams (1 foot 8 inches apart) taken as its lower limit in the west of the Island, crosses the eastern side of the bay at the caves, and runs through the Arched Rock at the south-eastern end of Freshwater Bay. The upper limit, about 50 feet higher, is drawn by Dr. Rowe at a marl-seam 6½ feet above a pair of tabular flint-seams which, with an underlying bed of flintless chalk, make a noticeable feature in the cliffs of the above-named bays. The richly fossiliferous chalk of the lower part of the zone can be studied to advantage in the well-weathered surfaces at Watcomb Bay, and in the cutting of the Military Road (between the posts numbered 21 and 24) above Compton Bay. In Freshwater Bay it is much obscured by rain-wash and sea-weed.

Cropping out high on the southern slope of the Central Downs, and unsuitable for marling purposes, the Cortestudinarium Chalk has been less quarried than any other sub-division of the formation, and there seem to be only two tolerably good exposures inland. One of these is in a disused pit at Bowcombe Barn Farm, on the Shorwell road south-west of Clatterford. The surface is not good, but *Micraster cortestudinarium* and *M. praecursor* are readily procurable.

The other is in a road-cutting pit above Knighton Farm, north-east of Newchurch. Examples of *Micraster cortestudinarium* abound in the lowermost 12 feet of hard, nodular chalk, at the southern end of the section. With them, but less frequently, there occur *M. praecursor*, *Echinocorys scutatus* (Leske.), *Holaster placenta* Agas., *Spondylus spinosus* (J. Sow.), and *Inoceramus involutus* J. de C. Sowerby. The character of the lowest specimens of *M. praecursor* indicate the proximity of the junction with the Planus Zone, while in the softer, poorly-fossiliferous chalk, about 45 feet higher, the rare Micrasters are of the transitional forms characterising the beds about the junction with the Coranguinum Zone.

At Culver the Cortestudinarium Zone forms the face of the sheer cliff which ends eastward at the Nostrils, opposite the Shag Rock islet. There are fairly good surfaces at the Nostrils, accessible at low tide. The lithological features which serve as guides to the zonal limits in the western coast sections, are not here discernible. Dr. Rowe, observes,[1] "The southern Nostril is entirely in the [Cortestudinarium] zone, and the junction with the beds of *Micraster coranguinum* may be placed at the point where the out-jutting cliff called the White Horse joins the surface in which the northern Nostril is cut". The zonal index fossil is not uncommon by the southern Nostril, in the roof of which there appears a bed, a foot thick, full of a species of *Membranipora*.

ZONE OF MICRASTER CORANGUINUM

Some doubt exists as to the thickness of this zone in the western part of the Island. According to Dr. Rowe, it is 310 feet thick at Scratchell's Bay, the

[1]*Op. cit.*, p. 242.

upper limit being drawn, as usual, at the first observed occurrence of *Uinta-crinus*. But it would appear from Mr. Brydone's subsequent measurement of the Uintacrinus Subzone, in the same locality, that remains of *Uintacrinus* occur 26½ feet below the horizon adopted as the upper limit of the Coranguinum Zone by Rowe. Deducting this thickness from Rowe's 310 feet, we have 283½ feet, which approximates more nearly to Rowe's figures for the thickness of the Coranguinum Zone in Freshwater Bay, *i.e.* 278 feet 3 inches.[1]

Except at the base, where it contains nodular and lumpy bands, the chalk of this zone is smooth and massive. The flint-nodules are disposed in numerous regular courses, which are more closely spaced near the base and about the middle than in other parts of the zone. Internally the flints are frequently cavernous, and may have a violet tinge: the rinds vary in thickness. There are occasional seams of tabular flint, and a few of grey marl.

As developed in the Isle of Wight, the substage under consideration might be aptly named the "Zone of *Inoceramus cuvieri*", for pieces of the shell of that large pelecypod abound throughout, and in the lower and middle beds occur in great sheets along the planes of stratification. In the coarse, faintly-greyish chalk of the lower part of the zone the *praecursor-coranguinum* passage-forms of *Micraster* are fairly well represented. The concomitant change in *Echinocorys*, from the gibbous to the ovate shape, is much less apparent, owing to the comparative scarcity of this echinid. *Conulus conicus* Agas. occurs sparsely in bands in the higher part of the zone: *Hagenovia rostrata* (Forbes) is seldom seen. The regular echinids (*Cidaris perornata* Forbes and *Cyphosoma koenigi* Mant. (*Phymosoma*), &c.), brachipods (*Kingena lima* (Defr.), &c.), pelecypods (*Chlamys cretosus* (Defr.), &c.), bryozoa, *Serpulae*, and sponges (especially *Porosphaerae* and *Plinthosellae*) are all fairly well represented. In all, 90 species of megascopic dimensions were identified by Dr. Rowe.

Notes of Exposures

In Scratchell's Bay the base of this zone is fixed by Rowe at a marked band of tabular flint about 15 feet above the grass-slope on the ledge south of the Grand Arch. This impressive section is accessible only by boat, and the condition of the surfaces within reach is indifferent. The Grand Arch is worn in the Coranguinum Chalk, something in the structure of which is favourable to the development of overhung recesses. Rowe calls attention to an "incipient Grand Arch" in this zone at Culver Cliff, and the small beginnings of similar recesses are to be seen in quarries.

In the western part of the Island, Watcomb Bay is probably the best place in which to examine this zone. Of the lower beds here Rowe remarks,[2] "we find a rich fauna passing right down to the junction and blending imperceptibly with that of the zone of *Micraster cortestudinarium*", and, "but for the presence of *Micraster* and *Echinocorys*, we could not have separated the base of one zone from the top of the other". The position of the junction has already been noted (p. 68). The section in Freshwater Bay is dirty. A feature of the base of the Coranguinum Zone here is the abundance of *Serpula ilium* Goldfuss. Exposures of fossiliferous chalk (yielding *Conulus* and *Hagenovia rostrata*) occur at the top of the cliff on the eastern side. The western part of the Military Road-cutting is in this zone.

---

[1]Rowe, *op. cit.*, pp. 223, 228. Brydone, *Geol. Mag.*, 1914, pp. 406, 407.
[2]*Op. cit.*, p. 225.

Inland sections are not numerous and few call for more than passing notice. There are two small pits in Idlecombe Down between the British Village and the Roman Road, and two more to the north, at and north-west of Rowridge Farm. All show abundant fragments of *Inoceramus*, and Rowe records the zonal echinid from the first two and the last one. The pit south-west of the Anglo-Saxon Cemetery on Bowcombe Down has an unpromising surface, but has yielded the zonal echinid, *Conulus vulgaris* (Lam.), *Echinocorys*, and *Chlamys cretosus* (Defr.).

The highest beds are indistinctly seen near the south-eastern corner of the great Downend quarry near Arreton, which cuts into four zones of the Upper Chalk. The section is described below (p. 71).

The quarry just south of the Newport road on the eastern end of Brading Down takes in, but does not fully show, about 200 ft of Coranguinum Chalk, up to the junction with the Uintacrinus Band. The bedding-planes forming the southern face of the quarry are veneered with fragments of *Inoceramus cuvieri* J. de C. Sow., among which are many small fossils (asteroid ossicles, *Bourgueticrinus*, bryozoa, &c.) and a few tests of *Micraster coranguinum*. The last-named species is common about the middle of the western face of the quarry, where *Echinocorys* (ovate) is most often met with, and *Inoceramus digitatus* Schlot., has been observed. In the higher beds *Conulus conicus* Agas. appears, but is rare. The top of the zone is reached in a shallow embayment in the overgrown northern face.

At the western end of Bembridge Down a small pit, just above the high road from Sandown to Bembridge, gives one of the few exposures of the lowest beds of this zone. Micrasters of the transitional type mentioned above are not uncommon in the lumpy chalk, which is crowded with rough violet-tinged flints and stout pieces of *Inoceramus*.

At Culver Cliff the zone comes down to the shore between Whitecliff and the Nostrils, and can be worked at the White Horse. Much of the accessible surface, however, is obscured by dust from falls. The seams of broken *Inoceramus* are conspicuous. Dr. Rowe notes the presence of *Epiaster gibbus* (Lam.) and *Hemiaster minimus* Agas. near the zonal base.

ZONE OF MARSUPITES TESTUDINARIUS

Owing to the unwonted scarcity of fossils, and the unfavourable condition of the surfaces in the principal sections, the limits of this zone are difficult to determine exactly, and we accordingly find considerable discrepancy in the published measurements. Dr. Rowe's measurements at the western end of the Island are:—Scratchell's Bay, 81½ feet; Freshwater Bay, 116 feet; the former being regarded by him as the more reliable. Mr. Brydone, however, finds the distance between the horizon at which *Uintacrinus* first appears and that at which *Marsupites* is last seen, at Scratchell's Bay, to be 129 feet. Inasmuch as Brydone's measurement has a definite lithological feature as a starting point; exceeds Rowe's figures for the Freshwater section by only 13 feet; and more nearly agrees with the present writer's measurement of about 120 feet at Arreton (Downend), we accept it as the approximate thickness of this zone in the western part of the Island.[1] At Culver Cliff, Dr. Rowe measured 95 feet of the zone, the base not being seen.

[1]Rowe, 'Zones of the White Chalk', *Proc. Geol. Assoc.*, vol. xx, 1908, pp. 223, 224, 230. Brydone, *op. infra cit.*, *Geol. Mag.*, 1914, pp. 406, 407.

The Chalk is pure white, compact, and contains a few marl-seams. Flint courses are less closely spaced than in the zone below, and are scarce or wanting in the highest beds towards the east. The flints are mostly rather small, solid and black, with short, hornlike, projections and thick cortices of a faintly pink hue externally. The tabular variety is common in oblique veins and almond-shaped lenticles.

Ossicles of *Uintacrinus* cf. *westphalicus* Schlüt. come in gradually, are rather common in some 40 feet of chalk, and then gradually disappear; an interval of five to ten feet usually separating their last occurrence from the first appearance of *Marsupites testudinarius* Schloth. The scutes of the latter crinoid, which become common more quickly and disappear more slowly than those of *Uintacrinus*, exhibit their usual progressive, climacteric, and retrogressive phases in size and ornamentation as they range through the 50 to 60 feet of beds which form the upper half of the zone, and when last seen have become so small and featureless as to be hardly recognizable by the unaided eye. Like *Uintacrinus*, this crinoid reaches its acme at a horizon well above the middle of its range. Among other characteristic fossils of this zone are *Echinocorys scutatus* var. *elevatus* Bryd., papilliform *Bourgueticrinus*, *Terebratulina rowei* Kitchin, *Caryophyllia cylindracea* Reuss.

Notes of Exposures

In Scratchell's Bay, Mr. Brydone draws the base-line at a strongly-marked marl-seam, 2½ feet above a layer of tabular flint which forks as it approaches the foot of the cliff east of the Grand Arch. The marl-seam is 182 feet south-east of the concrete platform on the shore. For details (mostly lithological) of this section we must refer the reader to Mr. Brydone's paper.[1]

The sections in Freshwater Bay are much stained by wash from the rubbly gravel above. The position of the zone on the eastern side of the bay is roughly marked by the truncated end of the old coast-road at the top of the cliff (Fig. 40, p. 167).

Inland, poor exposures of Uintacrinus Chalk are to be seen on Westover Down, a mile north-north-east of Mottistone; at and north of Swaintondown Gate Farm; and in a lane-cutting a quarter of a mile north-west of Bowcombe.

The Downend quarry, north of Arreton, shows in its eastern face the succession diagrammatically represented in Fig. 16. The southern (right-hand) part of the section, up to the first salient angle, has been trampled into a slope by sheep, and it is possible that the upper limit of the Coranguinum Zone lies a few feet lower than is indicated in the figure. The zonal Micraster, *Conulus conicus* Agas., and bits of *Inoceramus* are among the more noticeable fossils in this part of the section.

Plates of *Uintacrinus*, accompanied by characteristic forms of *Bourgueticrinus* and angulate *Echinocorys elevatus* Bryd., occurs with varying frequency northward to a point a little beyond the first salient angle in the quarry-face, where they become abundant. A few feet farther on they are scarce, and seem to die out entirely before *Marsupites* appears, about 10 feet short of the second salient. The remains of *Marsupites* are similarly distributed in the Marsupites Subzone. Here *Echinocorys elevatus* is common; *Kingena lima* (Defr.), and

---

[1] 'The Zone of *Offaster pilula* in the South English Chalk,' *Geol. Mag.*, 1914, pp. 405–409.

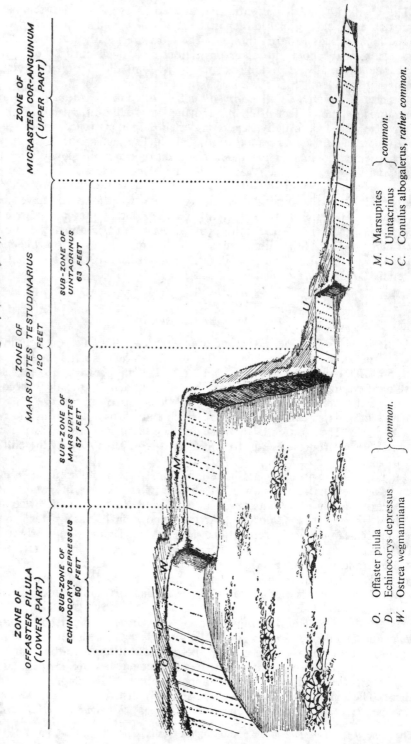

Fig. 16.　Section in Downend Chalk Quarry (eastern face), Arreton

ZONE OF
OFFASTER PILULA
(LOWER PART)

SUB-ZONE OF
ECHINOCORYS DEPRESSUS
50 FEET

ZONE OF
MARSUPITES TESTUDINARIUS
120 FEET

SUB-ZONE OF
MARSUPITES
57 FEET

SUB-ZONE OF
UINTACRINUS
63 FEET

ZONE OF
MICRASTER COR-ANGUINUM
(UPPER PART)

O.　Offaster pilula
D.　Echinocorys depressus } common.
W.　Ostrea wegmanniana

M.　Marsupites
U.　Uintacrinus } common.
C.　Conulus albogalerus, rather common.

other distinctive forms, mentioned in the introductory remarks above, also being represented. Near the third salient angle *Marsupites* dies out, and *Echinocorys*, decreasing in size, displays the tentative shape-variations usually observable at this horizon; a sub-elevate form predominating. In the same part of the section, nodular flints become scarce, and the chalk contains thinly-scattered green, earthy concretions, up to about 15 mm. in diameter—the first sign that one meets with, going eastward, of the green nodule-bands so conspicuous at the same and at rather higher horizons in the beds of nearly flintless chalk at Culver Cliff.

The remainder of the eastern face of Downend quarry is in the Zone of *Offaster pilula* (see p. 75).

A few feet of the basal beds of the Uintacrinus Band, with the name-fossil and *Septifer lineatus* J. de C. Sow., appears in the northern face of the quarry at the eastern end of Brading Down (see p. 70).

At the western foot of Bembridge Down, a pit containing a chalk-built shed, gives some patchy but interesting exposures of chalk, ranging from the upper part of the Uintacrinus Band into the lower part of the Zone of *Offaster pilula*. Working northward along the degraded face, one sees first about 25 feet of flinty chalk, with few remains of *Uintacrinus*, rostrate *Micraster coranguinum*, &c., followed by about 10 feet of similar chalk, in which *Uintacrinus* is rare or missing. In the succeeding 60 feet, where there is some tabular flint, scutes of *Marsupites* and tests of *Echinocorys elevatus* occur sparingly. Beyond this, at the top of the talus, an example of *Actinocamax granulatus* Blainv. was noted by the writer about 10 feet above the observed range of *Marsupites*. Near the northern end of the working, a little opening in the talus shows chalk about 40 feet higher, with *Offaster pilula* (Lam.), two marl-seams $1\frac{1}{2}$ feet apart, and a layer of rusty, slightly greenish nodules with sponge-impressions, immediately below the lower marl: presumably the spot where Dr. Rowe found *Actinocamax granulatus* and a "gibbous" *Echinocorys*.[1]

The layer of rusty nodules in the pit just described probably represents one of the less distinct of the upper group of nodular bands which occur in the 69 feet of hard, marl-seamed, nearly flintless chalk in the little promontory north-east of the White Horse at Culver Cliff. Here the upper limit of the Marsupites Zone is drawn by Rowe midway between the lowest distinct green-nodule band and that which succeeds it, between two and three feet higher; leaving about 45 feet of the flintless and nodular chalk to the Zone of *Offaster pilula*. The accessible surfaces are hard and worn smooth by waves.

ZONE OF OFFASTER PILULA

This sub-stage, as defined by Mr. R. M. Brydone in 1914,[2] comprises in the western part of the Isle of Wight about 110 feet of the Chalk formerly assigned to the zone of *Actinocamax quadratus*, and some 20 feet of beds equivalent to those which Dr. Rowe, when dealing with the Mainland coast-sections, usually referred to the upper part of the Zone of *Marsupites testudinarius*.[3] The title of the new zone is open to criticism, but is not easily to be improved upon and the beds to which it refers are sufficiently characterised

[1] Rowe, *op. cit.*, p. 259.
[2] *Op. cit.*
[3] A course adopted by the writer in the Geological Survey Memoirs on the Hungerford, Basingstoke, Alresford, and Winchester sheets of the one-inch map.

F

by their fauna to justify the separation of them from the mass of Quadratus Chalk above.

The base of the *Offaster pilula* Zone is the upper limit of the range of *Marsupites*; the summit is marked by a thin band of exceptionally large examples of *Offaster pilula* (Lam.), and between these horizons there occur distinctive forms of *Echinocorys*, *Bourgueticrinus*, and bryozoa. In the Isle of Wight, *Actinocamax granulatus* (Blainv.) appears to be confined to this zone.

Two sub-zones are recognizable. The lower one is characterised especially by the small, squat *Echinocorys scutatus* var. *depressus* Bryd. (one of several forms to which the term "gibbous" has been applied). The upper sub-zone is marked by the prevalence of *Offaster pilula*, which occurs most freely in two bands, with an intervening thicker band containing *Echinocorys scutatus* var. *cinctus* Bryd.—a variety not common in the Isle of Wight. In the two succeeding zones of the Upper Chalk, *Offaster pilula* occurs sporadically, and is generally of small size.

The chalk of the Pilula Zone contains numerous marl-seams. Nodular flints, in courses and scattered through the chalk, are less frequent in the lower than in the upper half of the zone at the western end of the Island, and become fewer eastward, till, at Culver Cliff, as already stated, the lowest 45 feet of the zone is devoid of them, a few thin seams of the tabular variety only being present.

Notes of Exposures

At Scratchell's Bay, the descending (north to south) sequence in the zone, made out by Mr. Brydone, is as follows:

Section of the Offaster pilula Zone, Scratchell's Bay[1]

	ft in.	ft in.
Marl seam		
Chalk with *O. pilula* of maximum size	1 6	
Flint seam		
Chalk with *O. pilula* of large size	1 0	
Marl seam		
Chalk with *O. pilula* and three marl seams ..	11 0	
Marl seam		
Chalk with *O. pilula*	1 0	
		14 6
Marl seam emerging from fall at base of cliff		
Chalk hidden by fall at base of cliff (about) ..	27 0	
Chalk with six marl seams	22 0	
		49 0
Chalk with *O. pilula*, two marl seams, and two flint tabulars, 3 feet apart	11 0	
Strong marl seam		
Chalk with a marl seam	4 0	
Strong marl seam		
Flintless chalk, apparently the belt mentioned by Dr. Rowe [*op. cit.*, p. 231]	5 6	
Marl seam		
Chalk with eight marl seams and two flint tabulars	39 0	
Strong marl seam		
Chalk	4 0	
		52 6
Strong marl seam		
Total		127 0

Left-margin bracketing labels: Zone of *O. pilula*; Sub-zone of abundant *O. pilula*; Upper belt of *O. pilula*; *Cinctus* belt; Lower belt of *O. pilula*; Sub-zone of *E. scutatus*, var. *depressus*.

[1]Brydone, *op. cit.*, p. 408.

In the cliffs near the head of Freshwater Bay this part of the Chalk is deeply weathered, and little is known about its contents, beyond the fact that both *Echinocorys depressus* and *Offaster pilula* are present.

Inland, there seem to be no sections west of the Medina.

In the Downend quarry (Fig. 16, p. 72) the Subzone of *Echinocorys depressus* is shown in a poor surface in the northern part of the eastern face. The index-fossil first appears in the highest few feet of the Marsupites Zone, along with other forms of *Echinocorys*, but is not common much below the pair of thick marl-seams (D), between and in the vicinity of which is easily procurable. About 10 feet higher, *Offaster pilula* is common, and occurs sparingly in the next 40 feet of chalk, with many marl-seams and scattered small flints. Most of this chalk is in the northern face of the quarry, which intersects the beds in such a way as to make accurate measurement difficult. The one-foot band containing large tests of *Offaster*, at the top of the zone, comes down to the quarry floor 35 yards east of the cave. An example of *Actinocamax granulatus* has been found just below that band.

The pit north-east of the crossways on Mersley Down (dip "63°" on map) shows in its short western and southern faces the following descending succession:

	ft	in.
Firm chalk with flints and casts of sponges: little exposed	—	—
Ventriculites radiatus Mant., *Offaster pilula*, *Echinocorys truncatus* Bryd.		
Marl-seam	0	3
Firm chalk	0	10
O. pilula, *Ostreae*, *Aptychus leptophyllus* Sharpe, *Enoploclytia leachi* (Mant.).		
Marl-seam	0	0½
Chalk with flints	2	4
Chalk with rare, scattered flints	12	0
Echinocorys depressus, *Rhynchonella limbata*, &c.		
Nodular ironstained chalk in grey marl	0	4
Echinocorys depressus		
Chalk with rare flints .. .. seen for	2	0
Echinocorys depressus		

The section evidently includes the junction of the Depressus and Pilula Subzones, and shows in its lower part an approach to the flintless and nodular conditions of Culver Cliff. More of the Pilula Subzone (but not its upper limit) appears in the eastern face of the pit, the chalk in which has been shifted a few feet (relatively) southward of that seen in the southern and western faces, by a vertical dip-fault.

The small exposures at the western end of Bembridge Down are described above (p. 73).

In the Culver section, the frequent marl-seams, the bands of nodules, and the arresting dearth of flints, which occur in clustered courses on either hand, impart a Turonian aspect to this subdivision of the Chalk. Owing probably to the unfavourable state of the surfaces within reach, the band of large *Offaster pilula* marking the top of the zone has not yet been found. The abnormal lithological conditions suggest that the zone is thinner here than in the west of the Island and at Downend. The few more or less distinctive fossils observed are the index echinid (sparingly, throughout), *Crateraster quinquelobus*

(Goldf.) var., *Actinocamax granulatus* (lowest beds), and *Coelosmilia laxa* Edw. & Haime (highest nodule-bed).

The green nodules, to which small *Ostreae* and *Dimyodon nilssoni* (Hag.) often adhere, were examined by the late William Hill, who "found them to consist mainly of the fine amorphous material of the chalk, with a somewhat unusual number of large and perfect foraminifera, and with many sponge spicules, the silica of which had been replaced by calcite. The colouring appeared to be sometimes due to a green material, much of which had accumulated in the interior of foraminiferal cells, but the whole of the amorphous material was sometimes tinted green with no apparent change in its constituent particles. There were no isolated grains of glauconite, such as appear in the somewhat similar nodules of the Chalk Rock. After treatment of the nodules with hydrochloric acid, the residue was a dull-greenish soft and earthy-looking material, a large part of which occurred as the casts of foraminifera and the canals of sponge spicules."[1]

ZONE OF ACTINOCAMAX QUADRATUS (restricted)

At the western end of the Island, the thickness of this zone is 216½ feet, according to Mr. Brydone; at the opposite end it is probably more, the combined thicknesses of the *Actinocamax quadratus* and *Offaster pilula* Zones at Culver Cliff, according to both Mr. Brydone and Dr. Rowe, being 400 feet, compared with their respective measurements of 327 feet and 343 feet at Scratchell's Bay.[2] The chalk is massive and white, though traversed by minute veins of marl. Seams of marl are numerous and flint-courses more so; the flints being mostly black and solid, and often of large dimensions.

With the detachment of the beds now assigned to the Zone of *Offaster pilula*, this substage loses much of its interest, for the greater part of what remains is poor in stratigraphically significant life-forms. The characteristic belemnoid is not often met with. *Echinocorys*, increasing in size as it ranges upwards, varies so much in shape that one cannot indicate a dominant type, though an ovate form, more inflated than that of the Coranguinum Zone, and a gibbous form resembling an overgrown *E. depressus*, are of common occurrence. Other noteworthy fossils are *Crania egnabergensis* Retz., *Serpula turbinella* J. de. C. Sow., at least one characteristic form of *Bourgueticrinus*, *Porosphaera pileolus* (Lam.), and *P. nuciformis* (Hag.).

Notes of Exposures

The Scratchell's Bay section seems to have yielded no fossils of particular interest beside a few examples of *Actinocamax quadratus* (Defr.).

There are upwards of a dozen inland sections, the majority of which we can no more than indicate in the present Memoir.

A pit south of Farringford House, and another 600 yards east of the Waterworks at Freshwater Gate, are noteworthy as showing Quadratus Chalk closer than usual to the boundary of the Eocene Beds. A third pit, to the east of the latter, also appears to be in the higher beds of this zone.

---

[1] 'Geology of the Isle of Wight,' *Mem. Geol. Surv.*, 2nd Ed., 1889, p. 78.
[2] Brydone, *op. cit.*, pp. 406, 409; Rowe, *op. cit.*, pp. 231, 248.

The large quarry south-west of the pond at Shalcombe shows, at its south-western corner, the passage into the *Belemnitella mucronata* Zone, the index-fossil of that zone coming in about 15 feet above a fossiliferous band in the Quadratus Chalk, of which some 40 feet is exposed.

We pass over small pit-exposures in Calbourne Bottom; south and a quarter of a mile east of Gotten Lees; half a mile south-east of Newbarn; and on the eastern side of High Wood, near Apesdown; and notice the large quarry north-east of Shide Station merely to observe that this, like the Shalcombe quarry, is cut southward through the Mucronata Beds to the Quadratus Zone, which has here yielded its characteristic belemnoid.

In the Downend Quarry, the thickness of the lower Quadratus Beds exposed in the northern face is roughly estimated at 100 feet. The chalk is poor in fossils other than *Porosphaerae*. A few examples of *Echinocorys* and some bryozoa have been noted, and a rusty impression of part of a large ammonoid, probably *Pachydiscus leptophyllus* (Sharpe), has been visible for some years on a projecting band of firm chalk, 40 yards east of the cave, and five feet above the lower limit of the zone.

Beds close to the top of the zone, with a conspicuous pair of marl-seams containing rolled pieces of *Inoceramus*, *Porosphaerae*, asteroid-ossicles, &c., can be seen in a pit near Duxmore Farm, north-west of Mersley Down.

The abandoned quarry (with a railway siding) near West Ashey includes the junction with the Mucronata Zone, but the beds in the transitional area are obscured by a belt of talus which has for a long time supported a vigorous colony of yellow horned poppy (*Glaucium luteum* Scop.), which possibly finds some congenial salinity in the chalk at this spot. *Echinocorys scutatus*, of divers forms, is among the commonest of the fossils in the Quadratus Beds, which occupy the southern parts of the section.

Approximately the southern half of the chalk-exposure above the siding at Brading Station is in this zone. The zonal name-fossil is present, but seldom to be found.

The same species occurs in the upper beds of the zone at Culver Cliff, where there are some workable surfaces. The ledge that runs out at the extreme eastern point of the cliff is taken as the upper limit of the Quadratus Zone.

ZONE OF BELEMNITELLA MUCRONATA

The highest of the Upper Chalk zones with which we are concerned in the present Memoir attains its maximum known thickness in Britain, 475 feet, at the western end of the Isle of Wight. In Whitecliff Bay, at the eastern end of the Island, however, only 150 feet of this Chalk is present. The rather rapid eastward dwindling which this implies is observable in the adjacent parts of the Mainland, where it leads to the complete failure of the zone, beneath the Eocene Beds, near the Hants-Sussex border. As there is nothing in the character of the Mucronata Chalk to suggest that this thinning is due to original defect of sediment, we may safely attribute it to the widespread erosion which is known to have preceded the deposition of the oldest Tertiary strata. Besides this regional eastward attenuation, a good deal of local variation in the thickness of the Mucronata Chalk occurs along the southern boundary of the Eocene Beds in the Isle of Wight, though not so much as was supposed by

Dr. A. W. Rowe and Mr. C. D. Sherborn, who first drew attention to this phenomenon in 1908.[1]

The chalk of this zone is white and massive, with numerous rather irregular flint-courses and many seams of marl. The flints, which not infrequently attain a great size, vary much in character but are often greyish within. Small spheroidal nodules, with mealy or quartz-lined cavities, are abundant in places.

The fauna is probably richer in species than that of any other Chalk zone, but varies little from bed to bed (as far, at least, as its megascopic elements are concerned), and no divisions of sub-zonal importance have yet been recognised. *Belemnitella mucronata* Schloth. is usually forthcoming in fair-sized exposures, and, failing that, there is the commoner small, *Conulus*-like *Echinocorys scutatus* var. *subconicus* Bryd., and the less frequent massive, domed variety, tending to a point at the apex. Among other more or less distinctive fossils are *Cardiaster ananchytis* Leske, *Cidaris serrata* Desor, *C. pleracantha* Agas., *Bourgueticrinus* varr., many bryozoa, *Magas pumilus* J. Sow. (mostly in the upper beds), *Crania costata* G. B. Sow., *Kingena lima* (Defr.) (pentagonal).

Notes of Exposures

In Scratchell's Bay the lower limit of this zone is drawn by Rowe at the horizon where *Belemnitella mucronata* and *Echinocorys subconicus* make their first appearance. At the foot of the cliff it is marked by a marl-seam at the south-eastern end of a big fall of Mucronata Chalk. The surface is passably good in this part of the bay, so that bryozoa and other small forms are clearly seen. Towards the northern horn of the bay the chalk becomes increasingly hard, and reaches its maximum induration in the southern face of the shore-ward Needle,[2] where it has been converted into a semicrystalline limestone.

---

[1] 'Zones of the White Chalk, &c.,' by A. W. Rowe and Note on the accompanying maps by C. D. Sherborn, *Proc. Geol. Assoc.*, vol. xx, 1908, pp. 285, 330–334.

Rowe mentions (p. 285) three localities where, to the best of his belief, the Quadratus Chalk "has a junction with the Tertiaries", viz.—at or near the four pits "Nos. 11 High Down, 4 and 8 Afton Down [for "8" read 3], and 23 Mersley Down [for which read 45 Ashey Down, *cf. ibid.* p. 267 and Plate E];" and four other localities in which "only a comparatively thin layer of *mucronata* chalk intervenes between the *quadratus* chalk and the Eocene", viz.—near the five pits "Nos. 10 High Down, 60 Carisbrook, 19 Pan Down [for '19' read 49], and 46 Ashey Down".

In preparing the maps which illustrate this paper C. D. Sherborn ventured to cut out the Mucronata Chalk near Burnt House (near Shide) and at N.W. end of Bembridge Down, as well as in the three localities where Rowe believed it to be missing.

Since the publication of this paper, the presence of Mucronata Chalk has been proved at No. 45 Ashey Down by the present writer, and near Burnt House by R. M. Brydone, who gives reasons for suspecting the existence of this chalk at No. 11 High Down, and No. 3 Afton Down as well. ('The thickness of the Zone of *Belemnitella mucronata* in the Isle of Wight', *Geol. Mag.*, 1918, pp. 350–354). The present writer, having visited the latter two pits, is of opinion that No. 3, while in the Quadratus Zone, is not on the Eocene boundary. The age of the chalk in the northern part of No. 10 is doubtful, but here also there is room for higher beds between it and the boundary of the Reading Beds. In the case of Bembridge Down there are no critical sections, nor any good ground for inferring the non-occurrence of the Mucronata Chalk, of which there is over 200 feet at Brading, half a mile distant.

In the light of these later observations, it appears probable that the Mucronata Chalk, though greatly reduced in places, is continuous along the Eocene boundary from Alum Bay to Whitecliff Bay.

[2] A. W. Rowe, *op. cit.* p. 232. The progressive increase in the dimensions of the Needles stacks seaward seems to imply a broadening of the zone of induration in that direction.

It is to this local hardening, combined with the high dip, that the Needles owe their peculiar conformation. The ascending sequence of the beds in this zone is continued in the southern side of Alum Bay, where the cliff is cut along a stepped succession of bedding-planes. The chalk decreases in hardness eastward from the Needles, and can be easily cut with a knife near the line where it passes behind the upturned Eocene Beds at the head of this bay. At this spot the eminently characteristic brachoipod, *Magas pumilus*, is rather common.

Owing to its accessibility from the long-settled clayey country north of the Central Downs, the Mucronata Chalk has been more extensively quarried than any other subdivision of the formation, and its outcrop is followed by a line of pits stretching from one end of the Island to the other. As the number of workings which present fair to good exposures is upwards of thirty, we notice only a few of them here, and refer the reader to Dr. Rowe's paper (*op. cit.*) for short descriptions of the rest.

The southern pit at the Waterworks, Freshwater Gate, is noteworthy as affording one of the few known instances of *Actinocamax quadratus* mingling with a Mucronata-zone fauna. The chalk is close to the base of this zone, and has yielded many fossils. The northern pit, containing the pumping house, just reaches the junction with the Reading Beds.

The Shalcombe quarry, giving a clear section of beds about the junction with the Quadratus Zone, is noticed above (p. 76). Between this place and Shide over a dozen sections can be seen on the face of the Downs. Fossils from the northern part of the quarry north-east of Shide Station include *B. mucronata*, *Echinocorys* (at least three forms), *Offaster pilula* (dwarf), and *Magas pumilus*.

We pass to the Waterworks quarry south of East Ashey, where, contrary to Rowe's impression, the chalk visible in the small face above the talus proves to be in the Mucronata Zone; the name-fossil occurring both above and below the slide-plane, which he mentions. The chalk at the slide-plane, which follows the bedding, is at least 100 feet below the projected base of the Eocene Beds, whose boundary is clearly marked near the quarry (*see footnote*, p. 78).

Nunwell Rookery pit, besides many other characteristic fossils, has yielded *Cidaris pleracantha* Agas. (radiole), also found at Brading, and recorded by Rowe from other localities.

The northern part of the chalk-face above the siding at Brading Station is rich in bryozoa, asteroid ossicles, *Serpulae*, and calcisponges (including ramose forms, not identified). The thickness of Mucronata Chalk in the cutting here is approximately 240 feet, allowing for dip and obliquity, and taking as the zonal base a thick marl-seam 130 paces south of the point where the base of the Reading Beds meets the permanent way.

The short southern side of Whitecliff Bay, like the longer one of Alum Bay, presents a stepped succession of highly-inclined bedding-planes of the Mucronata Zone. Most of the surface is grey with micro-vegetation, but fossils are well seen in the fallen blocks at the Point and in other places, tests of *Echinocorys* being especially noticeable. Rowe notes the occurrence here of *Aptychus portlocki* Sharpe and *Salenia geometrica* Forbes.

Chapter VI

EOCENE BEDS

Early Eocene Erosion. In the South East of England the Chalk is succeeded by Eocene deposits with which it has hardly a feature in common. The purely marine Cretaceous limestone gives way to sands and clays of shallow salt, brackish, and fresh water origin, while the varied Senonian fauna simultaneously disappears and is not seen again.

Far more is implied in these changes than a mere decrease in depth of water. There is here a wide gap in the stratigraphical succession, attributable in some measure to non-deposition, but chiefly to denudation, during the period of emersion which followed the close of the Secondary era in Western Europe. In the course of this period the floor of the Upper Cretaceous sea in the English region was brought within reach of the agents of erosion, and whatever deposits representative of the late Cretaceous Chalks of Denmark had been formed there, were washed away, while the underlying Senonian and older stages, which escaped complete destruction, were wasted back for unknown but certainly considerable distances southward and eastward of their original limits, and ultimately worn down to an even surface disposed more or less obliquely to their bedding-planes. When, therefore, as a result of later depression, or rise in sea-level, a great part of the region was overspread by the shallow waters of an early Eocene sea (advancing, apparently, from the south-east), the first of the Eocene sediments to be formed there came to rest upon the bevelled edges of the Cretaceous and older Secondary strata.

The widespread unconformity (or, rather, disconformity) so produced is seldom sufficiently marked to be discernible within the narrow limits of individual exposures of the base of the Eocene Beds, but it is clearly envisaged when the collected data of a number of widely distributed sections are brought under review. By this means we learn that the Eocene base transgresses the upper beds of the Chalk in descending order over a large sector of the South of England lying eastward, northward, and north-westward of a point in the neighbourhood of the Needles; and we are thence led to infer that the Chalk itself, prior to or during its planation in early Eocene time, had acquired a slight convergent inclination towards a depression which centred in or to the south of the area now occupied by the Isle of Wight and Bournemouth Bay.

There is no need, however, to go outside the Island for evidence of this unconformity: it is seen in the local variations in the thickness of the Mucronata Chalk between the Needles and Whitecliff Bay, and, in a minor degree, in the coast-section at Alum Bay.

Cropping out in a nearly straight line, along which it has been highly tilted and distorted by late Tertiary folding, the contact-surface of the Chalk and Eocene Beds appears here under conditions which afford a certain amount of scope for conjecture with regard to its original conformation. Thus, the variations in the thickness of the Mucronata Chalk along the boundary of the Eocene (Reading) Beds have been held to imply the existence of a strong relief in the top of the Chalk at the time when the overlying strata were deposited; the zonal expansions and contractions being taken to mark the sites of early- or pre-Tertiary hills and valleys respectively; while a tendency to complementary variations here and there detected in the thickness of the Reading Beds has been brought forward in support of this hypothesis.[1]

In opposition to this view, however, there is to be urged, not only the strong *a priori* improbability of the early Eocene surface of the Chalk, habitually planed smooth on the Mainland, having retained so pronounced a relief in the Island, but also the circumstance that the phenomena so interpreted are susceptible of a different and not less plausible explanation. Marked local variations of zonal thicknesses in the Chalk just below the Eocene Beds are not uncommon in other parts of England, and wherever conditions permit one to form a true conception of their character and physiographical relations, their immediate cause is found in local accentuations of that regional discordance between the bedding and the planed surface of the Chalk, which has already been mentioned.

Viewed in this light, the alternate thinning and thickening of the Mucronata Chalk along its outcrop in the Isle of Wight assumes a structural instead of a palaeo-topographical signification; the supposed hills and valleys now appearing respectively as gentle synclines and anticlines, truncated by the basal surface of the Eocene Beds. That this is the actual state of things, the present writer entertains little doubt.

As for the supposed sympathetic behaviour of the Reading Beds, these yielding strata have suffered so much compression and deformation in the neighbourhood of their existing outcrop, that a considerable amount of variation in their apparent thickness is to be expected; and even where the incidence of this variation meets the requirements of the first hypothesis, the amount of it admittedly falls far short of reasonable anticipation on the assumption that the beds in question were laid down on a markedly undulating surface.

1. READING BEDS

In the Isle of Wight this series is almost wholly composed of mottled, red and purple, structureless clays, such as are met with in freshwater formations of various ages in divers parts of the Earth. Such brightly-coloured clays are seldom fossiliferous, and save for rare bits of lignite the Reading Beds of the Island seem devoid of remains of contemporary organisms, though ostracods are stated to have been found in them.[2]

Resting on the worn surface of the Chalk, there is usually a thin bed of coarse, loamy, ferruginous sand, corresponding to the glauconitic bed with oysters and sharks' teeth often observed in this position on the mainland. Gnarled and deeply ironstained flint nodules occur in the sand, together with small flint-pebbles, and a few small pebbles of quartz. Where not completely decalcified the sand also contains microzoa derived from the Chalk. There is usually little else but mottled plastic clay between this bottom-sand and the slightly uneven upper limit of the Reading Series, but bands of sandy clay are intercalated in places, especially in the western part of the Island.

---

[1] C. D. Sherborn, 'Note . . . on the Physiography of the Tertiary Sea-Bottom' in A. W. Rowe's 'Zones of the White Chalk, &c.'. *Proc. Geol. Assoc.*, vol xx, 1908, pp. 330–334.

[2] *Vide* H. W. Monckton, *Proc. Geol. Assoc.*, vol. xiv, 1895, p. 100.

The thickness of the Reading Beds is about 150 to 160 feet at Whitecliff Bay, but less than 90 feet at Alum Bay. Much of the variation observed in their thickness, and in the width of their outcrop-surface, between these places, is doubtless due to accommodative movements in the clays, under pressure.

Notes of Exposures

At Whitecliff Bay a few square yards of the early Eocene surface of the Chalk, in a nearly vertical position and bordered by adhering masses of the Reading bottom-bed, can be seen on the southern side of the path to the shore at the head of the bay. The top of the Chalk is nearly smooth, save for scattered, hemispherical hollows or pot-holes, up to a foot in diameter, containing loose flints and chalky sand from which little springs exude. Lithodomous borings seem wanting.

The sandy bottom-bed, 4 feet thick, is charged with broken unworn flints and relatively few flint-pebbles, its aspect reminding one of the sandy sort of Clay-with-Flints often met with on Chalk uplands. This flinty and loamy sand not improbably includes the relics of old subaerial accumulations, but the character of the surface on which it rests discountenances the notion that the deposit has been formed *in situ* by weathering of the Chalk. It is probably of shallow marine origin, as is the normal type of Reading bottom-bed, on the Mainland; and the ochreous colouring (which heightens the resemblance to Clay-with-Flints) may be ascribed to the decomposition of an original glauconitic constituent.

Above the sands, and passing into them, there is a foot or two of laminated, grey, sandy, marl, in which the calcareous matter consists of fine washings from the Chalk, partly replaced by minute concretions of "race". The remainder of the Reading section here is occupied by slips, in which, however, one can trace the grey marl passing quickly into dark purplish-grey plastic clay, with red ochreous concretions and mottlings, succeeded by red plastic clay holding concretions of the same kind. The top of the red clay, visible *in situ* at the northern margin of the slips, has a sharp and gently undulate contact with the hard, conglomeratic sandstone in the basement-bed of the London Clay.

Following the boundary of the Series inland, one notes a small exposure of the bottom sand at the entrance to Longlands chalkpit, but in the overgrown river-bluff east of the Yar at Brading no sand is indicated at the junction with the Chalk, which is marked by a layer of large, loose flints. Across the Yar Valley, the loose flints at the same horizon are still larger, a broken cylindrical nodule which projects through the turf in the shallow railway-cutting at Brading Station measuring 1 × 2½ feet. At this spot, when the railway was in course of construction, Mr. W. Whitaker noted the section shown in Fig. 17. All that can now be seen there, besides the basal flint-layer, is a little mottled clay.

Farther west, there are abundant indications of red clay in fields and road-banks, but no good exposure is to be seen until one reaches the coast.

The junction with the Chalk is well displayed in the cliff at the head of Alum Bay (Fig. 18), and presents a different appearance from that seen at the opposite end of the Island. As at Whitecliff, the surface of the Chalk, newly stripped of its Eocence covering, is shown on a nearly vertical face; but here it is rugged and deeply furrowed, while the pot-holes attain much greater dimensions, and their sides, often undercut, in many cases open laterally into sand-filled fissures, some of which follow the bedding-planes. The general aspect of the surface is that of a foreshore worn in an approximately horizontal limestone, as more than one observer has remarked.

Fig. 17. *Section of Reading Beds in the Railway-Cutting south of Brading Station*

Scale, 1 inch = 48 feet

After W. Whitaker in "Geology of the Isle of Wight" (*Mem. Geol. Surv.*), 2nd ed., Fig. 17, p. 96.

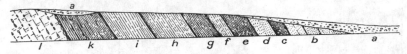

"*a*. Wash.

	b.	Buff and brown fine clayey sand, with layers of clay.
	c.	Purple-grey plastic clay, mottled crimson.
	d.	Buff and light-grey fine sand.
"Reading	*e*.	Grey and purple plastic clay.
Beds	*f*.	Crimson and grey plastic clay.
[130 ft seen]	*g*.	Greenish and crimson plastic clay.
	h.	Red plastic clay, mottled grey.
	i.	Grey and crimson plastic clay.
	k.	Brown grey and purple plastic clay.

"*l*. Chalk with flints; showing a dip of 60°, and on the other (eastern) side of the cutting as much as 80°.

"The junction of the Reading Beds and the Chalk was not clearly shown, but must be somewhat irregular. Some huge roundish flints occur at the junction, as in Alum Bay, partly projecting into the Clay."[1]

The bottom-sand of the Reading Beds, though seemingly devoid of glauconitic grains, has a pale, diffused, greenish tint in the deeper pot-holes, and there contains scattered dark-green flint-pebbles, besides the unworn flint-nodules. Angular flint is much less abundant than at Whitecliff. The bulk of the sand is of a light ochreous tint. In places it is cemented into hard calcareous sandstone.

Above the sand comes two or three feet of pale purplish loam, which passes up into the usual red and mottled clays. The rest of the Reading section is seldom unencumbered by slips, and the following account of it, dating back to about 1852, gives more complete measurements than are now obtainable.

Section of the Reading Beds in Alum Bay

	ft	in.
"Red and white mottled clay, with a ferruginous parting at 4 feet ..	25	0
Ferruginous-brown clayey sand..	14	0
Bright-red and white mottled clay (pipeclay)	20	0
Brown and grey sandy clay (with a bed towards the middle of dark-red clay 3 feet thick), most sandy in the upper 5 feet	10	0
Tenacious, wet, red and white mottled clay	3	0
Tenacious blue and brown ferruginous clay	8	0
Brown sand covering an uneven eroded surface of Chalk	3 to 4	0
	84	0"[2]

The contact with the London Clay is slightly uneven.

[1]"Geology of the Isle of Wight,' *Mem. Geol. Surv.*, 2nd ed., 1889, p. 96, Fig. 17.
[2]"Geology of the Isle of Wight,' *Mem. Geol. Surv.*, 2nd ed., 1889, p. 95.

FIG. 18. *Early Eocene surface of the Chalk, Alum Bay*

After a photo, by H. E. Armstrong in A. W. Rowe's "Zones of the White Chalk, &c.", *Proc. Geol. Assoc.*, vol. xx, 1908, Pl. XIV

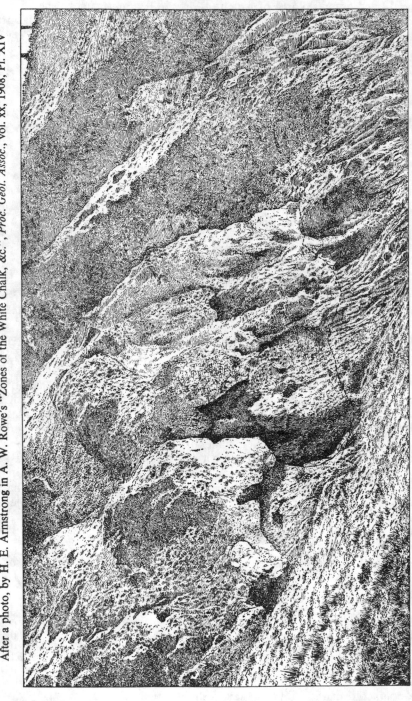

A newly-exposed surface of the Chalk is seen about the middle of the figure. Above and to the right, the surface has been modified by recent weathering and erosion. The Reading Beds form the foreground, and their sandy bottom-bed, scored by little rain-gullies, adheres to the Chalk below the dotted line.

2. LONDON CLAY

This formation is made up of alternations of blue to brown clays and grey to buff sands, the change from one kind of sediment to the other being gradual in some cases and in others abrupt. There is a well-marked glauconitic basement-bed, the lower part of which shows oblique bedding, and contains, in addition to the usual flint pebbles, a variable amount of rounded and angular pieces of red, ochreous plastic clay, the presence of which, coupled with the uneven bottom of the London Clay, indicates contemporary erosion of the Reading Beds, presumably by currents.

Concretionary cement-stones, some of which are septarian, occur in layers in a few of the less sandy beds. Thin loamy bands with scattered flint-pebbles appear at irregular intervals, and seem not to be restricted to definite horizons, as has been supposed. Fossils occur in bands in the clays, but are usually in a fragile condition.

Section of London Clay, Whitecliff Bay

ft

Bagshot Sands: Band of red sandstone, underlain by yellow and white sands, &c. (about 40 feet)

		ft
London Clay	Grey and brown clay, laminated at top . . . . . . *Protocardia nitens* (J. Sow.), &c.	9
	Dark grey and light brown sandy clays with three courses of septaria in the lower half. Pebble bed at base (marked P in Division 3 of Fig. 20, p. 92) . . . . *Pinna affinis* J. Sow., *Vermicularia bognoriensis* (Mant.), *Arctica scutellaria* (Lam.), &c.	28
	Light and dark sands and laminated loam. (Near the middle of this division seams of laminated clay are contorted around lenses of sand, 2 feet thick)	44
	Brown laminated clay with spheroidal concretions at top . . *Axinaea brevisostris* (J. de C. Sow.), *Meretrix suessoniensis* (Wat.), *Arca impolita* J. de C. Sow., &c.	17
	Grey and brown clay, less sandy than above, with bands of loamy sand. Fossils (fragile) in top 5 feet, and between 27 and 22 feet above base. (Slip obscures middle third of this division)	102
	Yellow and white sand with scattered pebbles passing down into dark grey sandy clay	56
	Laminated grey clay with open layers of cement-stones in upper part. Pyrites and lignite scattered throughout . . *Glycimeris corrugata* (J. Sow.), *Pholadomya margaritacea* J. Sow., &c.	52
	Basement Bed { Dark green glauconitic loam with pyrites and lignite. Two seams of small *Ditrupa plana* J. Sow. at base . . . . . . 12 ft Greenish glauconitic loam with small pebbles of flint and pieces of Reading red clay. Partly hardened into sandstone (non-calcareous) 2 ft Layer of pebbles at uneven base }	14

Reading Beds: red clay . . . . —

322

The only sections are those in the cliffs of Whitecliff and Alum Bays, at either end of the narrow belt of ground in which the formation crops out along the northern foot of the Central Downs. According to the classification here adopted, the thickness of the London Clay is 322 feet on the east coast of the Island and about 400 feet at Alum Bay on the west, but in the latter locality the upper limit is naturally indefinite; one may draw the line anywhere in the thick unfossiliferous sands and clays which lie between the beds with marine shells and those with leaf-bearing pipe-clays clearly of Bagshot age.

The contortions about 60 feet below the top of the London Clay seem to be due to irregular settlement occurring soon after the deposition of the beds affected by them.

With reference to the following description of the Alum Bay section (Fig. 19) it should be stated that in the last edition of the Geological Survey Memoir on the Isle of Wight (1889, p. 99), the division now numbered [6] is taken as the highest of the London Clay series, the total thickness of the formation being given as 233 feet, compared with 322 feet at Whitecliff Bay. It is necessary, however, to go 172 feet higher in order to find clean, light-coloured sands of Bagshot aspect, and the present writer prefers to follow Mr. J. Starkie Gardner[1] in assigning the intervening beds to the London Clay. Some of the sands in these beds resemble those in the London Clay at Whitecliff Bay, and the group as a whole has a more loamy aspect than could be inferred from the following table, which is copied (with some re-arrangement) from the above-mentioned Geological Survey Memoir (pp. 99 and 103). The Alum Bay cliffs waste rapidly, and lithological details change from time to time, but the writer has thought best not to burden the literature of the section with a new description of the varied assortment of strata comprised in the Eocene system in this locality.

Section of London Clay, Alum Bay

		ft in.	ft
[13–11]	Grey laminated sands and clays; mostly sands ..	18 0	
	Do. nearly all clay; very carbonaceous	11 0	32½
	Grey laminated sands and clay; clay predominating ..	3 6	
	Iron sandstone band and tawny ironsand with ferruginous veins and strings, and pebbles of quartz	0 6 to 3	
	Grey sands, &c.		
	Details:—		
	Pale yellow and bluish white sand, darker in the upper part and with a vew laminae of clay	16 0	
	Blue clay with thin (¼ inch) sandy laminae; carbonaceous matter	27 0	104
[10–8]	Grey and yellow sands, with thin laminae of blue clay; much pyrites and carbonaceous matter	61 0	
	(N.B.—These beds have a slightly reversed dip towards the top of the cliff.)		
[7]	Bright yellow and white sands, more laminated and clayey than the bed above, and containing much carbonaceous matter. The lower 5 feet sand	23 0	
	Iron sandstone	3 0	
	Parting of pale clay of variable thickness	0 2	33
	Very thinly laminated white and yellow sand	1 10	
	White sand and blue clay, becoming more clayey towards the lower part	5 0	
[6]	Dark blue loamy clay, with ironstone nodules. Becomes sandy in the upper part		46

[1]'Description and Correlation of the Bournemouth Beds,' *Quart. Journ. Geol. Soc.*, vol. xxxv, 1879, p. 226.

		ft
[5]	Laminated dark grey loam	13
	Loam, passing upward into fine sand	23
	Blue clay becoming more loamy above	17
	Line of large septaria full of *Cardita* [*sp.*] (a conspicuous bed)	
[4]	Dark blue clay	62
	Loam with scattered small flint pebbles. *Panopea intermedia* [*Glycimeris corrugata* (J. Sow.)], *Tellina, Cassidaria, Fusus, Turritella imbricataria, Natica labellata*	2
	Brown and bluish clay, with lines of septaria	35
	Septaria full of *Pinna affinis* (a conspicuous bed)	
	Brown and bluish clay, sandy in places, with lines of septaria ..	20
	Basement Bed—Sandy glauconitic loam with a little pyrites. *Ditrupa* at the base	15
	Total	405½

The numbers prefixed to the beds and groups of beds in the above table correspond, as nearly as may be, to those in Joseph Prestwich's classical description of the whole Alum Bay section.[1]

3. BAGSHOT SANDS

In the current edition (1903) of the Geological Survey Map of the Isle of Wight on the One-inch Scale the four series of strata between the London Clay and the Headon Beds are represented by one colour, and described as "Bagshot Beds" in the index; the only divisions distinguished by name being the Bracklesham Beds and the Barton Sand. In the present Memoir the term "Bagshot" is applied to the lowest only of the four series, which are dealt with under the several headings, Bagshot Sands, Bracklesham Beds, and Barton Beds, the last comprising the Barton Clay and overlying Barton Sand.

According to the classification here adopted, the Bagshot Sands are white and coloured micaceous sands with seams and lenses of pipeclay, some of which yield remains of the characteristic plants *Ficus bowerbanki* de la Harpe and *Aralia primigenia* Heer. At the eastern end of the Island these Sands are 138 feet thick, and their upper limit is sharply defined by the pebble-bed at the base of the marine Lower Bracklesham Beds. In the Alum Bay section, in the west, the beds which we refer to the Bagshot Sands comprise the white and coloured sands with pipe-clay, 76 feet thick, immediately succeeding the beds which we have above assigned to the London Clay, and separated from the more or less glauconitic beds with remains of a marine fauna of Upper Bracklesham facies by about 540 feet of other coloured sands and clays with lignite, which are believed to represent the greater part of the Bracklesham Series of Whitecliff and Bournemouth Bays. In the last Geological Survey Memoir on the Isle of Wight (1889, pp. 101–103), no less than 662½ feet of Eocene Beds in the Alum Bay section are classed as "Lower Bagshot", leaving only 388 feet of strata to be divided between the London Clay and the Bracklesham Beds, which have an aggregate thickness of over 900 feet at Whitecliff Bay; an arrangement which has met with little approval.

The Bagshot Sands of the Isle of Wight are, for the most part, evenly stratified, and have a less fluvial aspect than the corresponding set of pipe-clays,

[1]'On the Tertiary or Supracretaceous Formations of the Isle of Wight, &c.' *Quart. Journ. Geol. Soc.*, vol. ii, 1846, pp. 255–259, and Plate IX, Fig. 1.

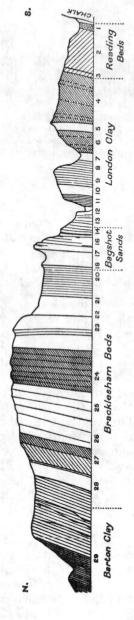

FIG. 19. *Section of the Eocene Beds in Alum Bay*

J. S. Gardner after J. Prestwich in *Quart. Journ. Geol. Soc.*, vol. ii, 1846, Pl. IX, Fig. 1, with slight alterations. The numbers of the beds are those used by Prestwich.

The brightly-coloured sands and clays for which this bay is famous are distributed through the divisions numbered 14 to 28, inclusive.

Features especially serviceable for purposes of identification are, the sharp ridge formed by the ironstone at the base of No. 16, the thin bed of coal or bituminous lignite in the upper third of No. 24, the group of lignite-beds in the lower half of No. 27, and the pebble-bed at the junction of Nos. 28 and 29.

sands, and gravels in Dorsetshire. Although they seem to contain no fossils besides the remains of land-vegetation and of a few insects, it appears probable that they were deposited in a broad, shallow, brackish lagoon or sheltered embayment on the low-lying coast of the land whence the Corfe pipe-clays and the Dorchester gravels were derived.

Writing about the year 1888, Mr. J. Starkie Gardner characterised the pipe-clay flora of the Bagshot Sands of Alum Bay as "the most tropical of any that has so far been studied in the northern hemisphere".[1] Elsewhere he observes that its distinctive character "is due to the size and variety of the leaves ascribed to the genus Ficus and Leguminosae, in a scarcely less degree to a deeply cleft palmate Aralia, a trilobed leaf resembling Liquidambar, a deeply serrate Banksia, and other leaves referred to Comptonia, Dryandra, and Myrica. Few, if any, of these have been found in the Middle Bagshot [*i.e.*, Bracklesham] division at Bournemouth".[2]

DESCRIPTION OF SECTIONS

We follow the outcrop across the Island, beginning on the east with the:

Section of Bagshot Sands, Whitecliff Bay

		ft
Bracklesham Beds: pebble-bed		—
Bagshot Sands	Yellow and white micaceous sands, with numerous seams of grey pipe-clay and a few inpersistent seams of small flint-pebbles in the upper half; and red ironsand and sandstone (to 3 feet) at the base	101
	Yellow, grey, and white sands, evenly bedded, with partings of sandy pipe-clay (much obscured) (No. 4, Fig. 20) ..	37
London Clay: brown, laminated sandy clay		—
		138

The red sandstone, from 37 to 40 feet above the junction with the London Clay, forms the most conspicuous of the foreshore reefs between the Chalk and the Bembridge Limestone in Whitecliff Bay. The ironstaining and induration, however, vary greatly within the narrow limits of the section, and constitute no sufficient grounds for excluding (as some authors do) the underlying 37 feet of light-tinted sands from the Bagshot Series.

Inland, light-coloured sands are dug in many places near the outcrop of the London Clay, but owing to the high and varying dip, it is not always easy to decide whether they belong to the Bagshot or some other series.

The pit at Longlands is in micaceous sand with bits of lignite and a seam of little pebbles. The dip is 85° S.W., showing the beds to be overturned. Yellow and brown sands, with a high southward dip, are exposed in a small pit at Beech Grove in Brading. At Downend, farther west, similar sands, overlain by clay with a pebble-bed at the junction, have been worked in Saltmore Copse. The pebble-bed is about 150 feet above the London Clay, and may be the same as that which marks the base of the Bracklesham Beds in Whitecliff Bay. The like sequence has been observed in a pit half-a-mile north of Calbourne.

[1]In 'The Geology of the Isle of Wight', *Mem. Geol. Surv.*, 2nd ed., 1889, p. 106.

[2]'British Eocene Flora, Pt. I,' *Palaeont. Soc.*, 1879, p. 16.

The pipe-clay now becomes more noticeable. Seams of it occur in the sands exposed in the road-cutting between the two lodges belonging to Westover, and thicker bands of the same material were formerly dug near East Afton. Sands with pipe-clay can be seen in a pit above the eastern bank of the Yar north of Freshwater Gate. Across the river there is a sand-pit at Easton, and a ferruginous sand (? Bracklesham) appears in the road-cutting south of Farringford House.

Section of Bagshot Sands, Alum Bay (Fig. 19, p. 88)

		ft	in
Bracklesham Beds: grey sandy clay			
[18] Fawn coloured and whitish sands, slightly variegated with red: the upper 10 feet slightly laminated			

Details (within [18]):

	ft	in.
Slightly laminated white sand	9	5
Irony band	0	1
White, pink and yellow laminated sand, with veins of white pipeclay and bright red laminae of iron	7	6
Fine light yellow sand	23	0

[18] total: 40 ft 0 in

	ft	in
[17] Pipeclay (full of leaves) between yellowish-white and variegated laminated clays. The lower 2 inches are composed of sandy white pipeclay, with laminae of yellow and crimson sand, becoming thicker towards the upper part of the cliff	6	0
[16] Bright yellow sand, with thin laminae of blue clay	13	0
Iron band	2	0
[15, 14] Yellow and grey sands	15	0

[London Clay: grey laminated clays and sands]

Bagshot Sands

76 0[1]

The leaf-bearing parts of the pipe-clay are lenticular, and not always to be seen in the cliff. They seem to have been missing from the section during the last quarter of the 19th century, but in recent years they have at times been well exposed. The general character and condition of the plant-remains is thus described by J. S. Gardner[2]:—"They consist principally of most delicate impressions of leaves, rarely presenting traces of colour, and giving little indication of their texture when living. They lie with the planes of bedding and are rarely twisted or rolled. The leaflets of compound leaves, of which there are many, are almost always detached, though a few specimens exist in which they still adhere to the axis. With the leaves are twigs of a conifer, shreds of fan-palm and reed, small leguminous pods, drupes and other bodies too decomposed for identification, and very rarely, a flower like *Porana* or *Kydia*, and the detached elytron of a beetle. All bear the appearance of long immersion and tranquil deposition, and the sediment is so fine that the disturbance in it caused by the formation and passage of gas bubbles is distinctly visible. Every trace of carbon has been chemically removed".

[1]Details from 'Geology of the Isle of Wight', *Mem. Geol. Surv.*, 2nd ed., 1889, p. 102.
[2]*Ibid.*, in note, pp. 104, 105.

4. BRACKLESHAM BEDS

In the east of the Island this series—by far the thickest of the Eocene System—is mainly composed of glauconitic sandy clays and loams with abundant marine shells. A few beds of pure sand occur between the shell-beds, and there are also thicker groups of interlaminated selenitic clay and sand with lignite. While much of the lignite evidently represents small vegetable refuse that had drifted from a distance and had sunk on becoming water-logged, it is clear, from the occurrence of root-beds or under-clays, that part of it is the remains of local plant-life. The roots are all small; those most in evidence are of uniform character, and seemed to have belonged to a reed-like plant, growing in mud. The prevalence of sulphur compounds in the lignite-beds points to accumulation in salt water.

The junction with the Bagshot Sands is marked in Whitecliff Bay by the only conspicuous bed of flint-pebbles which the Eocene System affords on that side of the Island. The contact with the Barton Clay above coincides here, as in other places, with the incoming of *Nummulites elegans*. Unfortunately, this horizon is marked by no distinct lithological feature.

The Bracklesham succession in Alum Bay presents a strong contrast to that on the eastern coast, for the massive shell-beds, so far from being distributed throughout, are confined to the highest 30 feet, and the bulk of the formation is made up of coloured sands and laminated clays with disseminated carbonaceous matter and some definite bands of lignite.

We owe our knowledge of the Marine Bracklesham Beds of the Isle of Wight chiefly to the researches of the late Osmund Fisher, the main results of which were published in 1862.[1]

Fisher divides the Bracklesham Series on the eastern side of the Island into four groups (lettered A to D), each containing one or more beds rich in fossils.

The highest group, A, generally abounds in Gasteropods, and one (at least) of its fossil-beds is full of *Nummulites variolarius* (Lam.).

Group B, more sandy than the last, also contains *N. variolarius* in its principal shell-bed, and is marked by the presence of *Cerithium giganteum* Lam. (*Campanile*).

These two groups comprise what is now known as the Upper Bracklesham (Auversian).

Group C, also sandy, is characterised by an abundance of *Nummulites laevigatus* Brug., and

Group D, mostly less fossiliferous than the higher groups, is distinguished by the occurrence of *Cypraea tuberculosa* Duclos, and *Cardita acuticosta*? (Lam.).

The latter two groups form the Lower Bracklesham (Lutetian).

Description of Sections

In the following account of the succession at Whitecliff Bay, Fisher's grouping and numeration of the bed are retained, but some of the details given in his table are excised for the sake of brevity, and others are altered where emendation has become necessary as a result of more recent researches. The place-names and other appellations by which the most fossiliferous beds are known to collectors are inserted in parentheses.

[1] On the Bracklesham Beds of the Isle of Wight Basin,' *Quart. Journ. Geol. Soc.*, vol. xviii, 1862, pp. 65–93.

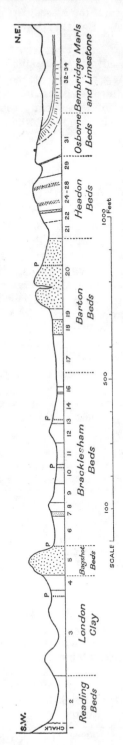

Fig. 20. *Section of the Eocene and Oligocene Beds in Whitecliff Bay*

W. Topley after J. Prestwich in *Quart. Journ. Geol. Soc.*, vol. ii, 1846, Pl. IX, Fig. 2, with slight alterations. The numbers of the beds are those used by Prestwich.

P. Pebble-bed. Only one of the beds so marked is conspicuous, namely, that at the junction of Nos. 5 and 6, the base of the Bracklesham Series. The rest are either pebbly seams or beds of sand and loam in which flint-pebbles are thinly scattered. More pebbly episodes than are here indicated can be discerned in the cliff.

The reef-making red sandstone in the lower part of the Bagshot Sands (at their base, according to this figure, but see p. 89); the coal-bed in No. 10; and the Tellina Sandstone, No. 15, are useful as guides to the other stratigraphical divisions near the middle of the cliff-section.

The Arabic numerals in parentheses refer to the diagram-section, Fig. 20.

Section of the Bracklesham Beds, Whitecliff Bay

ft

Barton Beds.—Green and blue clays with Zone of *Nummulites elegans* (1 foot) at base .. .. —

Upper Bracklesham Beds.

A, 184 ft

- (17) XIX.—("Huntingbridge Beds," lower part of). Greenish and blue clays[1] 94
- (16) XVIII.—Dark blue and green sandy clay 22
- XVII.—("*Nummulites variolarius* Zone"). Blue clay crowded with *N. variolarius* (Lam.), also *Alveolina sabulosa* (Montf.) *Turbinolia sulcata* Lam., *Obitulifera petiolus* (Lonsd.) *Fusus longaevus* (Sol.) (*Clavalithes*), *Pleurotoma denticula* Bast., &c. 10
- (15) XVI.—("*Tellina* Bed.") Light-coloured sand and sandstone with *Tellina donacialis* Lam., *T. plagia* Edw. .. 6
- (14) XV.—Sandy clay, passing into lead-coloured clay with *Ancillaria canalifera* Lam. (*Ancilla*) 10
- XIV.—("Brook Bed.") Dark sandy clay, full of *Corbula pisum* J. Sow. above, and *Pecten corneus* J. Sow. (*Pseud-amusium*) below. *Nummulites variolarius* (Lam.), *Cytherea lucida* J. de C. Sow. (*Meretrix*), *Voluta modosa* J. de C. Sow., &c. 3
- XIII.—Dark-green clay and sand with *Pecten corneus* J. Sow., passing into light-coloured loamy sands[2] .. .. 39+

B, 27 ft

- XII.—Sands, white and yellow 10
- XI.—Sandy clays with *Sanguinolaria hollowaysi* J. Sow. (*Gari?*), *Pecten corneus* J. Sow., *Pectunculus pulvinatus* Lam. (*Axinaea*) 4
- X.—Sand, yellow and grey 7
- (13) IX.—("*Cerithium giganteum* Bed"). Brown sandy clay with scattered pebbles. *Numm. variolarius* (Lam.) *Cerithium giganteum* Lam. (*Campanile*), *Turritella sulcifera* Desh., *Murex minax* Sol. .. 6

Lower Bracklesham Beds.

C, 123 ft

- (12) VIII.—Laminated sandy clays with lignitic seams in upper part, and fossiliferous band with *Nummulites laevigatus* Brug., &c., near the middle[3] 46
- VII.—("*Nummulites laevigatus* Bed"). Green sand with *Sanguinolaria hollowaysi* J. Sow. Mass of *N. laevigatus* Brug. four feet above base 15
- (11) VI.—Green sands with *Nummulites laevigatus* Brug., *Cardita planicosta* Lam., *Natica labellata* Lam., (*Ampullina*), *Turritella sulcata* Lam., *T. sulcifera* Desh. 62

---

[1]Fisher (*op. cit.*, p. 70) makes this division (XIX) 162 feet thick, as he includes in it 68 feet of clays now referred to the Barton Beds.

[2]Described by Fisher,—"Beds not exposed, apparently clays, 39 feet". The upper 12 feet naturally belongs to division XIV, above; and the thickness appears to be about 50 feet.

[3]Fisher mentions no fossils from this division. Attention has since been called to the existence of the fossiliferous bed near the middle by J. Boussac. *Ann. Soc. Géol. du Nord*, tom. xxxvi. 1907, p. 361.

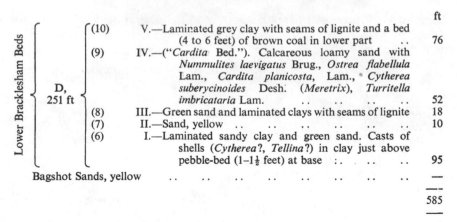

					ft
	(10)	V.—Laminated grey clay with seams of lignite and a bed (4 to 6 feet) of brown coal in lower part		..	76
	(9)	IV.—("*Cardita* Bed."). Calcareous loamy sand with *Nummulites laevigatus* Brug., *Ostrea flabellula* Lam., *Cardita planicosta*, Lam., *Cytherea suberycinoides* Desh. (*Meretrix*), *Turritella imbricataria* Lam.			52
	(8)	III.—Green sand and laminated clays with seams of lignite			18
	(7)	II.—Sand, yellow			10
	(6)	I.—Laminated sandy clay and green sand. Casts of shells (*Cytherea?*, *Tellina?*) in clay just above pebble-bed (1–1½ feet) at base :			95

Bagshot Sands, yellow .. .. —

585

Mr. J. S. Gardner correlates divisions I to III with the Bournemouth Freshwater Beds,[1] of which they are probably the equivalent, though deposited under different conditions. The stratification is more regular than in the Freshwater Beds exposed between Bournemouth and Poole Harbour, and division I, at least, is marine. Plant-remains are plentiful in III, and include impressions of leaves and legumes, which, however, are rarely to be found in a good state of preservation.

Fig. 21.   *Coal-bed in the Bracklesham Series, Whitecliff Bay*

Scale: 1 inch = 16 feet

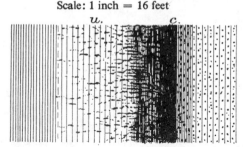

The strata are vertical, the older being on the left.

c.   Brown coal, passing into lignitic silt below.

u.   Underclay with roots. In the actual section, the disturbance of the lamination in this bed, by the intrusion of the roots, is perceptible.

The coal-bed in V is based on a bleached, shaly underclay, containing selenite, and penetrated by roots (¼ to ½ inch in diameter) to a depth of 10 feet. (Fig. 21.) Some of the roots are casts in pyritic clay, and most have an external film of lignite which frequently exhibits fine longitudinal ribs. Roots occur abundantly in the coal itself, which is partly, and perhaps mainly, composed of remains of plants that grew on the spot—probably in a salt-marsh.

At the base of IX a change occurs in the fauna, mainly arising from the introduction of new species of Upper Eocene (Bartonian) character. A slight stratigraphical break is suggested by the frequency of water-worn shells and the presence of pebbles.

---

[1]*Op. cit., Quart. Journ. Geol. Soc.*, vol. xxxv, 1879, p. 209.

Most of the Upper Bracklesham part of this section has lately become obscured by slips. The junction with the Barton Clay is still to be seen on the foreshore, but it is not easy to locate when the Tellina Sandstone, 126 feet below (and south of) it, is hidden.

A few inland sections which seem to include the base of the Bracklesham Beds have been noticed (p. 89). The only locality in which determinable fossils have been obtained is the railway-cutting leading to the chalk-quarry near West Ashey (p. 77). The cutting, now completely overgrown, showed the following abnormal succession:

"*Section in the railway cutting south of Ashey*

		ft	in.
"Bracklesham Beds	⎧ Light-blue or greenish loamy sand, crowded with Bracklesham fossils (IV of Fisher?)	7	0
	⎨ Dark blue loamy clay with a little lignite	33	0
	⎩ Blackish shaly clay with a little lignite	18	0
	Probable position of a strike-fault		
"London Clay	⎰ Clay overgrown	11	0
	⎱ Sand (Basement Bed of the London Clay)	6	0
"Reading Beds:	Red and mottled clay	92	0
	Chalk, nearly vertical"[1]		

About a dozen species of mollusca, characteristic of Bracklesham and younger strata, were found in the shelly sand 160 feet above the Chalk, together with a smaller number of species which range down into the London Clay. The Bagshot Sands and most of the London Clay have, almost certainly, been cut out by a strike-fault, which is indicated on the Geological Map. A bed of coal or lignite was formerly exposed in a pit close to the railway-siding. It lies at a horizon about 260 feet above the shell-bed just described, and therefore probably higher than that of the coal-bed of Whitecliff Bay.

Westward of Ashey, Bracklesham loams are worked at Gunville Brickyard and a few other places, but nothing of special interest is met with short of the coast at Alum Bay. There the Bracklesham Series has so changed in character that satisfactory correlation of its divisions with those of the Whitecliff Bay section is difficult, if not impossible.

The horizon now adopted as the lower limit of the Bracklesham Beds at Alum Bay is that indicated by J. S. Gardner in 1879,[2] namely, the bottom of Prestwich's "Bed 19".[3] It seems as good as any, and, in view of the thickness of the series at Whitecliff Bay and on the Bournemouth coast, preferable to the base-line selected by the Geological Survey ten years later. In the following tabulated description, the details of which are taken from the last edition of the Geological Survey Memoir on the Island (pp. 101, 102, 115, 116), the numbers in brackets (*e.g.* [29]) refer to Figure 19, p. 88.

---

[1]'Geology of the Isle of Wight,' *Mem. Geol. Surv.*, 1887, pp. 114, 115.

[2]*Op. cit.*, *Quart. Journ. Geol. Soc.*, vol. xxxv, p. 226.

[3]Prestwich, *op. cit.*, p. 258, Pl. IX, Fig. 1.

Section of the Bracklesham Beds in Alum Bay

	ft	in.

[29] BARTON CLAY.—Dark sandy clay with fossils (principally small bivalves). [Zone of *Nummulites elegans* at base.] — —

Dark sandy clay 15 6

Indurated, dark-greenish, sandy clay, with impressions of fossils .. 1 0

Fusus undosus?	[Corbula pisum *J. Sow.*]
Murex asper.	Sanguinolaria hollowaysi.
Pyrula nexilis.	Modiola sp.
Turritella imbricataria.	Tellina plagia.
Natica ambulacrum.	—— filosa?
Dentalium sp.	—— branderi?
Cardium parile.	—— sp.
Cardita sp.	Arca aviculina.
Cytherea lucida.	[Nummulites variolarius (*Lam.*)]
—— suberycinoides.	

Dark, sandy clay containing a bed of septaria 11 0

Indurated, greyish, sandy clay, with impressions of fossils 0 7

Fusus undosus?	Cardita 2 sp.
Voluta nodosa.	Cytherea obliqua.
Natica sp.	—— suberycinoides.
Phorus agglutinans.	—— lucida.
Turritella sulcifera.	Tellina tumescens?
Dentalium sp.	—— 2 sp.
Teredo sp.	Sanguinolaria hollowaysi.
Pecten corneus.	Panopaea corrugata.
Cardium parile.	Leda sp.
—— sp.	Modiola (or Mytilus) sp.

Dark sandy clay, weathering greenish grey, containing bands of lignite 16 0

Conglomerate of flint-pebbles, cemented by iron-oxide. The pebbles are of various sizes, up to a foot in diameter .. .. .. 1 foot to 1 6

[28] Sands (principally white), light tawny-yellow in the upper part; the lower 3 feet crimson 45 0

[27] Whitish marly clay 25 0

Dark chocolate-coloured marls and carbonaceous clay, with much lignite and selenite

	ft	in.		
Clay and marls	15	3		
Lignite band	1	6		
Clays and marls	3	3		
Lignite band	1	3	39	6
Clays and marls	6	0		
Lignite band	2	3		
Clays and marls	4	3		
Lignite band .. .. 9 in. to	1	0		
Clays and marls	5	0		

[26] Very thinly laminated pale yellow sand 10 0

White, crimson, and rose-coloured variegated sand passing into pale brownish-yellow sand 50 0

Thinly laminated light grey pipe-clay 1 6

[25] Pale yellow sand, and white laminated clay, with crimson streaks

Details of the upper part of this subdivision—

	ft	in.	
Yellow sand	14	6	
Pipe-clay parting	—		104 0
White sand	11	6	
Yellow sand	12	0	
White and crimson sand	—		

ft in.

[24] Thinly laminated clay, chocolate-coloured in the upper part
    Details:—

	ft in.	
Clay	27 0	
Lignite (very bituminous)	0 6	
Clay, with a band of lignite 5 or 6 feet from the base	44 0	} 99 0
Thinly laminated yellow sandstone, with much car-bonaceous matter .. .. .. 4 inches to	0 6	
Clay: white, hard and marly	27 0	

[23–21] Tawny, variegated, pink and white sands, with brown laminae: white
    sand predominates   ..   .. } 90 0
    (Iron bands 1 inch thick occur at 52 feet and 79 feet from the bottom)

[20] Pale grey and yellowish-brown sands, with thin laminae of a darker
    grey clay, containing pyrites and carbonaceous matter   ..   ..
(Some of the laminae, when newly broken, are of a greenish colour. } 60 0
    These beds are darker and most laminated in the lower part, and
    are most sandy towards the upper part)   ..   ..

[19] Light grey sandy clay, with vegetable matter lying across the bedding   2 0
[Bagshot Sands: laminated white sand] ..   ..   —

                                                                 571 7

The lignite occurring in definite beds in the divisions numbered 24 and 27 resembles the brown coal of the Whitecliff Bay section, and each of the lignite beds in No. 27 has a thin underclay penetrated by rootlets similar to those seen in that section, but of more slender shape and less conspicuous. Leaves have been observed in a seam of lignitic clay at the base of No. 24.[1]

Crimson-mottled grey pipe-clay, like that to be seen in exposures of the higher parts of the Bagshot Sands near Poole, occurs at the top of No. 28.

Above the strongly-marked pebble-bed at the base of No. 29, shells first appear as ill-preserved casts in green loam with large burrows. A solitary *Nipa*-like fruit was noted by the writer in the 11-foot bed, farther up.

The position of the pebble-bed with respect to the base of the Barton Clay corresponds to that of the lower and more persistent of the two pebble-beds in the upper part of the Highcliff Sands of the Christchurch Bay section.

The correlation of the Bracklesham Beds of Alum Bay with those of the opposite coast of the Mainland, indicated in the subjoined table, was proposed by Mr. Starkie Gardner in 1879.[2] It is to a large extent conjectural, but has not been seriously impugned.

Alum Bay				*Poole Harbour—Highcliff*
Group Nos. 29 (lowest 47 feet), 28		..		Highcliff Sands
27, 26	..	..	..	Hengistbury Head Beds
25	..	..	..	Boscombe Sands
24	..	..	..	Bournemouth Marine Beds
23—19 ..	..	..	..	Bournemouth Freshwater Beds

5. BARTON BEDS

The Barton Clay and Barton Sand form a stratigraphical series broadly comparable to the Selbornian of the Cretaceous system, and divisible on a palaeontological basis into three stages. As in the Selbornian Series, though to a less degree, sands replace clays, and *vice versâ*. In the Mainland area of the Hampshire Basin, the Upper Barton corresponds to the Barton Sand, whereas,

[1] R. S. Herries and H. W. Monckton. *Proc. Geol. Assoc.*, vol. xiv 1895, pp. 104, 106.
[2] *Op. cit.*, p. 226.

in the Isle of Wight, it includes not only the Sand but also the highest part of the Barton Clay. Conversely, the Lower Barton Stage, which is mainly argillaceous in the Hampshire Basin, seems to be represented in the London Basin by the eminently sandy Upper Bagshot Beds. As the Barton Clay and Barton Sand are not distinguished by appropriate colouration in the current edition (1903) of the Geological Survey Map of the Isle of Wight,[1] no inconvenience will be caused to the reader by the adoption in the present Memoir of the three-fold division of the Barton Beds recognised by Messrs. Gardner, Keeping and Monckton, and defined by them in their paper on "The Upper Eocene, &c.,"[2] in 1888.

The Barton Beds are thicker in the Isle of Wight than in their type-locality, but their nearly vertical position in the Island sections, while reducing accessible surfaces to the minimum, has facilitated decalcification by percolating soil-water, so that stages and zones which are famed for the variety and good condition of their fossil marine molluscs at Barton, here yield relatively few and fragile shells representative of a much smaller number of species.

The following table shows the variation in thickness of the three stages between Barton Cliff and Whitecliff Bay, a distance of about 25 miles, the measurements being in feet:

		Barton	Alum Bay	Whitecliff Bay
	Upper	90 ..	.. 114 ..	.. 221
Barton Beds ..	Middle ..	53 ..	.. 167 ..	.. 92
	Lower ..	49 ..	.. 57 ..	.. 55
		192	338	368

The *Lower Barton*, consisting mostly of bluish and greenish sandy clay, begins below with a coarse, gritty clay, 1 to 1½ feet thick, which abounds in *Nummulites elegans* T. R. Jones (*N. wemmelensis* var. van den Broeck and de la Harpe); and ends in loamy beds with patches of drifted small shells, as at Barton. Characteristic fossils include *Voluta athleta* Sol. (*Athleta*), *Cassis ambigua* (Sol.), *Hippochrenes amplus* (Sol.), *Cominella canaliculata* (J. de C. Sow.), *Mitra parva* (J. de C. Sow.), *Volvaria acutiuscula* (J. and G. B. Sow.), *Crassatella sulcata* (Solander).

The *Middle Barton* also is mainly argillaceous, but (at Alum Bay) is distinguished by the presence of layers of septarian clay-ironstone concretions, which are likewise confined to the same stage at Barton. This stage is less fossiliferous than the preceding one, and the species represented are mostly common to the Lower and Middle Barton.

The *Upper Barton* embodies the thick mass of almost unfossiliferous, light-tinted, fine-grained sands, formerly termed "Headon Hill Sands", and now known as Barton Sand. It also takes in 15 to 24 feet of bluish fossiliferous sandy clay, representing the Chama Bed (or Beds) of Barton Cliff, but forming in the Island the highest parts of the "Barton Clay". From the Chama Bed a fairly large number of fossil species have been recorded, such as *Seraphs sopitum* (Sol.), *Voluta humerosa* F. E. Edw., *Pyrula nexilis* (Sol.), *Calyptraea aperta* (Sol.), *Axinaea deleta* (Sol.), *Chama squamosa* Sol., *Cardium porulosum*

---

[1]Except in the small tract of Mainland, near Lymington, appearing therein.

[2]*Quart. Journ. Geol. Soc.*, vol. xliv, 1888, pp. 578–635.

Sol., *Crassatella tenuisulcata* F. E. Edw., MS. S. V. Wood, *Hemiaster branderi* (Forbes), (often recorded as *Schizaster d'urbani* Forbes, a Bracklesham species).

DESCRIPTION OF SECTIONS

We begin with the Alum Bay section, which is nearest to the type-locality on the opposite coast of the Mainland.

Section of Barton Beds, Alum Bay[1]

			ft
Barton Sand, 90 ft	Upper Barton, 114 ft	White sand, becoming clayey and yellow towards the base	90
		Dark blue clay, with one band of ironstone a foot thick, 6 feet from top, and a similar band 4 feet lower down; numerous fossils	24
Barton Clay, 248 ft	Middle Barton, 167 ft	Pale and ferruginous yellow sandy clays, green in the upper part. Lignite, corals, *Dentalium*, *Ostrea*, *Corbula*, *Pleurotoma*, common and of several species. Pale yellow sand at base ..	70
		Layer of tabular septaria, with many sharks' teeth, pebbles, fragments of wood, &c., and layer of scattered pebbles beneath, in green sand	10
		Grey and brown sandy clay, with numerous casts of fossils of Middle Barton species, the shells being preserved in the lower 7 feet only ..	29
		Drab clay, with band of septaria at top, and a second one 16 feet lower down. *Corbula*, sharks' teeth, and lignite	58
	Lower Barton, 57 ft	Dark bluish-green clay, with sands in patches at the top, containing *Buccinum canaliculatum* (*Cominella*), *Volvaria acutiuscula*, *Mitra parva*, &c. The whole capped with 9 feet of pale grey loamy sand	56
		The same, with *Nummulites elegans*	1
Bracklesham Beds		Glauconitic sandy clay	47½
		Pebble-bed	0½

The *Nummulites elegans* Zone and succeeding fossiliferous beds of the Lower Barton are usually well shown a little southward of the pier approach, which, with a retaining wall, obscures much of the Middle Stage of the series. The shelly parts of the Chama Bed seem to be represented by ironstone bands in the cliff, but are to be seen at times in a less altered condition on the foreshore.

Fine sands at the top of the Upper Barton and their junction with the Headon Beds are sometimes exposed just above the beach north-east of Headon Hill, about 170 yards south-west of the boat-house at Widdick Chine.

The sands of the Upper Barton are, or have been, dug inland at Five Houses near Calbourne, at Gunville, at Thornhill near Stapler's Heath, and other places. They are remarkable for their purity and fineness of grain, which fit them for use in the manufacture of glass.

---

[1]From Gardner, Keeping and Monckton, *op. cit.*, p. 600, with slight alterations.

Section of the Barton Beds, Whitecliff Bay,[1] (Fig. 20, p. 92)

			ft
Headon Beds: light-green clay		.. ..	—
Barton Sand, 206 ft	Upper Barton, 221 ft	Buff sand, with darker clayey beds towards the base	206
		Bluish sandy clay, with *Chama squamosa, Terebellum sopitum* (*Seraphs*), *Vulta humerosa*, &c.	15
Barton Clay, 162 ft	Middle Barton, 92 ft	Blue sandy clays, with mottled-brown patches of soft earthy ironstone and ironstone band 3 ft thick at base	38
		Greyish-blue clays, with fawn-coloured bands near base	36
		Stiff laminated clay with few, if any, fossils ..	18
	Lower Barton, 55 ft	Blue and yellow sandy clays, with few badly-preserved fossils	54
		Dark-green glauconitic sandy clay crowded with *Nummulites elegans*	1
Bracklesham Beds ..		Dark-green glauconitic sandy clays with *Nummulites variolarius*	126
		Sandstone ("*Tellina* Bed")	—

Both here and at Alum Bay there is nothing in the general appearance of the Lower Barton Clays to distinguish them from the Upper Bracklesham Clays, into which they pass.

The Lower and Middle Stages, and the Chama Bed of the Upper Stage, are all fossiliferous. Casts of shells (*Cardita oblonga* and *Cytherea sp.*) have been observed in the Upper Sands about 66 feet from the well-marked junction with the Headon Beds.

---

[1]Gardner, Keeping, and Monckton, *op. cit.*, p. 604, with some alterations.

Chapter VII

OLIGOCENE BEDS

THE OLIGOCENE BEDS of the Isle of Wight were subjected to such minute investigation by able observers during the latter half of the last century, and were so fully described in the second edition of the Geological Survey Memoir on the Island, published in 1889, that little fresh information of importance concerning them has since been forthcoming. The task of preparing the necessarily brief account of these strata for the present work, therefore, has been, almost exclusively, one of abridgment.

The "Fluvio-marine Beds" of the Island were first described by Thomas Webster in 1816,[1] but it was not till 1853 that the complete succession was satisfactorily established by Prof. Edward Forbes,[2] whose divisions and measurements are adopted, with but little modification, in the present memoir.[3]

TABLE of the OLIGOCENE BEDS of the ISLE OF WIGHT

					ft
Hamstead Series ..	..	..	..	about	260
Bembridge Marls	..	..	..	„	100
„ Limestone	..	..	..	„	10
Osborne Series ..	..	..	..	„	100
Headon Series ..	..	..	..	„	150
Total ..	..	..		„	620

The propriety of retaining the Headon Series in the Oligocene System has been questioned, but the point cannot well be decided until the palaeontology of the Tertiary Rocks of the Island has been revised.

1. HEADON BEDS

This series consists of thinly-bedded marls and clays, with subordinate bands of limestone and sand; the total thickness varying from 147 feet at Headon Hill to 212 feet at Whitecliff Bay. At the western end only of the Island does this series make much show at the surface: elsewhere it is confined to two narrow belts of ground; one of them following the outcrop of the Eocene Beds throughout the length of the Island; the other lying on the coast near Norris Castle and Osborne.

The Headon Beds are divided into three stages, namely:

Upper Headon: Freshwater and brackish.

Middle Headon: Brackish and marine—the latter thickening eastward.

Lower Headon: Brackish and freshwater.

[1] In Sir H. C. Englefield's 'A description of the Principal Picturesque Beauties, Antiquities, and Geological Phenomena of the Isle of Wight', (London, 1816), p. 226.

[2] 'On the Fluvio-marine Tertiaries of the Isle of Wight,' *Quart. Journ. Geol. Soc.*, vol. ix, 1853, p. 259 *et. seqq.*

[3] A summary of the views of various geologists, concerning the age and relations of the strata under consideration down to 1889, is given in the Geological Survey Memoir above referred to (pp. 124–127).

All three divisions are highly fossiliferous. The freshwater and brackish (or estuarine) pelecypods most abundantly represented are species of *Erodona* (*Potamomya*) and *Cyrena*, which swarm in the Lower and Upper Stages: *Unio* is comparatively scarce, and normally occurs in thin seams. In the freshwater limestones the mollusca are nearly all gasteropods, of which *Limnaea longiscata* (Brongn.) and *Planorbis euomphalus* J. Sow. are most conspicuous. *Viviparus lentus* (Sol.) and *Stenothyra parvula* (Desh.) (*Nematura*) also are common and widely distributed in the freshwater marls. Several species of land-shells are scattered through the limestones.

Among the marine bivalves, *Meretrix incrassata* (J. Sow.), *Nucula headonensis* Forbes, and *Ostrea velata* S. V. Wood, are noteworthy. The first of them, ranging from the Middle Barton to the Bembridge Marls, attains its maximum abundance in the Middle Headon. Formerly assigned to the genus *Venus*, it gave the name to the wellknown "Venus Bed". The other two species abound in Colwell Bay, where the third forms a thick oyster-bed.

The most plentiful gasteropods in the marine and estuarine beds are several species formerly referred to *Cerithium* (such as *Batillaria concava* (J. Sow.) and *Potamides vagus* (Sol.)), *Melanopsis fusiformis* (J. Sow.), *Pisania labiata* (J. de C. Sow.), *Murex sexdentatus* (J. de C. Sow.), *Neritina aperta* (J. de C. Sow.), *N. concava* (J. de C. Sow.), *Ancilla buccinoides* (Lam.), *Melania acuta* (J. Sow.) (*muricata* S. V. Wood), and several species of *Cancellaria*, *Natica*, *Pleurotoma* and *Voluta*. The last-named genus includes *V. suturalis* (Nyst.) and *V. geminata* (J. de C. Sow.); two species characteristic of the Royden and Brockenhurst Beds of the New Forest. They are associated with corals in the most purely marine bed of the Middle Headon, at the junction with the lower Headon, in the eastern half of the Island.

A large number of the marine mollusca range downward into the Barton Beds, but about half of the species are peculiar to the Oligocene of British geologists.

"Of other fossils the most commonly found are valves of *Balanus unguiformis* in the marine beds, and nucules of *Chara*, generally *C. wrighti* in almost any part of the series, but especially in the *Neritina*-bed at the base of the Middle Headon Beds. Vertebrate remains are comparatively scarce. Except *Chara*, there are few recognisable plants.

"Every variation in the amount of salt in the water seems to have been marked by a change in the fauna. The purely freshwater beds contain few mollusca except *Limnaea*, *Planorbis*, *Paludina* [*Viviparus*], *Unio*, and land-shells. The different species of *Potamomya* [*Erodona*], *Cyrena*, *Cerithium* (*Potamides*), *Melania*, and *Melanopsis* appear nearly all to have liked water containing more or less salt. So we have a gradual change to beds containing Oysters, and then to beds with Volutes.

"Besides these indications of varying conditions, it is interesting to observe a general tendency in the beds to become more freshwater towards the south-west, while tufaceous limestones appear in that direction. The land-shells also point to the proximity of land, as do the pebbles of flint."[1]

Description of Sections

"The following section, measured during the original survey of the Island, will give a good idea of the nature and fossils of these beds. It must not be

[1]'Geology of the Isle of Wight,' *Mem. Geol. Surv.*, 2nd ed., 1889, pp. 146, 147.

forgotten, however, that each of the minor divisions is extremely variable, and many of them are found to die out or entirely change their character in short distances.

"Section of the Headon Series of Headon Hill, measured by Edward Forbes in October, 1852 (*with a few Corrections made in* 1888)

		ft	in.
	Blue and yellow clays and marls, passing into grey laminated clays with crushed *Paludina lenta* [*Viviparus*] and *Potamomya gregaria* [*Erodona*]	15	0
	Variegated clays with *Potamomya*, especially in the lower part. A 6-inch band of ironstone with *Paludina* occurs in the centre of the bed. *Serpula*	3	3
	Brown and green clays. *Potamomya, Paludina lenta, Melanopsis fusiformis*	3	4

"Upper Headon Beds, 46 ft 7 ins.

	Limestone, carbonaceous at top; details:—		
	Carbonaceous 1 0		
	Sandy, with crushed *Limnaea longiscata* and *Planorbis euomphalus* 2 0		
	Full of fine shells; *Limnaea longiscata, Planorbis euomphalus, P. lens, P. obtusus, P. rotundatus, P. platystomus, Paludina,* &c. 2 0	8	0
	Rubbly, with *Planorbis euomphalus* 3 0		
	Bluish and purplish clays, passing into Limestone. *Melanopsis carinata, Limnaea longiscata, Planorbis platystoma, P. obtusus, Bulimus politus*	5	0
	Limestone, compact in places, with many shells and lines of nodular concretions in places. Shells as in the limestone above	10	0
	Greenish white compact sands, carbonaceous at the base. *Serpula tenuis*	2	0

"Middle Headon Beds, 33¼ ft

		Blue clays and sands, crowded with univalve shells. *Cerithium ventri-cosum* [*Potamides*], *C. concavum* [*Batillaria*], *C. pseudo-cinctum* [*Potamides vagus*] *Cyrena obovata, Ostrea, Natica.* The shells are much broken at the lower part (at 2 feet down) and larger than further northward	3	3
		Yellow sand, with bands of lignite and clay. *Cerithium concavum*	2	0
		Blue-green clay with lignite. Fossils few:—*Cyrena obovata*, scattered *Ostrea*	2	0
		Limestone. *Planorbis euomphalus, Limnaea longiscata* ..	1	0
	Venus Bed	Blue, green, and brown sandy clay, with oysterbeds at about 5 feet from the top. A few fossils in blue clay above; fossils mostly in the middle and lower part. Occasional flint pebbles. *Ostrea, Cyrena obovata, Cytherea incrassata* [*Meretrix*], *Nucula, Natica depressa* [*Ampullina*], *Melania, Fusus,* small species. The oysters in this bed are smaller and fewer than at Colwell Bay; the other marine shells are also fewer	15	0
	Neritina Bed	Sand, clay, and lignite; with bands full of bivalves and scattered univalves. *Cyrena obovata, Cerithium ventricosum, C. concavum, C. pseudo-cinctum, Neritina concava, Melanopsis fusiformis*	10	0

		ft	in.
	Cream-coloured limestone in one bed. *Limnaea longiscata, Planorbis euomphalus, P. lens*? This corresponds with the limestone of How Ledge	3'	0
	Sand, clay, and lignite, with seeds. At the bottom 2 feet 9 inches of strong carbonaceous bands with seeds and univalves. *Carpolithes, Melania*	20	0
	Limestone with shells (much broken) probably brackish water? *Limnaea longiscata, Nematura*	1	6
	Green clays; fossils few or none	8	0
	Zones of lignite and sand	2	0
	Ferruginous bands, alternating with clays full of *Paludina*	3	0
	Pale sands with bands of lignite	4	8
	CYRENA PULCHRA BED.—Green clays, carbonaceous at the base. *Cyrena pulchra, Potamomya* [*Erodona*], *Limnaea*	0	6
	Limestone, very shelly in the middle, and divided into two beds by a clayey parting. *Limnaea longiscata, L. caudata, Planorbis euomphalus*, fragments of *Paludina*	5	4
"Lower Headon Beds, 61 ft	Green clays with purplish streaks (from this clay to the base of the Headon Series the beds vary much at different places)	1	4
	Sandy limestone, very shelly and ferruginous at the base. Shells crushed	0	6
	White and yellow sand, with a carbonaceous band at the top	0	4
	Blue clay with shells; becomes sandy below. *Potamomya, Cerithium*	4	6
	Sandy limestone, passing upwards into sand. *Planorbis euomphalus, Limnaea longiscata* (shells much broken) ..	1	6
	Strong band of ironstone 2 inches to	0	4
	CYRENA CYCLADIFORMIS BED.—Sandy green clays, *Potamomya, Cyrena cycladiformis, Cerithium elegans* [*Potamides*], *C. duplex* [*Potamides*]	3	0
	White sands with harder bands	1	6
	Green clays with a thin ferruginous band one inch thick at the base. No fossils?	6	0
	Total	146	10
[Barton Sand]	Bright yellow sands, with white sand, forming lenticular patches in yellow sand	11	0"[1]

A section of the Middle Headon Beds, in the north-eastern part of Headon Hill, is illustrated in Fig. 22.

The succession shown in the cliffs of Totland and Colwell Bays, to the north, is generally similar to that above described, though differing in detail, owing to lateral variation in the character of many of the beds. The marine element in the Middle Headon fauna, too, becomes more pronounced northward of Headon Hill. These changes, in conjunction with slight undulations in the prevailing northward dip, the obliquity of the sections thereto, and local obscuration by landslip, account for the difficulty experienced by some observers in correlating the Headon Beds of Headon Hill with those of Colwell Bay. The connection becomes clearer if certain marked horizons be followed through the intervening ground, after one has noted the disposition of the cliff-outcrops when viewed from the sea.

The How Ledge limestone, with its perfectly preserved freshwater shells, at the top of the Lower Headon, is a well-marked bed, conspicuous in the broken ground of Headon Hill, and readily traceable, through the cliff in the

---

[1]*Ibid.*, pp. 128–130.

FIG. 22. *Vertical section in the Headon Beds, at North-East corner of Headon Hill*

H. Keeping and E. B, Tawney, *Quart. Journ. Eeol. Soc.*, vol. xxxvii., 1881p .91.

(Space does not permit the interpolation of revised nomenclature.)

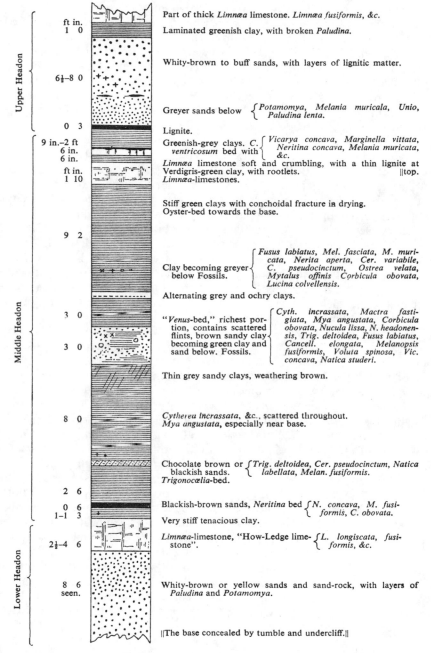

Part of thick *Limnæa* limestone. *Limnæa fusiformis, &c.*

Laminated greenish clay, with broken *Paludina*.

Whity-brown to buff sands, with layers of lignitic matter.

Greyer sands below { *Potamomya, Melania muricala, Unio, Paludina lenta.*

Lignite.

Greenish-grey clays. C. { *Vicarya concava, Marginella vittata,* *ventricosum* bed with { *Neritina concava, Melania muricata, &c.*

Limnæa limestone soft and crumbling, with a thin lignite at Verdigris-green clay, with rootlets. ‖top.
Limnæa-limestones.

Stiff green clays with conchoidal fracture in drying.
Oyster-bed towards the base.

Clay becoming greyer { *Fusus labiatus, Mel. fasciata, M. muri-* below Fossils. { *cata, Nerita aperta, Cer. variabile,* { *C. pseudocinctum, Ostrea velata,* { *Mytalus offinis Corbicula obovata,* { *Lucina colvellensis.*

Alternating grey and ochry clays.

"*Venus*-bed," richest por- { *Cyth. incrassata, Mactra fasti-* tion, contains scattered { *giata, Mya angustata, Corbicula* flints, brown sandy clay { *obovata, Nucula lissa, N. headonen-* becoming green clay and { *sis, Trig. deltoidea, Fusus labiatus,* sand below. Fossils. { *Cancell. elongata, Melanopsis* { *fusiformis, Voluta spinosa, Vic.* { *concava, Natica studeri.*

Thin grey sandy clays, weathering brown.

Cytherea incrassata, &c., scattered throughout.
Mya angustata, especially near base.

Chocolate brown or { *Trig. deltoidea, Cer. pseudocinctum, Natica* blackish sands. { *labellata, Melan. fusiformis.*
Trigonocælia-bed.

Blackish-brown sands, *Neritina* bed { *N. concava, M. fusi-* { *formis, C. obovata.*
Very stiff tenacious clay.

Limnæa-limestone, "How-Ledge lime- { *L. longiscata, fusi-* stone". { *formis, &c.*

Whity-brown or yellow sands and sand-rock, with layers of *Paludina* and *Potamomya*.

‖The base concealed by tumble and undercliff.‖

Upper Headon
Middle Headon
Lower Headon

ft in.
1 0
6½–8 0
0 3
9 in.–2 ft
6 in.
6 in.
ft in.
1 10
9 2
3 0
3 0
8 0
2 6
0 6
1–1 3
2½–4 6
8 6
seen.

H

northern part of Totland Bay into Colwell Bay, where it comes down to the shore a little north of Colwell Chine. The calcareous sand and sandstone of Warden Ledge, 19 feet lower, is unrecognisable in the Headon Hill sections. Comparatively soft in the cliff south of Warden Point, it hardens on immersion in salt water, and forms a stronger reef than the more noticeable How Ledge limestone above it. Still lower, a group of thin limestones, forming a minor reef below Warden Fort, can be traced southward nearly to Widdick Chine.

Another marked division, of greater interest, is the exceedingly fossiliferous Oyster Bed included in the "Venus Bed" of the Middle Headon. This is about 95 feet above the sea at Widdick Chine, and still at approximately the same altitude half a mile to the north, in the hillock east of Totland Pier (the prevailing dip being interrupted hereabouts by a low anticline), but declines through the cliff from the Coastguard Station in Totland Bay into Colwell Bay, gaining in thickness in that direction (Fig. 23, p. 107). East of How Ledge the base of the Oyster Bed (there about 12 feet thick) passes below the beach, but emerges abruptly about 70 yards farther north, when it becomes evident that the obliquely-stratified mass of drifted oyster and other shells occupies a hollow eroded in the underlying sandy clay with abundant *Meretrix incrassata*.

At Brambles Chine the Oyster Bed, now reduced in thickness to 3 feet or less, is about 10 feet above the beach, to which it again descends—in this case, as a result of the general dip—a few yards south of Linstone Chine. It reappears, for the last time, at the foot of the cliff some 50 yards north of Linstone Chine, being brought up there by a remarkably sharp ∧-shaped anticlinal fold, which is slightly overturned towards the south in the overlying freshwater sands and clays of the Upper Headon.

The Upper Headon Beds fall to sea-level between the anticline last mentioned and Sconce Point. Most of the cliff on this stretch of coast is badly foundered and overgrown. The massive Limnaean limestone in the lower part of the Upper Headon at Headon Hill seems to be represented by the thin bed (1½ to 3 feet) which occupies the foreshore under Cliff End Fort.

Inland sections yielding evidence of definite horizons are scarce.

Highly fossiliferous sandy marl, apparently near the base of the Middle Headon, is cut into by a little ravine near the north-eastern corner of the grave-yard of All Saints' Church, Freshwater. The included specimens of *Neritina concava* are unusually large, and have their colour well preserved.

Middle Headon Beds were proved in a well-boring at Messrs. Mew, Langton, & Company's brewery at Newport, and were completely traversed in a boring at West Cowes Waterworks near Broadfield, where they appear to be about 116 feet thick.[1] The Cowes boring is interesting in this connection as revealing the presence in abundance of the characteristic Brockenhurst Beds species, *Voluta geminata* J. de C. Sow. and *Cardita simplex* Wood.

The Upper Headon Beds crop out in a small area at the extreme northern point of the Island, and were formerly well displayed at the foot of the cliff near Norris Castle, but are now almost entirely hidden by a sea-wall and groynes.[2] Shells of *Erodona*, *Cyrena*, *Cerithium* and other brackish- and freshwater molluscs abound on the beach.

---

[1]*Ibid.*, pp. 313, 314.

[2]The section there is described in the first and second editions of the *Geol. Surv. Memoir* on the Island (pp. 141, 142 of second ed.).

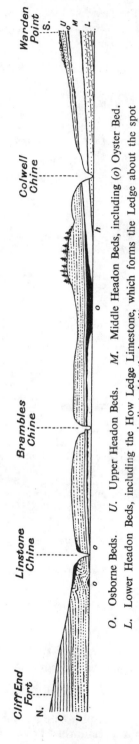

Fig. 23. *Section in Colwell Bay*

Distance about ¾ mile.   Vertical scale exaggerated.

O. Osborne Beds. *U.* Upper Headon Beds. *M.* Middle Headon Beds, including (*o*) Oyster Bed.
L. Lower Headon Beds, including the How Ledge Limestone, which forms the Ledge about the spot
indicated by the letter (*h*).

The dark patches shown in the upper part of the cliff at Linstone Chine represent gravel left by the brook
which has cut that chine.

The following section of the Headon Beds on the east coast of the Island is that measured during the original Survey, with some corrections and additions made in 1888 (*see* Fig. 24, p. 109):

Headon Beds in Whitecliff Bay

	ft	in.
"Upper Headon Beds, 58 feet — Grey, reddish, bluish, and ash-coloured laminated clays, Layers of *Potamomya gregaria* [*Erodona*], with occasional *Paludina lenta* [*Viviparus*], *Melania* 2 *sp.*, Fishscales, *Serpula* on the *Paludina* and *Potamomya*	12	0
Grey laminated clays. *Unio*, *Cyrena obovata*	5	0
Sandy clay with calcareous concretions. *Limnaea caudata*, *Chara wrighti*	1	0
Ferruginous sands and calcareous hard bands. *Hydrobia* [*Nystia*], &c.	1	0
Green clay, with *Cyrena obovata*	5	0
Brown clay, without fossils		
Yellow sand, without fossils	10	0
Marl and green clay with calcareous concretions. *Cyrena obovata*, *Limnaea longiscata*, *Planorbis euomphalus*, pieces of wood	15	0
White sand with thin layers of whitish clay	4	0
Alternations of carbonaceous clays and greenish sands. *Cyrena obovata*, *Potamides*, *Chara wrighti*	5	0
"Middle Headon Beds, 126 feet — Green sandy loam, with a few casts of marine shells. *Psammobia compressa* [*Psammotaea*], *Cytherea incrassata* [*Meretrix*] *Cyrena*	12	0
Blue sandy clay. *Cytherea incrassata* very abundant at the top; *Cerithium pseudo-cinctum* [*Potamides vagus*]	20	0
Stiff blue clay, full of fossils. *Cytherea incrassata*, *Psammobia compressa*, *Cyrena obovata*, *Fusus labiatus* [*Pisania*], *Cancellaria elongata*, *C. muricata*, *Natica labellata*	4	0
Sand or sandy greenish clay weathering brown. Ironstone nodules. Casts of marine shells	76	0
Brown sandy clay, often with nodules containing marine shells and fish-remains. *Cardita deltoidea*, &c.	12	0
Brown clay, containing pieces of the underlying clay and flint-pebbles, and full of marine shells. *Ostrea*, *Modiola*, *Cardium*, *Cardita deltoidea*, *Cytherea incrassata*, *Calyptraea sp.*, *Fusus*, *Voluta spinosa*, *V. geminata*, &c. (Messrs. Keeping and Tawney record 62 species of mollusca from this bed and compare it with the Brockenhurst zone of the New Forest)	2	0
"Lower Headon Beds, 28¼ feet — Green freshwater marls, with seams of *Potamomya plana*, *Planorbis*, *Limnaea*, &c.	8	0
Grey sandy clay	7	0
Hard ferruginous sandstone	0	3
Pale-green clays, with seams of lignite, and ironstone nodules. *Paludina lenta*, *Limnaea*, *Planorbis euomphalus*, *P. obtusus*, &c.	8	0
Carbonaceous clay and lignite	1	0
Green clay, ferruginous at the base. No fossils observed	4	0
Total	212	3"

"Here, as at Cowes, there seems to be a tendency in the marine bands to thicken at the expense of the estuarine Lower Headon Beds. These marine bands become more thoroughly marine, losing to a large extent the admixture of freshwater shells which is so conspicuous at the west end of the Island. The tufaceous fresh-water limestones have all died out, and most of the purely freshwater beds seem to be largely replaced by beds of estuarine origin. However, the occurrence of derivative fragments of the underlying freshwater clays at the base of the marine beds, shows that the thinning out of the lower

FIG. 24. *Vertical Section of the Headon Beds, Whitecliff Bay*

Scale: 1 inch = 40 feet

Adapted from "Geology of the Isle of Wight" (*Mem. Geol. Surv.*),
2nd Ed., 1889, Pl. 5

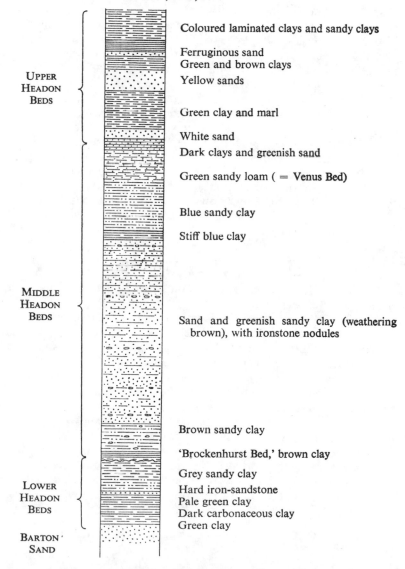

UPPER HEADON BEDS

Coloured laminated clays and sandy clays

Ferruginous sand
Green and brown clays
Yellow sands

Green clay and marl

White sand
Dark clays and greenish sand

Green sandy loam (= **Venus Bed**)

Blue sandy clay

Stiff blue clay

MIDDLE HEADON BEDS

Sand and greenish sandy clay (weathering brown), with ironstone nodules

Brown sandy clay

'Brockenhurst Bed,' brown clay

Grey sandy clay

Hard iron-sandstone
Pale green clay
Dark carbonaceous clay
Green clay

LOWER HEADON BEDS

BARTON SAND

series may be due to actual erosion, and not to a replacement by contemporaneous beds of marine origin. Messrs. Keeping and Tawney record the occurrence of a similar line of erosion at the base of the Brockenhurst Beds in the New Forest."[1]

Ill-preserved corals referable to *Lobopsammia, Solenastra, &c.*, are occasionally to be found at the base of the Middle Headon in Whitecliff Bay. This part of the section is seldom clearly exposed. The blue sandy clay with abundant *Meretrix incrassata*, 92 to 112 feet higher, apparently represents the Venus Bed of Colwell Bay.

2. OSBORNE BEDS

Between the Upper Headon Beds and the Bembridge Limestone there lies a series of brackish-water sediments, of more varied lithological character than those just described. The series alluded to was originally termed the "St. Helen's Series" by Professor E. Forbes, because of the "conspicuous features formed by them [on the coast] between St. Helen's and Ryde", but he altered their title on its becoming apparent that their relations with the beds above and below them were more clearly discernible in the cliff and grounds of Osborne House than in the locality after which they were named in the first instance. The change, however, proved unfortunate, for, not many decades after it had been made, the new type-section was obliterated by the erection of a sea-wall. The name "St. Helen's" is still used in connection with the Osborne Beds, to denote the higher members of a group of predominantly sandy beds appearing in the middle and upper part of the formation on the north-eastern shores of the Island; the lower, coarser, and more indurated members of the group being known as the Nettlestone Grits.

The clays and marls of which the Osborne Series mainly consist are more brightly coloured than those of the Headon Beds, and the bands of green and red, reminiscent of the Wealden Marls, are a striking feature of the cliff-sections. The series thickens from about 80 feet at each end of the Island to about 110 feet under Newport and Cowes.

The included shells, massed in bands disposed at irregular intervals, are referable to but few species, most of which occur both in the underlying and in the overlying Series: as far as is known, not one is peculiar to the formation. There are, however, a few recorded fish (*Lepidosteus sp., Amia colenutti* Newton, *Diplomystus vectensis* (Newton) (*Clupea*), and prawns (*Propalaemon*), which appear to be distinctive; and the appearance here of the two mammals, *Palaeotherium minus* ? Cuv., and *Theridomys aquatilis* Aymard, is of importance for purposes of correlation with the Continental deposits.[2] Plant-remains have been observed, but seem not to have been described.

"The paucity of [molluscan] species seems to be mainly due to the conditions under which the beds were deposited. There is an absence of truly marine beds, though a few marine shells occur. Purely freshwater strata are also rare. The mass of the clay seems to have been deposited in lagoons, varying in saltness, in which could live brackish-water molluscs like *Melania* and *Potamomya*, and a few of the more hardy freshwater and marine species. Lagoons of this

[1]*Ibid.*, pp. 143, 144.

[2]G. F. Dollfus, 'On the Classification of the Beds of the Paris Basin,' *Proc. Geol. Assoc.*, vol. xxi 1909, p. 111.

character are at the present day favourite places for turtles and alligators, like those so abundant in this deposit."[1]

Description of Sections

We follow the north coast of the Island, beginning in the west.

"Osborne Series at Headon Hill

	ft	in.
"Whitish (passing into red and blue) marls, with occasional hard bands, and courses of nodular concretions of light-grey argillaceous limestone in which occur traces of shells and turtle bones. In the concretions are *Limnaea longiscata, Planorbis discus, P. obtusus, P. obigyratus, Paludina sp.*	40	0
Grey shale, with crushed *Paludina lenta* [*Viviparus*], fish-vertebrae, &c. ..		
Ferruginous and nodular band ..	7	0
Grey shale, *Paludina lenta, Melanopsis carinata, Melania costata.* ..		
The FISH and PLANT BEDS ..		
Yellow, red, and blue sandy clays ..	3	0
Thick concretionary limestone, with siliceous concretions sometimes of large size and used for building. This band almost disappears northward. Fossils scarce. *Limnaea longiscata, Planorbis euomphalus, P. lens, Paludina lenta* ..	18	0
Greenish-white calcareous clay ..	4	0
Sandy ferruginous band ..	2	0
	74	0

"The concretionary limestone can be traced inland towards Middleton, forming a bold feature in the hill. At the old limekilns near Greens it contains *Bulimus ellipticus* [*Amphidromus*], *Limnaea*, and teeth of *Palaeotherium minus ?* This rock was formerly referred to the Bembridge Limestone, but both its lithological character and its continuity with the concretionary limestone of the coast show that it ought to be referred to the Osborne Series.

"Between Headon Hill and Linstone Chine the Osborne Series has been removed by denudation, and the cliffs consist of the subjacent Headon Beds. At Cliff End it reappears beneath the battery and can then be traced at short intervals along the coast nearly to the river Yar . . .

"Osborne Beds at Cliff End

	ft
"Bluish sandy and marly clays. *Cyrena obovata* (this bed is now invisible) .. About 10	
Red and blue marls, with lines of nodular concretions of argillaceous limestone in which fossils occur occasionally .. 25 to 30	
Dark-grey shales with an ironstone band in the centre. Leaves, Insects, and Fish; *Candona, Paludina lenta* [*Viviparus*], *Melanopsis carinata, Melania costata, Lepidosteus, Alligator.* (Probably the equivalent of the FISH BED.) ..	7
Reddish and bluish clayey marls, with greenish nodules containing shells; turtle; *Limnaea longiscata, Hydrobia,* and *Paludina globuloides* ..	40
	82 to 92"[2]

---

[1]'Geology of the Isle of Weight', *Mem. Geol. Surv.*, 2nd Ed. 1889, p. 157.
[2]*Ibid.*, pp. 148–150.

It will be noticed that the thick concretionary limestone of the Headon Hill section is wanting at Cliff End, its place in the sequence being occupied by part of the marls with remains of turtle, and nodules containing *Limnaea* and *Viviparus* (*Paludina*). A trial shaft sunk in the southern part of Cliff End Fort in 1920 proved nearly 50 feet of coloured marls and clays, including only one band of broken shells, a few feet down.

From Norton eastward to the mouth of Newtown River the Osborne Beds are below sea-level. East of Newtown River the green and red marls reappear from beneath the Bembridge Limestone and are exposed for a depth of about 30 feet in the cliff and a brickyard. Half a mile farther east they again sink below sea-level, and are lost for two and a half miles. Between Gurnard Ledge and Cowes the cliff is generally much obscured by slips, and the beds exposed are poor in fossils.

The cliff at Osborne was long ago sloped and planted, and no useful purpose would be served by reproducing Forbes's discursive account of what he saw there. The beds exposed would seem to have been of the usual types.[1]

"A section in red and mottled clays of the Osborne Series is seen in the East Cowes Park Brick-yard. Here J. Rhodes obtained *Chara*, impressions of plants, casts of *Limnaea*, Fish vertebræ, scales of *Lepidosteus*, *Chelone*, *Trionyx*, Crocodile, and the astragalus of a small mammal."[2]

The small fish, *Diplomystus vectensis* (Newt.) (*Clupea*), which occurs so abundantly in a thin bed of shaly clay near the middle of the Osborne Series, was first observed near Ryde House by Mr. G. W. Colenutt,[3] who subsequently traced the horizon westward to King's Quay, and eastward to Sea View. The position of this bed with reference to the Bembridge Limestone at King's Quay is indicated in the subjoined section. At present, the best exposure is on the shore near the boat-house west of the mouth of Wootton Creek.

"Section east of King's Quay

(Clement Reid and G. W. Colenutt)

		ft
"Bembridge limestone		
Red and mottled clay (only seen in landslips) .. .. About		40
Green clay, with scattered fish bones. Scales and vertebræ *Lepidosteus* abundant, *Alligator*, *Emys* [*Ocadia*?], *Trionyx*, and *Chelone*, *Theridomys* and snake vertebra .. .. About		4
[Fish-bed] Hard grey shaly clay, full of fish bones, and whole fish (*Clupea vectensis* [*Diplomystus*])		2
Similar clay with grass-like leaves and lenticular masses of cement stones ..		3
Blue clay, with abundance of mollusca. *Paludina lenta* [*Viviparus*], *Melanopsis carinata*, &c.		6
Unfossiliferous green clay, to low water.		
		55"[4]

---

[1]*Vide ibid.*, pp. 151, 152.

[2]*Ibid.*, p. 152.

[3]Colenutt, 'On a Portion of the Osborne Beds, &c.', *Geol. Mag.*, 1888, p. 358. See also *id.* 'Note on the Geology of the Osborne Beds', *ibid.*, 1903, p. 99; H. Woodward 'On some Fossil Prawns from the Osborne Beds', *ibid.*, 1903, p. 97; and E. T. Newton, 'On the remains of *Amia*, &c.', *Quart. Journ. Geol. Soc.*, vol. lv, 1899, p. 1.

[4]'Geology of the Isle of Wight,' *Mem. Geol. Surv.*, 1889, p. 152.

The fish-bed crops out just below high water-mark. It is slightly harder than the other clays and often projects through the beach.

"West of Binstead Point, thirty feet of red and green marls are displayed at the base of the cliff, supporting hard light-green marl with small white concretions (*d*, Fig. 25); above this succeeds a thin band of decayed shells (forming a soft shelly limestone, the greater portion of which is composed of fragments of bivalve shells), with a sort of laminated appearance. The calcareous band contains comminuted *Cyrena*, *Limnaea longiscata*, *Unio*, *Melania excavata*, *Melanopsis*, *Planorbis discus*, &c., with two feet of interstratified sands and sandstones and grits (*c*) above it, which are probably the equivalents of the siliceous beds beneath the Bembridge Limestone at the Binstead quarries. Two feet of soft sand (*b*) complete the section.

FIG. 25. *Section in the Osborne Beds, Binstead*

From "Geology of the Isle of Wight" (*Mem. Geol. Surv.*), 2nd Ed., Fig. 50, p. 153.

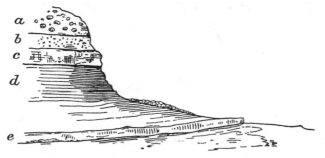

a. Gravel. *b*. Sand. *c*. Grits. *d*. Marl. *e*. Grit.

"At Ryde House a ripple-marked flaggy sandstone (probably bed *e*, Fig. 25) immediately overlies the fish-bed.

"At Binstead Point the upper calcareous portion of the thick bed [seen] at Nettlestone comes to the shore, capped with green marls, and assumes the character of a hard and compact white limestone with *Melania excavata*. Westward of the Point it forms a ledge on the shore, which strikes nearly due west in the direction of Osborne. About a quarter of a mile east of the Point, sandstone appears, dipping 10° W. of S. at 5°."[1] Hence eastward to Ryde the strata are concealed by gravel and enclosure.

East of Ryde, a slight arching of the strata, which culminates near the old salterns in the marsh east of Spring Vale, brings into view all but the lowest beds of the Osborne Series, between Apley and Node's Point. As implied in the introductory remarks, the middle and upper beds of the series hereabouts present a sandier facies than in the other coast sections. A short abstract of Prof. Forbes's account of the descending succession,[2] observed, for the most part, in shore exposures, is given below.

---

[1]*Ibid.*, p. 153.
[2]'On the Tertiary Fluvio-marine Formation, &c.,' *Mem. Geol. Surv.*, 1856, pp. 74, 75.

Bembridge Limestone, in 3 bands

			ft
OSBORNE BEDS	St. Helen's Sands, 45 to 50 feet	Beds 1, 2. Dark green clay and yellow and white marls, with concretions	9½
		Beds 3 to 6. Green, white, and yellow sands and sandstones, with siliceous concretions; a layer of purple nodules (manganiferous?) near middle	29
		Beds 7, 8. White sandy and greenish blue clay (contains the Fish-bed), about	10
	Nettlestone Grits, about 20 feet	Beds 9, 10. Yellow limestone and marls, with calcareous nodules	6
		Bed 11. Freestone: hard calcareous sandstone, with siliceous concretions: conglomeratic in places ..	8
		Beds 12 to 15. Sand and sandstones, calcareous ..	5½
		Green marls, base not seen—estimated	30

Most of these beds are fossiliferous. The green marls below the Grits form the shore about Puckpool and Spring Vale. The Grits can be seen to the west of Puckpool Point, but they are better displayed on the eastern side of the low anticline, about Nettlestone Point, and immediately below the sea-wall at Sea View, to the west of the pier.

"The rocks at Nettlestone Point are thick-bedded concretionary limestones, in some places soft and composed of comminuted *Paludina lenta*, in others passing into hard siliceous grit. They constitute large blocks on the shore, eight feet thick, which weather very unequally into irregular cavities, and contain a few small rounded pebbles of flint, larger fragments of subangular flint, Turtle bones, and fossils with the shells preserved. The lower four feet become more indurated and cavernous (honey-combed) and pass into hard grit; while in the freestone, about two feet six inches from the top, there is a well-defined band of *Limnaea*, six inches in thickness. Green sand, with large flat lenticular concretions of a yellow colour, which have an irregular surface and resemble *septaria*, overlies the limestone.

"Round the Point, the upper part of the thick grit becomes an indurated marl of an ochreous colour, with greenish-grey, argillocalcareous concretions; while further east, a short distance west of the boat-house, it becomes a limestone (containing *Chara* and *Limnaea longiscata*), which has been quarried on the shore for building stone. This change of mineral character apparently escaped the notice of Professor Forbes, who has described the bed, both under its normal and altered aspect, in his section of the Nettlestone Grit (at pages 74 and 75 of his Memoir on the Fluvio-marine formation of the Isle of Wight), as two distinct and separate strata, Nos. 9 and 10.

" . . . At Sea View the fish-bed occurs at the base of the cliff a short distance east of the Pier; and as the Nettlestone Grits sink beneath the sea-level close to the Pier, it is probable that the fish-bed is in the clay at the base of Forbes's higher division, or St. Helen's Sands. At this locality, as near Ryde House, ripple-marked flags are found immediately above it.[1]

At Horestone Point, the Nettlestone Grits are brought up by a small fault, running S. 30° E. along the coast, and form a group of large rugged boulders on the shore. At this spot, the massive freestone-bed (No. 11 of Forbes's succession, summarized above), which contains scattered pebbles at Nettlestone Point, becomes markedly conglomeratic; "containing in some parts bands of small rounded flint pebbles; in others, layers of partially decomposed angular

[1] 'Geology of the Isle of Wight,' *Mem. Geol. Surv.*, 1889, pp. 154–156.

flints. The upper part is full of broken shells, and patches of comminuted shells occur about two feet from the top, which is calcareous, and less hard than the lower portion of the bed. There are also occasional fucoidal markings and large irregular concretions, which, weathering unequally, cause the rock to assume a honey-combed cavernous appearance."[1]

FIG. 26.   *Vertical Section of the Osborne and Bembridge Beds, Whitecliff Bay*

Scale: 1 inch = 40 feet

Adapted from "Geology of the Isle of Wight", *Mem. Geol. Surv.*, 2nd Ed., 1889, Pl. 5.

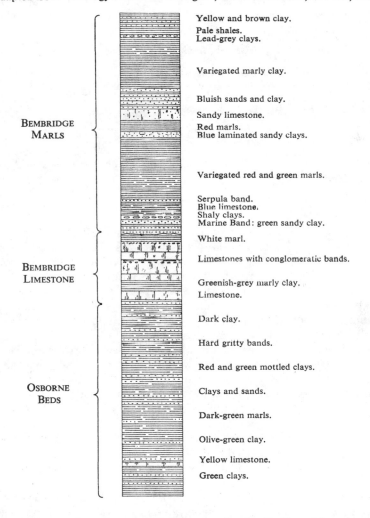

BEMBRIDGE MARLS
- Yellow and brown clay.
- Pale shales.
- Lead-grey clays.
- Variegated marly clay.
- Bluish sands and clay.
- Sandy limestone.
- Red marls.
- Blue laminated sandy clays.
- Variegated red and green marls.
- Serpula band.
- Blue limestone.
- Shaly clays.
- Marine Band: green sandy clay.
- White marl.

BEMBRIDGE LIMESTONE
- Limestones with conglomeratic bands.
- Greenish-grey marly clay.
- Limestone.

OSBORNE BEDS
- Dark clay.
- Hard gritty bands.
- Red and green mottled clays.
- Clays and sands.
- Dark-green marls.
- Olive-green clay.
- Yellow limestone.
- Green clays.

Fine white sands and green marls appear in the bluff at this point. The small cliff-exposures at Priory Bay call for no particular notice.

At Brading, tufaceous, gravelly, current-bedded sands, of fluvial aspect, underlie and appear to pass into the Bembridge Limestone. In the good section

[1]*Ibid.*, p. 156.

at Cliff Close, east of the Church, the gravelly bands consist of sub-angular flints (up to 3 inches), smaller flint-pebbles, and rolled pieces of concretionary clay-ironstone, in coarse, yellow quartz-and-flint sand.

"Section of the Osborne Beds in Whitecliff Bay (Fig. 26)

	ft
"Dark bituminous clay, with *Limnaea* in patches	2
Grit	1
Dark olive-green clayey sand	3
Red and green mottled clays, with 1 to 2 inches of clay-ironstone on the top of the bed	18 or 20
Green clays	3 or 4
Dark grey sandy clays	3
Shelly band, large *Paludina* [*Viviparus*] *Melanopsis carinata*	4½
Dark green marls	8
Olive-green clay, *Melanopsis carinata, Paludina lenta*	15 to 18
Fine cream-yellow limestone, running out to sea in a direction 10° N. of E. No fossils observed	1
Green clays; *Paludina, Melanopsis* .. .. About	15
"Total thickness of Osborne beds	79½"[1]

The cream-coloured blocky limestone, 15 feet up, serves as a guide to the base of this Series.

3.   BEMBRIDGE LIMESTONE

This division, comprising two or more bands of massive fresh water limestone and intercalated, shaly, greenish clays and marls, is the thinnest and most easily recognisable of the Oligocene formations. Formerly treated by the Geological Survey merely as part of a "Bembridge Series" (which, in a measure, it is), the Limestone has latterly been shown as a separate formation in the Survey maps; for its limits, as a rule, are sharply defined by lithological changes, and the upper limit also by signs of erosion, and by the incoming of marine shells at the base of the Bembridge Marls.

The Bembridge Limestone is usually to be distinguished from the Headon limestones by its whiteness and partly brecciate structure; also by the fact that the contained molluscs are normally represented by casts or moulds, the shell in some cases being replaced by calc-spar. The Headon limestones are of a darker cream tint, more earthy, and have the shells of *Limnaeae*, &c., preserved.

The thickness of the Bembridge limestone varies from 8 to 25 feet or more on the coast, and may average about 10 feet. Some records of inland well-sections, near the Medina line, mention only 2 or 3 feet of limestone, or 'rock', at this horizon.

Freshwater molluscs (*Limnaea longiscata* (Brongn.), *Planorbis discus* Edw., *P. euomphalus* J. Sow., and many others, ranging up from the Headon Beds) abound in, and largely constitute the Bembridge Limestone. Mingled with them, and in places occurring in great numbers, are more characteristic land shells, such as the well-known *Amphidromus ellipticus* (J. Sow.), *Achatina costellata* J. Sow. (*Glandina*), and *Helix globosa* J. Sow. (*H. pseudo-globosa*

---

[2]*Ibid.*, p. 157.

d'Orb.). About a dozen mammalian genera are recorded, including *Palaeo-therium, Hyopotamus, Chaeropotamus*, and *Anoplotherium*. Nucules of *Chara* (*C. tuberculata* Lyell, &c.) are plentiful, but determinable fruit or leaves of higher orders are seldom met with.

Description of Sections

The Bembridge Limestone includes the uppermost limestones of Headon Hill and Sconce; the limestones of Hamstead and Gurnard Ledges, and the once-famous building-stone of Binstead and Quarr.

Headon Hill and Sconce Outliers. The Bembridge Limestone plays but a minor part in the Headon section, as it appears only in small exposures in the broken ground on the upper slopes of Headon Hill. Where seen to the north of the summit, it is partly tufaceous, and contains layers of the ovoid concretions once supposed to be eggs of turtle. The fossils of the travertinous bands are mostly terrestrial, and include *Helices, Pupae*, and *Amphidromus* (*Bulimus*). The total thickness of the limestone hereabouts, including the associated freshwater marls, is estimated at 15 feet.

In the Hill Farm outlier, north of Freshwater, the limestone, with scattered land-shells, has been dug in several old pits, and can be seen in the road-cutting north of Hill Lodge.

In the adjacent outlier of West Hill, above Sconce Point, the limestone series is 16 to 20 feet thick, and forms a narrow platform, which is surmounted by a low ridge of the Marls. Much of it is highly travertinous, as at Headon Hill, and it has yielded several species of land-molluscs in an exceptionally good state of preservation. These shells occur chiefly in the upper part of the Series, but in places the irregular tufaceous bands with *Helix, Amphidromus*, and *Glandina* are intercalated in the lower hard rock full of *Limnaeae* and *Planorbis*. The section from which so many museum specimens of terrestrial species were obtained, long ago became obscured, but the Limestone can be studied in fallen blocks on the shore below.

Main Outcrop: Yarmouth to Bembridge. The Bembridge Limestone, dipping below sea-level in Yarmouth estuary, reappears in Hamstead Ledge, where it comprises three stone-beds with softer bands between. It can be traced thence in the overgrown cliff nearly to Newtown River, where it passes under the marsh.

East of Newtown River, beyond the crest of the low Porchfield anticline, it gradually declines along the cliff, and spreads out in the double reef of Saltmead or Thorness Ledge, north of Burnt Wood. Here the lower bed of limestone is of the usual character, with casts of *Limnaeae*. Above it lies dark-green marl (*a*, Fig. 27), the upper part of which is full of *Viviparus minutus* (J. Sow.) (= *Paludina globuloides*). The upper band of limestone (*b*) is a soft earthy stone, hardening on exposure, and is remarkable in that it contains abundant *Limnaeae* and other freshwater molluscs with the shell preserved, which, as already noted, is seldom the case in this Series. The top of the Limestone is much broken up and eroded, and in the crevices there occur marine bivalves with their valves united. In places, the erosion has cut through the upper band of Limestone, allowing the black base of the Bembridge Marls (*c*) to come in contact with the green marl (*a*).

"In Thorness Bay the Limestone rises again, showing the same three divisions. The bottom block forms Gurnard Ledge, and the thin upper block makes a minor ledge nearly opposite Sticelett Farm. From Gurnard Ledge the Limestone runs as a marked feature in the cliff as far as Gurnard Bridge, but on the east side of the marsh the sections are obscure and hidden by talus, though abundance of fallen blocks can be examined as far as Egypt Point. From this Point eastward through West Cowes another marked feature, now overgrown or hidden by buildings, shows the outcrop of the Limestone, which was fomrerly seen in the foundations of several of the houses. Near the West Cowes Gas Works the same rock is again met with, and from this point to Bottom Copse, where it sinks beneath the Medina, there is no difficulty in following its characteristic feature."[1]

FIG. 27. *Section in the lower part of the Cliff near Burnt Wood, Porchfield*
From "Geology of the Isle of Wight" (*Mem. Geol. Survey*), 2nd Ed. Fig. 55, p. 164.
Scale: 1 inch = 8 feet

Bembridge Marls: *c.* Black clay with marine shells
Bembridge Limestone { *b.* Upper bed of limestone
                      { *a.* Green marl

Between Cowes and Ryde, the Limestone can be seen at King's Quay, Fishbourne, and other places; and at the eastern end of Quarr Wood the upper band of it—light-brown, porous, and saccharoidal—has lately been worked in one of the long-disused quarries whence so much building stone was obtained during the Middle Ages. From this or a neighbouring quarry, "in the wood west of Binstead Church", teeth of *Anoplotherium* and claws of lobster were obtained, with other fossils, from laminated flaggy beds below the same band of stone.[2]

Small exposures can be seen by the railway south of St. John's Road Station at Ryde, in Apley Wood, and south of Sea View. At Node's Point, where the Limestone descends to the shore, we again meet with clear sections. On the south side of the Point the lower part of the cliff shows the following descending sequence:

"Bembridge Limestone at Node's Point

	ft	in.
"Limestone, irregular, marly, and most compact in the lower half of the bed, which is, also, the least fossiliferous. Full of *Chara*, with a few *Limnaea* and *Paludina globuloides* [*Viviparus*]. The upper 2 feet more ferruginous and less indurated, and frequently marked by the abundance of *Limnaea*	4	0
Dark laminated clay; the lower part of a lighter colour, and more sandy..	1	3
Compact greenish clay (slightly bituminous), with fragments of *Cyrena*, and now and then a perfect valve	0	9
Earthy limestone; the upper part soft and of variable thickness. *Planorbis discus* in the upper part, *Limnaea* throughout	1	6 to 2 0
Hard green marl, with concretions in the lower part..	2	6"[3]

---

[1]*Ibid.*, pp. 164, 165.
[2]*Ibid.*, p. 166.
[3]*Ibid.*, p. 167.

The top of the Limestone is uneven and covered by a thin bed of black oysters (*Ostrea vectensis* Forbes). By the tower of old St. Helen's Church, the Limestone dips below sea-level, to reappear at Bembridge Point, on the farther side of the Harbour.

From Bembridge Point to the Foreland, the Limestone is nearly horizontal and spreads out in extensive ledges on the foreshore. Between the Foreland and Whitecliff Bay it occupies much of the shore, dipping slightly inwards and landwards, with a dish-like concavity, on the east and south-east; the broken margin of this shallow trough forming the dangerous reef known as Bembridge Ledge.[1] In the northern part of Whitecliff Bay, the Limestone, in four principal bands, rises from the shore to the top of the cliff in a sweeping cycloid curve, and is displayed to better advantage than in any other locality.

"*Bembridge Limestone at Whitecliff Bay* (Measured in 1856 by Professors Ramsay and Morris, and H. W. Bristow)

		ft
"[Bembridge Marls: green marl.]		
	Hard white crumbly marl, with a few concretions and scattered shells, and becoming harder and more shelly for the lower 6 inches. Throws out water at the top. *Planorbis discus, Limnaea* in places. Passes gradually into the bed below	2½
	Hard, compact, very shelly limestone, sometimes forming two beds, with a harder and darker-coloured parting between. *Chara tuberculata* and *Ch. sp.*—very abundant. *Paludina orbicularis* [*Viviparus*] at 2 feet from the top. *Limnaea, Planorbis discus, Planorbis* [*sp.*]	5
	Hard bed of compact sandy limestone, weathering white; plant-like markings. *Limnaea* (a few); *Paludina* (sm. sp.) ..	1
"[Bembridge Limestone]	Dark grey and carbonaceous clays, laminated with sand in the lower part; light green in the upper 2 feet where they are compact and marly, and separated from the lower 12 inches by a band of *Cyrena obtusa* with both valves joined..	3
	Cream-coloured cavernous limestone, with a hard brecciated concretionary cap, 6 to 9 inches thick, on the top of the bed, which weathers to a very irregular surface. *Limnaea*, numerous *Taxites* and *Planorbis* (sm. sp.), *Chara tuberculata*, especially 2 feet from the top. Emits a bituminous odour when struck	4 to 6
	Soft, white, earthy limestone, with a few casts of shells; *Planorbis, Limnaea*, Fish	2
	Concretionary cream-coloured limestone, with an uneven surface above and below; weathering irregularly, and emitting a bituminous odour when struck. *Chara, Limnaea longiscata*	4 or 5
"[Osborne Beds: dark-grey clay]		—"[2]

Inland Exposures: Beginning in the west; the outcrop-surface of the Bembridge Limestone expands south-east of Yarmouth, and forms, between Thorley and Shalcombe, a pronounced dip-slope feature, or cuesta, of about three square miles, such as one would hardly expect from so thin a group of beds. Despite its size, this tract affords no considerable section, and the few pits open at Thorley Street, Wellow, and Newbridge show neither the upper nor lower limit of the Series.

---

[1] A fertile source of shipping casualties in foggy weather.

[2] *Ibid.*, p. 168.

"Other sections are seen in the old pits between Newbridge and Fullholding, and for nearly a mile the road runs along a ridge formed by the Limestone. From Fullholding eastward the bedding becomes vertical. The limestone, therefore, occupies a very small area at the surface. There seems also to be a tendency for it, like other thin limestones, entirely to disappear for a depth of several feet from the surface, where exposed to the solvent action of rain water. For these reasons it is often difficult to follow the outcrop; but limestone has been seen south of North Park Farm; north of Swainstone; at Great Park; for nearly three-quarters of a mile west of Gunville; and in an old quarry half-a-mile east of Gunville."[1]

In and about Newport the Limestone has been proved in several wells, its thickness being generally much less than on the coast. East of Newport it was formerly quarried near Great and Little Pan Farms, and has been proved in a boring at Durton Farm. From Combley Farm it is traceable as far as Little Duxmore, where it is vertical; and it has been observed in temporary exposures near Ashey and Nunwell, where it makes no appreciable feature.

At Brading, where the outcrop has receded into an area of lower dips, the Limestone forms a marked ridge which supports the Church and Wall Lane. On the southern side of Wall Lane it has been quarried, with the gravelly top-beds of the Osborne Series, at Cliff Close (see p. 116); and on the northern side of that lane it is well exposed in the quarry of the Cement Works. Casts of *Helices* are common in the upper and softer layers of the stone in the last-mentioned excavation. The southward increase in the dip here indicates a flexure as pronounced as that seen in Whitecliff Bay.

East of the Yar the Limestone reappears at two spots in the low bluff at the edge of the marsh, and from Peacock Hill eastward it forms a perceptible ridge.

4. BEMBRIDGE MARLS

Above the Bembridge Limestone there lies a series of shelly brackish and freshwater clays and marls, having at its base a bed, or thin group of beds, containing marine fossils. Certain minor divisions, such as the Insect Bed in the lower part of the Series, and a seam of marl with abundant *Nystia duchasteli* (Nyst) (*Hydrobia, Tomichia*) close to the top, have a fair measure of persistence, but, save for the basal marine beds, or Zone of *Ostrea vectensis*, no well-marked substages have been recognised.

Brightly-coloured lagoon-clays with remains of turtles and crocodiles or alligators, are less developed than in the other argillaceous Series of the Oligocene, and purely freshwater episodes are confined to thin seams. The general facies of the Bembridge Marls and their fauna point to deltaic, brackish-water conditions of deposition. The Marls are about 70 feet thick in the west of the Island. Like most of the other Older Tertiary formations, they expand eastward, and attain a thickness of about 120 feet near St. Helen's.

Rich in individuals, the brackish and freshwater molluscan fauna of the Bembridge Marls is rather poor in species. The commoner genera are *Cyrena* (*C. semistriata* Desh., *C. obtusa* Forbes, &c.) *Melania acuta* J. Sow., *Potamaclis turritissima* (Forbes), *Melanopsis* (*M. fusiformis* J. Sow., &c.), and *Viviparus* (chiefly *V. lentus* (Sol.)). A few land-molluscs also occur. The non-marine shells are well preserved, those of *Cyrenae* often retaining their colour-markings.

[1] *Ibid.*, p. 163.

In the marine beds, the shells, though in a less presentable condition, are of greater interest, for not a few of them—including *Ostrea vectensis* Forbes, the elegant *Arca websteri* Forbes MS., Morris, and *Panopaea minor* Forbes (*Mya*)—are either restricted to that horizon, or appear there for the first time.

The mammals of the Bembridge Marls are little known, but said to be "apparently the same as those of the Limestone": the other vertebrates are reptiles and fish, "such as occur throughout the Oligocene Beds".[1]

Drift-wood, seeds, and fruits are of common occurrence, especially near Yarmouth and Hamstead. The insectiferous limestone (noticed below, p. 123) seems the only good leaf-bed so far observed. Among the plants recorded are *Chara lyelli* Forbes, *Chrysodeum lanzaeanum* Visi., *Arthrotaxis couttsiae* Heer, *Carpolithes spp.*, *Cinnamomum*, *Ficus*, *Pinus*, *Viburnum*, and *Zizyphus*.

Description of Sections

We begin in the west, but, since the most complete section of the Bembridge Marls is to be seen at Hamstead, it will be convenient to deal with that before noticing the less important developments at the western extremity of the Island.

At Hamstead, a complete ascending sequence of the beds which make up this Series can be seen on the shore when proceeding south-westward from the outcrop of Bembridge Limestone in Hamstead Ledge.

"Bembridge Marls of Hamstead

"Measured along the Shore at Low Water

	ft	in.
"Hamstead Series: Black Band	—	—
Green clays, with large bands of *Paludina lenta* [*Viviparus*]	4	6
Ironstone	0	9
Clay	4	0
Clay with *Paludina*	4	6
Concretionary ironstone	0	3
Clay with *Paludina*	4	6
Clay with two or three small black bands	2	6
Ferruginous brown sandy clay, with *Paludina* at base, thickness variable 0 to	0	6
Thin bituminous bands, with reed-like plants, and a layer of *Paludina lenta* below filled with green clay	0	1
Grey clay, with short zones of *Melania forbesi* [*Potamaclis*] and nodules containing *Paludina lenta*	3	0
Band of scattered nodules of iron pyrites, overlying verdigris green clays, with bands of *Paludina lenta* (occasionally of very large size), *Melania forbesi*	5	0
Dark-grey clays, with *Paludina* and numerous oval seed-vessels, and containing thin carbonaceous sandy bands, with (reed-like) plant impressions. *Cypris, Paludina, Planorbis* immediately overlying a layer of large *Limnaea*. This is altogether a freshwater deposit	3	0
Bands of *Melania turritissima* [*Potamaclis*], *Planorbis*, and *Paludina*	0	1
Greenish shaly clay, with concretions of indurated marl, and containing near the base a band of *Melania turritissima*, *M. costata*, *Melanopsis carinata, Paludina, &c.*	4	0
Hard shelly band chiefly made up of *Melania, turritissima*, a few *Melanopsis*, and fragments of *Fish*	0	3

[1]'Geology of the Isle of Wight,' *Mem. Geol. Surv.*, 2nd Ed., 1889, p. 182.

J

	ft	in.
Pale-grey clay, with bands of compressed shells, chiefly *Paludina*	2	0
Sandy band, full of *Cyrena obtusa* (with both valves), *Cerithium* and *Melanopsis fusiformis*	0	9
Pale greenish shaly clay, with a thin band of *Melania turritissima* 6 inches from the top, and a 1-inch bituminous band at 3 feet. Compressed *Carpolithes, Melania turritissima, Melanopsis carinata*	6	0
Sandy clay, with *Melania muricata* [*acuta*, (J. Sow.)] *M. turritissima, Melanopsis*, 3 inches thick, resting on sandy clay, almost entirely composed of *Melania muricata*, with a few broken *Cyrena* and some *Melanopsis* .. .. 0 4 to	0	7
Bluish irregular shaly clay, with selenite. A band of *Melania turritissima* and *Melanopsis carinata*, 2 inches from the top, *Paludina*	3	0
Indurated, greenish marly clay, with bands of *Paludina lenta*	4	6
Greenish clay, with two bands of broken *Cyrena obtusa* and *C. semistriata*, and on the top of a bed of *Melania muricata*, with scattered *Melanopsis* and occasional *Cerithium*	0	9
Green clays, *Melania turritissima*, with scattered *Melanopsis* and *Melania muricata*, mixed with patches of *Cyrena semistriata C. obovata*, Fish remains, &c., about the middle 4 inches	1	0
Green clays, with *Melania muricata, M. turritissima*, and numerous *Melanopsus carinata* and *Paludina lenta*	1	6
Verdigris-green clay, with *Cyrena semistriata*	1	0
Bright-green clays, with *Cyrena semistriata* on the top	2	0
Bluish-green clays, with bands of *Melania muricata* and *Cyrena obovata*	1	6
Hard, sandy green marl, with scattered *Cyrena semistriata*	0	6
Verdigris-green clays, with 5 bands of *Cyrena semistriata* and *Melania* ..	1	6
Greenish clay, with 2 marked bands 1 and 2 inches thick, full of *Melania muricata* (small var.), occasional *Cyrena pulchra*, and a few *Cyrena semistriata*	1	0
Green clays, with *Cyrena semistriata* (finely preserved), *C. pulchra*, and *Melania*	0	9
Dark clay with soft green sandy concretions, 6 inches; greenish clay 1 foot. Scattered *Cyrena obovata*	1	6
Blue clay, with small *Cyrena* (*obovata*?), *Melania muricata*, and *Melanopsis*	1	0
BEMBRIDGE LIMESTONE in three beds, with softer beds between, forming a ledge (Hamstead Ledge), out at sea, in the direction of the Buoy, and containing numerous *Limnaea longiscata, Chara*, &c.		
Total of Bembridge Marls	[67	9]"[1]

About five feet below the Black Band at the base of the overlying Hamstead Series, and not mentioned in the above account of the section, there is a thin seam of *Nystia duchasteli* (Nyst) (*Hydrobia*), a little gasteropod long thought to be confined to the Hamstead Beds. Though barely two inches thick, this seam is usually to be found between three and ten feet below the upper limit of the Bembridge Marls.

The Marls dip below the shore about a quarter of a mile south-west of Hamstead Ledge, and reappear half-a-mile east of Yarmouth. Here, in the low cliff and on the foreshore, the *Nystia duchasteli* Bed can be seen, with the underlying marls down to the beds with abundant *Potamaclis turritissima* (*Melania*), 10 to 15 feet above the Bembridge Limestone. The base of the Marls cannot be examined here, but the Limestone out-crops·on the other side of Yarmouth, at the Station.

---

[1]*Ibid.*, pp. 179, 180. The total is there given as 69 feet 6 inches. Other measurements make the thickness 75 to 82 feet.

"A good deal of drift-wood occurs in the Bembridge Marls between Hamstead and Yarmouth, and thin seams rendered quite black by the number of seeds they contain are often conspicuous on the shore or in the washed base of the cliff. The drift-wood does not occur as rafts, but generally as isolated trunks and branches, often of considerable size. One of these trunks, examined by [H.] Keeping and Clement Reid, was cleared for 18 feet without reaching the end. It measured $3\frac{1}{2}$ inches thick at the broken smaller end, only increasing to 5 inches 13 feet below. The thickness of the overlying clay prevented [them] from following the tree further, but its straightness and slenderness showed that it had probably grown in a forest—not in open ground. In the Marls near Yarmouth Toll Gate [they] also obtained portion of the bones of a large teleostean fish."[1]

East of Hamstead and of Newtown River, the Marls come down to the shore near Thorness Point (Saltmead Ledge), and the basal Oyster Bed, there well developed, is seen resting with a slight unconformity on the Bembridge Limestone, as described above (p. 117). The Lower and Middle Beds of the Bembridge Marls are well shown near the Point, and the upper beds, with the Nystia Band near the top, in the cliff near Sticelett.

In Thorness and Gurnard Bays, the lower beds include a seam of blue, insect-bearing limestone three feet above the Marine Bed with *Ostrea vectensis*. The Insect Band, discovered by E. J. A'Court Smith about sixty years ago, was traced by him from the vicinity of Newtown River to West Cowes. The thickness varies from two inches to about two feet (the latter thickness being exceptional), and its distance above the Bembridge Limestone ranges from four to nine feet. The insect fauna (beetles, flies, locusts, ants, &c.) includes representatives of seven orders. Spiders and small crustacea also have been obtained from this and adjacent beds.[2] The position of the Insect-limestone is indicated in the following section, seen in the lower part of the cliff west of Gurnard Ledge.

	ft	in.
"Blue clay	1	0
[Insect-bed.] Fine-grained blue-hearted limestone, like lithographic stone. Many insect remains, and occasional leaves and freshwater shells. This bed does not appear to be perfectly continuous, but forms large thin cakes dying out for a few feet and coming on again at the same horizon. One portion, a little further west, thickened to 2 feet, and was full of insect remains, but is now entirely destroyed	0	3
Blue clay	0	3
Sandy bed, full of *Cerithium mutabile*	0	3
Blue clay, with *Cyrena obovata, Melania muricata* [*acuta (J. Sow.*)], *Melanopsis carinata,* and *Paludina globuloides* [*Viviparus*]	2	6
[Marine Bed.] Ferruginous loam, with *Ostrea vectensis, Cytherea incrassata* [*Meretrix*], *Cyrena, Cerithium mutabile* &c.	0	10
BEMBRIDGE LIMESTONE."[3]		

North of Gurnard Ledge, in the cliff below the little outlier of Hamstead Beds, the upper part of the Bembridge Marls, with the shelly Nystia Band 8 feet below their upper limit, are exposed. Thence north-eastward to Cowes,

---

[1] *Ibid.,* p. 118.

[2] *Vide* H. Woodward, *Quart. Journ. Geol. Soc.,* vol. xxxv, 1879, pp. 342–350, and T. R. Jones and C. D. Sherborn, 'Supplement to the Tertiary Entomostraca', *Pal Soc.,* 1889.

[3] 'Geology of the Isle of Wight,' *Mem. Geol. Surv.,* 2nd Ed., 1889, p. 177.

the cliff-section is much obscured by slips and vegetation. At Werror brick-yard, south of Cowes, a phalanx of a bird was found just below the Hamstead Beds, the junction with which is cut into at Ashlake brickyard, on Wootton Creek. At the latter spot the Nystia Band is only three feet below the Black Band of the Hamstead Series.

Farther east, the lower part of the Marls appears in the cliff of Priory Bay, and near old St. Helen's Church. The Oyster-band of the Marine Beds is there overlain by thin brown clay, containing *Arca websteri* Forbes, *Modiola sp.*, *Mya minor* Forbes (*Panopaea*), *Fusus*, *Balanus*, &c. In the same bed occur *Potamaclis turritissima* Forbes, which is not usually met with so low in the Bembridge Marls, and *Terebralia plicata* (Brug.) (*Cerithium*), which becomes abundant in the Upper Hamstead Beds, at a horizon about 350 feet higher.

On the borders of Brading Harbour bones of turtle have been found at the brickyard, in the lower part of the Marls, near Carpenter's, and the Oyster Bed, which was met with about 23 feet below sea-level in a well close to St. Helen's station, is just discernible in the bluff north of Woolverton.

The lowest beds of the Bembridge Marls are well exhibited on the shore between the Foreland and Whitecliff Bay, but the description of these will be more easily followed if we take first the more comprehensive section presented in the cliff near the northern end of that bay (Fig. 26, p. 115).

"Bembridge Marls in Whitecliff Bay

	ft	in.
"Variegated yellow and brown clay (occasionally sandy) containing lines of nodular concretions, but no fossils	8	0
Pale shaly clays, the lower part with a band of septarian concretions, containing *Paludina lenta* [*Viviparus*] and other shells	3	0
Lead-coloured clays, laminated above, paler below, *Paludina lenta, Melanopsis, Melania turritissima* [*Potamaclis*] occasional *Cyrena*, and remains of Fish	20	0
Pale bluish sands and sandy clay, *Melania turritissima, Melanopsis fusi-formis, Paludina lenta*. Fish, Seeds	8	0
Sandy grey limestone occasionally passing into marl; sometimes very very fossiliferous, often concretionary, with few fossils *Bulimus ellipticus* [*Amphidromus*], *Achatina costellata* [*Glandina*] *Limnaea longiscata, Melania costata, Paludina lenta, Cyrena transversa, Unio, Chara wrighti* ..	4	0
Red marl, without fossils	5	0
Pale blue laminated sandy clay, containing a few pebbles of limestone and flint. Traces of Fish	3	0
Variegated red and green marls. *Cyrena*; fragments of *Trionyx incrassatus* ..	24	0
Clays with whitish streaks. *Melanopsis fusiformis, Paludina lenta*	2	0
Seam of *Serpula*		
Clay, with *Cyrena semistriata* C. *pulchra,* C. *obovata,* C. *obtusa, Cerithium mutabile* and *Melania costata..*	4	0
Hard unfossiliferous bluish septarian stone (probably the equivalent of the Insect Limestone further west)	0	6
Dark shaly clay. *Cyrena semistriata*	2	6
[Oyster Bed.] Green sandy beds. *Ostrea vectensis, Cytherea incrassata* [*Meretrix*], *Mytilus affinis, Nucula similis,* &c.	2	0
Whitish sands interstratified with fine stripes of clay; occasional pebbles. Lines of *Cyrena semistriata* and occasional *Cerithium*	2	0
Greenish marls, with lines of white nodules in the lower part	3	0
BEMBRIDGE LIMESTONE.		
	91	0

"Another measurement of the Marls, made near the same place in 1888, gave a total visible thickness of 93 feet; but about 15 feet of the upper part of the cliff are overgrown and hidden. Possibly there may be an outlier of Hamstead Beds here, but if not, the Bembridge Marls must be least 106 feet thick, with the top not reached. This computation agrees with the thickness proved at St. Helen's.

"The marine base of the Bembridge Marls is so variable that the following detailed notes of the beds seen on the coast will be useful, especially as portions are often entirely hidden by beach-sand or talus. The account is that given by Forbes, with some additions from notes made in 1888.

"The blue septarian limestone strikingly resembles in mineral character the harder insect-bearing limestones of the Purbeck beds. It is the thickest (about 1 foot) and finest about half-way between Whitecliff Point and the Foreland, where its upper surface forms part of the floor of the shore. Everywhere it preserves the same peculiar mineral character. Near the same place the finest display of the oyster bed is seen, the surface of which also, for some distance, forms the floor of the shore. There it is underlain by a pale concretionary blue marl, containing occasional pebbles, and abounding in casts of shells, especially of *Cerithium* (probably *C. mutabile*) occasionally mingled with casts of freshwater shells (*Limnaea longiscata, Planorbis discus* and *P. obtusus*), *Cyrenae* of more species than one, a small angulated *Corbula, Murex forbesi*, a curious pupa-like *Bulimus* ? occasional *Mytili, Hydrobiae*, a Tellinoid bivalve, occasional examples of *Melania muricata*, and traces of fish. Between this blue marl and the oyster band is a thin sandy bed, filled with comminuted shells, and on this rest numerous individuals of *Cytherea incrassata* [*Meretrix*], with their valves closed. . . . Then come the oysters, mostly, but not all, single valves, here and there mingled with good double specimens. They are thinly distributed, but occasionally occur in clusters of considerable number, bristling the surface of the shore. Individuals vary much in shape even in the same cluster. With them are *Mytili* (*M. affinis*), *Nucula similis*, a *Solecurtus*-like bivalve, and Forbes once met with a *Natica*. The *Mytili* and *Nuculae* retain the substance of their shells perfectly. Occasional pebbles are mingled with the oysters.

"In a few places interesting indications can be found that marine conditions lingered for some time. *Cliona*-bored oysters occur, on and in which *Serpula* and *Balanus* have grown, and the dead *Serpulae* and *Balani* have been subsequently covered by a growth of *Polyzoa*. The best preserved marine shells will be found at about half-tide level, a short distance south of the Foreland Inn, where even the *Cytherea* may occasionally be obtained in a perfect condition, though fragile. *Nucula similis* is abundant here, and uninjured specimens are sometimes washed up by the sea.

"At the foot of the cliff, half way between Whitecliff Point and Foreland Point, just beyond the place where the oyster bed is best displayed on the shore, the strata immediately surmounting the septarian stone-band are well exhibited. Dark blue clays, with scattered shells (double) of *Cyrena obtusa* and *C. obovata* first appear. Then come darker and more friable shaly clays, including a strongly marked band of *Cyrenae*, the species being *C. pulchra, obtusa*, and *obovata*, mingled with occasional large examples of *Cerithium mutabile*, of which now and then a specimen may be found with a *Balanus* attached. After some pale laminated clays, containing the same shells, succeeded by greenish marls, crowded with little knots of *Serpulae*, clays and shaly strata follow, including a thick band composed almost entirely of *Melania muricata* [*acuta*], associated with *Cyrena semistriata*, which latter shell forms also a band of its own. The specimens of all these shells are beautifully preserved. In the clays and mottled marls that follow, shells are scarce or wanting, but fragments of turtle occur, and Forbes had the good fortune to find *in sitû* the greater part of the carapace of a *Trionyx incrassatus*."[1]

The few inland exposures on the southern line of outcrop are of slight interest. Though mapped as Plateau Gravel, the small patch of flint-shingle on the crest of the low ridge east of Gunville seems rather to be the outcrop of a pebble-bed near the base of the Bembridge Marls.

5. HAMSTEAD BEDS

Over the greater part of the northern half of the Isle of Wight, between Yarmouth and Brading Harbour, the Bembridge Marls are covered by a thick series of coloured clays, loams, sands, and shales, known as the Hamstead Beds. These are mostly of brackish and freshwater origin, but include near their upper limit the vestiges of a marine stage, with which the local sedimentary record of the Oligocene, and of the Older Tertiary period, is brought to a close.

Taken in ascending order, the beds comprised in the Hamstead Series, indicate a typical submergence-sequence; beginning with a freshwater phase, and continuing through an alternation of fresh and brackish-water phases, which leads eventually to a truly marine phase. In the following table, showing the major divisions of the Series and their thicknesses in the type-section at Hamstead and Bouldnor, the grouping in the first column is that adopted by the Geological Survey in 1889, while the classification in the second column is a slight modification of that drawn up by Edward Forbes in 1853.[2]

		ft
Upper Hamstead Beds, 31¼ ft	Marine beds ("Corbula Beds") with *Ostrea callifera*, *Corbula sub-pisum*, *Voluta rathieri*, &c.	19½
	Upper estuarine and freshwater beds ("Cerithium Beds") with *Terebralia plicata* (*Cerithium*), *Nystia duchasteli*, *Cyrena*, &c.	11¾
Lower Hamstead Beds, 224½ ft	Middle estuarine and fresh-water beds, with *Melania fasciata* (*Bayania*, *Striatella*), *Nystia*, *Cyrena*, &c. ("White Band" at the base)	158¾
	Lower estuarine and freshwater beds, with *Melania acuta*, *Nematura pupa* (*Stenothyra*), *Nystia*, *Planorbis* &c. .. ("Black Band," with *Unio* and *Viviparus*, at the base)	65¾
		255¾

The mottled coloured clays which form the bulk of the Lower Hamstead Beds seem to have been laid down in slightly saline lagoons, and, like so many other deposits of their class, yield few fossils, and those mostly drifted plants and bones of reptiles; though seams of *Unio* and *Melania*, and rootlet-beds,

---

[1] *Ibid.*, pp. 170–173.

[2] Forbes, 'On the Fluvio-marine Tertiaries, &c.' *Quart. Journ. Geol. Soc.*, vol. ix, p. 259.

are not wanting. The intercalated blue clays often contain abundant fresh-water shells, with the addition of a few more distinctly "estuarine" forms, such as *Cerithium Terebralia*, *Modiola*, and *Mya*, at certain horizons. These, Ostracods, and multitudinous fruits of *Carpolithes* and *Folliculites*, are the fossils commonly met with in the clays of the Lower Stage.

The Lower Hamstead Beds contain hardly any molluscan species that are unrepresented in the underlying brackish and freshwater strata; they are the natural continuation of the Bembridge Marls, and might well have been grouped with them, as the lithologically distinguishable upper stage of that Series, as Clement Reid, in effect, pointed out.

Whether the Upper Estuarine Beds with *Terebralia plicata* (*Cerithium*) also should be assigned to the same series with the Bembridge Marls, is an open question. The distinction drawn between them and the marine "Corbula Beds" by Forbes was discountenanced by Clement Reid, on the ground that they "pass imperceptibly into each other, and form one marine division, with *Corbula* becoming scarcer below, and *Cerithium* dying out above".[1] With the object of simplifying the classification, Reid bracketed the two groups of beds together as "Upper Hamstead", though, it is to be noticed, he still drew a clear distinction between them when dealing with bore-hole sections inland.

The occurrence of *Corbula* in the "Cerithium Beds", on which Reid laid stress, appears to be a point of minor importance beside that of the restricted vertical range of the other marine shells with which *Corbula* is associated in the highest 20 feet of the Hamstead Beds in Bouldnor Cliff. These top beds, the most purely marine of the whole Series, and containing nearly all the characteristic Hamstead mollusca, seem to mark the beginning of a new epoch, and are included in the Upper Oligocene (*Stampien*) by M. G. F. Dollfus, who refers all the underlying strata, down to the base of the Osborne Beds, to the Lower Oligocene (*Sannoisien*).[2]

Possibly some such classification will eventually be adopted by British geologists, and the term "Hamstead" be restricted in its application to the few feet of marine beds with *Ostrea callifera* Lam., *O. cyathula* Lam., *Meretrix lyelli* Forbes M.S., Morris, *Voluta rathieri* Héb., &c., at the top of Bouldnor and Hamstead Cliff. In the following pages the Geological Survey's grouping into Lower and Upper Hamstead is adhered to, but the use of the expression "marine beds", as a synonym for the latter division, is dropped.

Description of Sections

We take first the coast-sections between Yarmouth and Gurnard Bay, beginning with Hamstead and Bouldnor Cliff (Fig. 28).

"*Section of the Hamstead Beds at Hamstead*
"(Measured by Clement Reid and Henry Keeping, 1888)

ft

"Drift ⎰ Irregular clayey gravel of subangular flint, flint and quartz
⎱ pebbles, &c. (0 to 5 feet) ..   ..

---

[1] In 'Geology of the Isle of Wight', *Mem. Geol. Surv.*, 2nd ed., 1889, p. 185.

[2] 'On the Classification of the Beds of the Paris Basin,' *Proc. Geo. Assoc.*, vol. xxi, 1909, p. 114. *See also*, *id.* 'Excursion to Paris', *ibid.*, vol. xxi, 1909, plate facing p. 24.

ft

"Upper Hamstead Beds (marine and estuarine) 31¼ feet

Corbula Beds

Pale bluish-green clay (much weathered), with seams of *Ostrea callifera* bored by *Lithodomus* and overgrown by *Balanus* .. .. — 11

Carbonaceous and ferruginous clays, full of broken and waterworn *Cyrena semistriata. Cuma charlesworthi* and *Voluta rathieri* also occur occasionally .. .. — 1

Stiff blue clay, full of *Corbula pisum* [*subpisum* d'Orb.], *Cerithium plicatum, C. elegans, Vuluta rathieri,* and *Strebloceras cornuoides.* A layer of flat septaria about the middle .. .. — 7

Cerithium Beds

Black clay, full of *Corbula vectensis.* Also *Cytherea lyelli* [*Meretrix*], *Cyrena semistriata, Hydrobia chasteli* [*Nystia*], *Cerithium plicatum* [*Terebralia*], *C. elegans* [*Potamides*], *Melania fasciata* [*Bayania*], *M. inflata* [*nysti* du Chast] .. .. — ½

Shaly clays, with *Cyrena semistriata, Cerithium plicatum, Hydrobia chasteli,* seam of *Mya minor.* Occasional *Paludina lenta* [*Viviparus*] and *Unio* towards the base .. — 4½

Shell-bed, full of *Cerithium plicatum, C. elegans, Hydrobia chasteli, Melania inflata,* and *Cyrena semistriata* .. — ¾

Shaly clays. Seams of *Paludina lenta* and *Unio* .. .. — 4

Stiff blue clay, carbonaceous at the base. Scattered *Cyrena semistriata.* At base, seams of *Mya minor,* with *Cerithium plicatum, C. elegans, Hydrobia chasteli, Melania inflata, Corbula vectensis, Cyrena semistriata* and *Balanus* .. .. — 1½

Laminated carbonaceous clay, and sand-partings with *Cyclas* .. .. — 1

"Lower Hamstead Beds (estuarine and lacustrine) 224¼ feet

Green clay, with *Paludina* .. .. — 3½

Carbonaceous clay, with *Chara* .. .. — ½

Mottled red and green clay. *Unio, Paludina,* seeds, &c., occasionally .. .. — 11

Obscure (mottled clays ?) .. .. — 18

Carbonaceous seams, with *Carpolithes ovulum, Unio,* and *Paludina lenta* .. .. — 2

Carbonaceous clays, with seams of *Melania inflata* var. *laevis, Unio, Paludina, Planorbis, Hydrobia chasteli,* and Seeds .. .. — 15

Bluish loam .. .. — 1

Clay, with *Paludina,* Seeds, &c. .. .. — 3

Obscure .. .. — 4

Clays, with occasional *Paludina* and *Melania,* and seams of *Carpolithes ovulum.* Fossils rare .. .. .. — 20

Obscure .. .. — 5

[WATER-LILY BED:] Laminated carbonaceous clay, with Seeds, Palm-leaves, leaves of Water-lily, *Unio, Paludina lenta, Melania* and *Candona* .. .. — 1¾

Green and red marls .. .. — 8

Obscure (?sparingly fossiliferous) .. .. — 60

WHITE BAND: Green clays and white shell-marls. *Melania fasciata, Cerithium inornatum, C. sedgwicki, Mya minor, &c.* .. .. — 6

Green clay, with lines of ironstone nodules at the base .. — 7

Obscure .. .. — 28

[NEMATURA BED:] Black or slate-coloured carbonaceous clay, full of *Cyrena semistriata* and *Nematura pupa* [*Stenothyra*]. Also *Bythinia conica, Cerithium* 2 `sp., and *Cyclas bristovi* .. .. — 3

Green clay .. .. — 1½

Black laminated clay, full of *Planorbis obtusus, P. sp.,* and *Cyclas bristovi* [*Sphærium*] .. .. — ½

		ft
"Lower	Green clays	4
Hamstead	Mixed black and green clay, full of *Melania muricata,*	
Beds	*Hydrobia chasteli, Limnœa, Planorbis,* &c.	¼
(estuarine	Green clays with *Paludina, Nematura sp.* (in the upper	
and lacustrine)	part), *Melanopsis carinata*	20
224½ feet	BLACK BAND, full of *Paludina lenta; Unio* at the base ..	1¼

Total   ..   ..   ..   255¾"[1]

It will be noticed that there are gaps in the Lower Hamstead of the above section. Beds corresponding in position to some of these here obscured by slips have been noted by other observers, and seem to have presented no features of especial interest.

The Black Band at the base is a dark-brown carbonaceous clay or loam, turning sooty black on short exposure, and containing abundant seeds of aquatic plants, freshwater shells (mostly *Viviparus lentus* (Sol.), *Melanopsis carinata* (J. de C. Sow.), and *Unio gibbsi* Forbes), and scattered fish-bones. Angular pieces of flint occasionally occur in it. The top of the underlying Bembridge Marls is penetrated by rootlets, and in places has a weathered aspect, which is more noticeable in samples from borings than in the coast-sections. Clement Reid remarks that, "repeatedly after boring through un-weathered Hamstead Beds we penetrated a carbonaceous soil (the Black Band), and then again entered weathered clays full of roots, like the surface soil many feet above".[2]

Though the Black Band and "weathered" zone are traceable throughout the area occupied by the Hamstead Beds, they are unaccompanied by more definite indications of a stratigraphical break, and appear to mark merely a lengthy pause in the deposition of sediment. There seems to have been no contemporary channelling of the underlying Bembridge Marls, such as one would expect to have occurred had the top of that Series been raised even a few feet above water-level.

The Nematura Bed, about 30 feet higher, is a laminated dark clay, liable to be mistaken for the Black Band in poor exposures. It is the first bed in which *Stenothyra pupa* Nyst (*Nematura*) is met with. Brackish-water conditions are implied by the presence of *Modiola* and *Cerithium.*

The White Band, 65 feet above the Black Band, is so named on account of its seams of white shell-marl (chiefly *Cyrenae* with *Cerithium inornatum* Morris (? = *Terebralia plicata* Brug.) and *C. sedgwicki* Morris (*Potamides*), both characteristic, *Mya minor* (Forbes), &c. The White Band has not been positively identified inland. In parts of East Medina, sands are developed at about this horizon.

The next markedly fossiliferous band, 70 to 80 feet higher, is that known as the Water-lily or Leaf Bed; a firm, dark clay full of a creeping root, and containing leaves of water-lily (*Nelumbium*), palm, &c. It forms a ledge in the cliff. This bed also has not been recognised away from the coast.

The characters of the Cerithium Beds and the Corbula Beds of the Upper Headon are sufficiently indicated in the foregoing remarks and section. The only open sections of them are in the bluff which rises above the wilderness

---

[1]'Geology of the Isle of Wight,' *Mem. Geol. Surv.*, 2nd ed., 1889, pp. 186, 187.
[2]*Ibid.*, p. 190.

FIG. 28. *Vertical Section of the Hamstead Beds, Hamstead Cliff*

Scale: 1 inch = 40 feet

Adapted from "Geology of the Isle of Wight" (*Mem. Geol. Surv.*), 2nd ed., Pl. V.

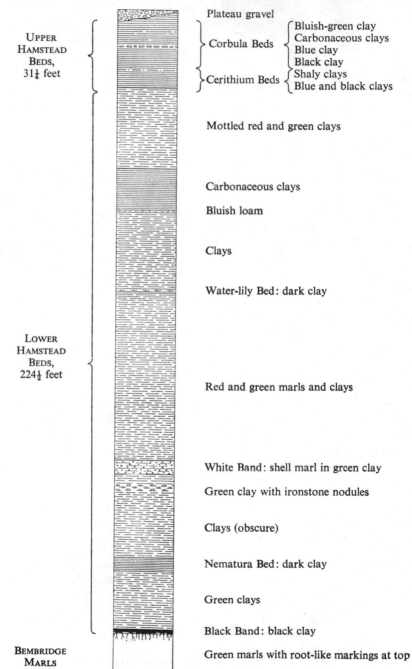

UPPER
HAMSTEAD
BEDS,
31¼ feet

Plateau gravel

Corbula Beds
- Bluish-green clay
- Carbonaceous clays
- Blue clay
- Black clay

Cerithium Beds
- Shaly clays
- Blue and black clays

Mottled red and green clays

Carbonaceous clays

Bluish loam

Clays

Water-lily Bed: dark clay

LOWER
HAMSTEAD
BEDS,
224½ feet

Red and green marls and clays

White Band: shell marl in green clay

Green clay with ironstone nodules

Clays (obscure)

Nematura Bed: dark clay

Green clays

Black Band: black clay

BEMBRIDGE
MARLS

Green marls with root-like markings at top

of landslides and fallen timber at Bouldnor Cliff (Fig. 29,). The beds occupy but a few acres of the hill-top, and as the ground there all slopes inland, the slipping of successive slices from the face of the bluff is somewhat quickly reducing the thickness of the Upper Hamstead division by the elimination of its highest and most interesting strata.

Hamstead Beds occupy more than two miles of shore and cliff between Yarmouth and Hamstead Ledge, and the Black Band, with some of the overlying beds of the Lower division, reappears in the cliffs farther east, at Thorness, near Sticelett, and to the north-east of Gurnard Ledge; but we must pass over these sections, and proceed to the brief description of the developments inland.

FIG. 29.   *Sketch of the upper part of Hamstead Cliff*
After Edward Forbes in "Geology of the Isle of Wight", (*Mem. Geol. Surv.*),
2nd Ed., Fig. 76, p. 193.

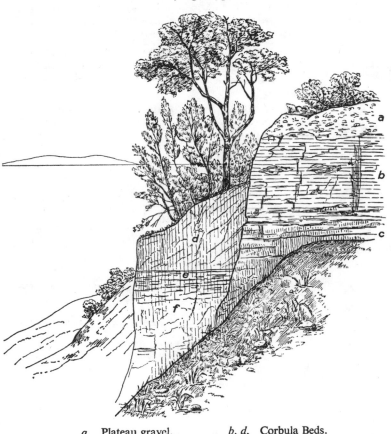

a. Plateau gravel.	*b. d.* Corbula Beds.
c. e. Lower Cyrena band	⎫
f. Shaly clays	⎭ Cerithium Beds

Exposures Inland. Much of the information concerning the distribution and character of the Hamstead Beds, which appeared in the last Geological Survey Memoir on the Isle of Wight, was obtained from a large number of trial-borings, made with the principal object of ascertaining the areal extent of the beds in question. These borings, carried down, in many cases, to the Black Band, or other marked horizons above it, made possible the tracing of the Hamstead-beds boundary in the featureless clayey ground on the outcrops of these strata and the Bembridge Marls: they also furnished additional proofs of the participation of the Hamstead Beds in the folding which affected the older rocks of the Island, and gave the *coup de grâce* to the moribund "Medina fault" hypothesis.

a. West Medina. In Parkhurst Forest, no sign of the Marine Beds with *Ostrea callifera*, supposed to occur there,[1] could be discovered. The greatest thickness of Hamstead Beds in the Forest area probably occurs in the vicinity of the Signal House, where a boring showed red mottled clays like those just beneath the Cerithium Beds at Bouldnor, about 220 feet above the Black Band. Part of a turtle, and freshwater shells, were found in a neighbouring trial-pit; and about 175 yards south-west of the Signal House the boring-tool brought up mammalian remains in the shape of a tooth of *Theridomys* and a small bone, from different levels.

North of the Forest, pits at Skinners Grove Tile-works show mottled clay with seams of *Cyrena* and ostracods. Here, too, bones of turtle were found, together with those of crocodile. These beds are inferred to be 30 to 40 feet above the Black Band.

At Werror Brickyard, on the left bank of the Medina, the junction with the Bembridge Marls seems to be shown. "Above a black seam were found *Melania turritissima* [*Potamaclis*], *M. forbesi*, *Melanopsis*, *Paludina lenta* [*Viviparus*], Fish-bones, and *Folliculites thalictroides* with other seeds, but the strata are so weathered that it is not easy to obtain details of the section, and it is possible that this black seam may be somewhat higher than the Black Band. . . .

"At the West Medina Cement Works, the *Nematura pupa* Bed [appears] at the sea-level near Dickson's Copse, but in the pit close to the Kilns it is nearly 10 feet lower. A good section may be seen at the latter place; and by means of boring (B.H. 93) it was carried 10 feet below the bottom of the pit and 8 feet below high-water level. It shows:

	ft
"Blue and yellow clay, with faint red mottling in the upper part; no mollusca observed. Turtle bones. (Seen in the pit)	25
Soft greenish clay (in B.H.)	3
Soft light-blue and yellow loams, with sand partings and selenite. Decayed *Cyrena* at 6 feet; Entomostraca from 7 to 7½ feet	7
Lead-coloured, dark-grey, or black laminated clay, full of shells between 11¼ and 12¼ feet. *Nematura pupa* [*Stenothyra*], *Hydrobia chasteli* [*Nystia*], *Neritina tristis*, *Melania muricata* [*acuta* (J. Sow.)], *Cyrena semistriata* ..	2¼
Green loam, with sandy partings	¾
	——
	38
	——

"The carbonaceous clays were at first taken to represent the Black Band, but there is now little doubt that they are really 20 or 30 feet higher in the series.

"South of Medina Cottage clays with *Melania muricata* and *Melanopsis carinata* are seen at several places in the river bank. They are the beds immediately above the lower *Nematura* Bed."[2]

---

[1] Godwin-Austen *in* Forbes, *op. cit.*, p. 37, footnote.
[2] 'Geology of the Isle of Wight,' *Mem. Geol. Surv.*, 1889, p. 198.

b. East Medina. "Alverstone Brick and Tile Works deserve notice as one of the few localities where the Hamstead Beds can be examined in an open section. The strata there visible belong, perhaps, to that part of the series which overlies the *Nematura* Beds, but the fossils are not sufficient to settle this point, though a boring was carried 17 feet below the bottom of the pit. The following is the section obtained:

"*Alverstone Brick Yard*

	ft
"Blue and yellow clay, with a thin seam of shelly marl. *Paludina angulosa, Hydrobia chasteli* [*Nystia*], *Melania muricata* [*acuta*], *M. forbesi, Melanopsis subulata,* Fish bones, and *Folliculites thalictroides*	6
Ferruginous clay and ironstone	¾
Laminated clay, with sand partings. *Folliculites thalictroides, Sequoia,* and other plant remains, *Trionyx?*	5
Blue and yellow laminated clay, with selenite, becoming stiffer below. *Paludina* and *Melanopsis carinata* at 20 feet from surface	17
	28¾

"The whole of the beds, except those reached in the lower part of the boring, are much weathered."[1]

On the eastern side of Wootton Creek, the Black Band runs through Ashlake Brickyard, the section showing the usual weathered soil beneath it, and the thin seam of *Nystia duchasteli*, already noticed (p. 122). The low position of the Hamstead Beds at this spot is attributed to an old landslip.

Near Newport a fine-grained sand appears at about the horizon of the White Band, and, expanding eastward, reaches a thickness of 30 to 40 feet about Haven Street and north of Brading. "This sand is so useful as fixing a definite horizon in a mass of clay, and also as a water-bearing bed, that wherever it could be traced it has been laid down on the [6-inch] map. It seems to form an obscure feature above Cross Lane (about half a mile north-east of Newport), but is apparently thin at that place. As this feature is traced to the south-east it becomes bolder, and the springs given out along its course make a belt of wet land near Heathfield and Buckbury, but no section is visible. Between Buckbury and Little Pan the sand seems suddenly to have expanded to a thickness of about 40 feet, for three borings (B.H. 112, 113, 114) at different levels were all in this bed, and another lower down (B.H. 103) also showed a trace of it. A pit at Staplers Brickyard affords the only open section of these beds in the neighbourhood. It shows alternations of loam, fine sand, and shaly clay, the only fossils being casts of freshwater shells, principally *Paludina* and *Limnaea*, and also some casts of cyprids.

"The same sand bed can be traced along Long Lane, till at Longlane Shute it approaches closely to the Downs. It is evident that at this spot the sharp monoclinal curve affects all the strata up to the middle part of the Hamstead Series. The high dip, however, dies away so suddenly that the beds flatten immediately and the sand can be traced for a long distance northward with only a gentle dip. Near Blackland the sand has sunk to near the stream level, but it re-appears in the cutting at Wootton Station, and also at several points on the eastern side of the gravel ridge.

[1] *Ibid.,* p. 201.

"Near Briddlesford two pits have been dug in sand, the one in the hollow showing at least 10 feet of very fine white sand and sandy loam. Further east this bed forms several small outliers on the hills around Haven Street. South of Binstead, in the upper part of Stroud Wood Brickyard, more than 7 feet of fine white sand overlie red and mottled clay, and the bed is probably of considerable thickness. On the high land at Upton Mill an old pit has apparently been dug for brick-earth. A boring (B.H. 185) at the bottom of this pit showed a considerable thickness of sand, but no fossils. In another outlier, at East Ashey, the sand has been dug, and it can also be well seen in several parts of the large outlier near Brading, especially in the road cutting between Ricketshill and New Farm."[1]

The beds overlying the sand in East Medina seem to be confined to the western part of that area, where they occur in the ridge east of Staplers Heath, and in that extending northward from Downend by Dorehill towards Wootton.

In the Staplers ridge, the highest beds proved were inferred to be near the top of the Lower Hamstead division, but in the Dorehill ridge clear evidence of the Cerithium Beds of the Upper Hamstead was obtained at the northern end of Little Lynn Common, and at Briddlesford Lodge; while at Dorehill the lowest of the succeeding Marine Beds seemed to be indicated by the presence of *Corbula pisum* and *C. vectensis* in material thrown out of a well. Clement Reid observes that, "still higher beds ought to be found on the top of the hill immediately west of Dorehill—unless the gravel is exceptionally thick. This seems to be the only place in the East Medina where there is any likelihood of the *Ostrea callifera* beds being found, but there is too much gravel to allow of a trial boring being made."[2]

A thin outlier of Lower Hamstead Beds may exist beneath the gravel and stony loam on the plateau north of St. Helen's.

---

[1] *Ibid.*, pp. 203, 204.
[2] *Ibid.*, p. 206.

Chapter VIII

POST-OLIGOCENE DISTURBANCES AND TECTONIC STRUCTURE: DEVELOPMENT OF THE EXISTING TOPOGRAPHY

POST-OLIGOCENE DISTURBANCES

THE COMPLETE stratigraphical discordance between the Hamstead Beds and the succeeding superficial gravels marks the passage of a considerable period of time, and definitely denotes the intervention of revolutionary changes in the tectonic structure and physiography of the Island. Of these impending changes, the Hamstead Beds give no intimation. So far, indeed, from affording any sign of the approaching termination of the intermittent subsidence that had been in progress since the early Eocene, the marine clays with *Corbulae* in the upper part of Hamstead Cliff rather suggest the indefinite continuance of the régime under which some 2,000 feet of alternating shallow marine and freshwater sediments had already accumulated on the sunken platform of the Chalk. It is probable that the Hamstead Beds were succeeded by strata contemporary with the higher stages of the Upper Oligocene of France, and that the physical conditions underwent no important change until the early or middle ages of the Miocene period.

The geological records of the adjacent parts of the European continent point to the Middle Miocene as the critical epoch when the accumulated stresses in the earth's crust there found relief in an outbreak of orogenic activity, such as had often occurred in earlier ages. In the British area the movements which then took place resulted mainly in widespread uplift, accompanied by localized plication, the latter being almost confined to a broad east-and-west zone, running through the South of England and the Channel, and giving rise to a system of folds which calls to mind the older and greater Armorican system of late Palaeozoic date, upon which it is superimposed.

The anticlinal domes and synclinal basins comprised in the Miocene fold-system are disposed *en échelon* on roughly parallel east-and-west axes, which have a slightly bow-shaped curvature, convex to the north. A notable trait in these folds is their transverse asymmetry, which is due, in the case of the anticlines, to the relatively steep inclination of the northern limb. Not infre-· quently, the contrast presented by the abrupt plunge of the strata north of the axis and their gentle dip on the south is sufficiently pronounced to give the flexure a monoclinal aspect. In extreme instances, the northern limb is overturned, or broken by thrust-faults. These faults are of various kinds, but the type associated with the most important individual displacements is that which tends to follow the bedding planes, and in which the main mass of rocks involved in the fold is pushed northward with respect to a partly detached and over-riding flake.

In the British area, the Miocene earth-movements, in so far as they found expression in folding and reversed faulting, attained their maximum known intensity in a belt of ground extending along the coast of Dorset, and the

135

Fig. 30. *Sketch Map of the Island, showing Axes of Folding*

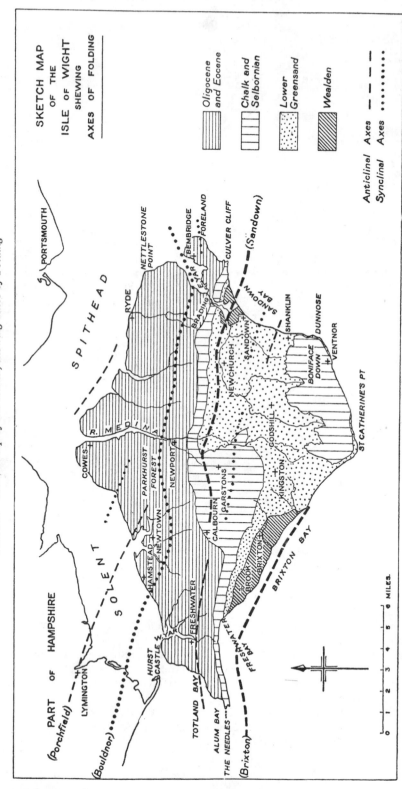

the effects of disturbances only a degree less powerful are to be seen in the Isle of Wight, which lies in north-eastward prolongation of that belt, and in probable tectonic continuity with it.

At the date when these movements began, the Tertiary Beds of the Island remained in the approximately horizontal position in which they were deposited, save for a slight tilt to the south-east. Nothing is known about the local physiographical conditions at that time, but it may be conjectured that the beds in question formed part of the substructure of a coastal plain laid bare by the definitive withdrawal of the shallow sea whose waters had so often overflowed the area since the beginning of the Eocene period.

As the movement progressed, the strata were gradually pushed northward and buckled up, and eventually, by a continuance of the process, were heaved into broad-backed, steep-fronted waves over the southern half of the Island area; bent down into a complementary trough on the north; and everywhere subjected to deformation on a smaller scale. Measured from crest to trough, the maximum vertical displacement of the base of the Eocene Beds by these movements amounts to about 4,800 feet, in the longitude of Brook.

We shall now describe the effects of these disturbances in some detail.

TECTONIC STRUCTURE

The dominant structural features of the Island (Fig. 30) are two strong, nearly-coincident folds known as the Sandown and Brixton anticlines, which overlap and replace each other a little to the west of the River Medina, and are responsible for the upturning of the strata in a belt of country extending the whole length of the Island, from the Needles to Culver Cliff.

The *Sandown Anticline* begins off-shore south-east of Culver Cliff. Its axis crosses the coast-line at Sandown Fort (where the Wealden Beds, dipping away on either hand, are for a short space horizontal), and runs thence in a direction about West 18° North, to Newchurch. Here it curves westward, and continues in that direction, with a slightly sinuous course, by Marvel Wood and the northern part of Gatcombe Down, to the neighbourhood of Calbourne, beyond which place the folding becomes feeble, though it is still discernible in the attitude of the Tertiary Beds as far west as Totland Bay.

North of the axial line the beds bend down, at first gently, and then with rapidly increasing curvature as the septal section of the northern limb is approached. In Whitecliff Bay the London Clay and Bagshot Sands are about vertical, while the middle beds of the Bracklesham Series are slightly overturned. The overturning is noticeable also in the Bagshot Sands at Longlands, in the highest beds of the Chalk exposed in the pit 200 yards west of Little Jane's Cottage at Brading, in the sand-pit at Beech Grove in that village, and in the chalk-pit a quarter of a mile south-east of Nunwell House. At Nunwell Rookery, where the dip has decreased to between 80° and 90°, the Chalk is much slickensided and many of the contained flints are crushed to powder; phenomena not uncommon on the northern side of the Central Downs.

Round the blunt northward salient of the Downs about Ashey the upturned beds of Eocene and Oligocene age are so compressed that the width of their outcrop, in places, is less than their true thickness. Further evidences of a local intensification of the earth's movements are afforded by sections now and formerly open in the neighbourhood. Thus, at the Ryde Waterworks quarry,

K

south of East Ashey, the Chalk is traversed by a thrust-fault which nearly coincides with the bedding (Fig. 31). Below the slide-plane the chalk is hardened, polished, and striated; above it, a thin fault-breccia is developed, passing in places into a crush-conglomerate, in which some of the larger pieces of broken flint have been roughly rounded by flaking, and in some cases resemble, the late Palaeolithic "*grattoir Tarté*". At West Ashey quarry, the Mucronata Chalk is so badly smashed and cleaved that the bedding is hardly distinguishable, and the crushed flints in places are drawn out into contorted wisps. Two nearly vertical strike-faults, accompanied by breccias, are seen in the eastern face of the working, and in the southern face there are indications of a horizontal shift along a vertical dip-fault. Close by, the cutting north of the tunnel under the road formerly showed the remarkable section, described on p. 95, in which the lower beds of the London Clay are succeeded by clays of Bracklesham age; whence it is inferred that over 400 feet of strata are cut out by a strike-fault, marked on the one-inch map. The occurrence of a horizontal shift along a dip-fault in the Chalk at Mersley Down has already been mentioned (p. 75). The eastern face of the same pit shows a little strike-fault on a nearly horizontal plane, the Chalk above which has shifted northward.

FIG. 31.   *Strike-fault at Ashey Down*
Scale—1 inch = 3 feet

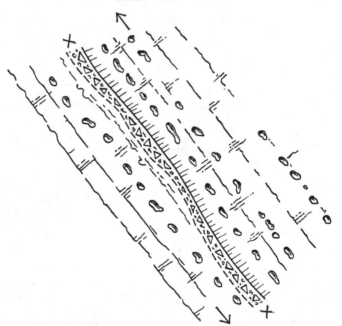

XX.   Fault and fault-breccia.
◄—.   Direction of movement.

Between Mersley Down and Calbourne there is little in the tectonic features that calls for particular notice. The dips in the Upper Chalk remain steep, and the Tertiary Beds, below the Bembridge Limestone, continue approximately vertical, though less compressed, as far as the Medina. At Carisbrook, the Convent quarry intersects a strike-fault (*see* p. 64), above which much of the normally massive, nodular chalk near the junction of the *Terebratulina lata* and *Holaster planus* Zones exhibits a coarse strain-slip cleavage. In the vicinity of Alvington Farm, near Gunville, the constriction of the outcrops of the Tertiary Beds opposite a northward bulge in the Downs suggests an approach to the conditions obtaining at Ashey.

Near Calbourne the strike curves southward. Simultaneously there is a marked reduction in the dips, which fall as low as 17° in the upper part of the Chalk, and a consequent widening of the outcrop-surfaces of all the beds; these changes being due to the rapid weakening of the Sandown fold towards its western termination. About a mile beyond Calbourne the east-and-west strike and high northward dips are resumed, but thenceforward, to the western end of the Island, the attitude of the strata is mainly determined by the folding on the Brixton axis.

True to type, the Sandown anticline develops only moderate dips on its southern limb. The gentle south-south-westward decline of the Lower Greensand is well seen in the cliffs of Sandown Bay. The interruption caused by the faulting at Little Stairs Point, and by the low anticline between the Point and Shanklin Chine, is described on an earlier page (34). These minor disturbances have not been traced through the Lower Greensand area inland, but, as Sir Aubrey Strahan has pointed out,[1] they may be continued in the sharp flexure, of similar trend, which is noticeable in the Selbornian Beds at Sibdown (or Gossard Hill), west of Rookley, at the same distance south of the Sandown axis.

In the Southern Downs the Cretaceous rocks have suffered little deformation. The few known faults (*e.g.* St. Catherine's Hill, p. 61) are small and of the normal type. The average dip is barely 2° under the northern summits of the Downs, but increases somewhat towards the coast near Ventnor; while the direction varies from south-south-west to east-south-east, the eastward element becoming more pronounced towards Chale, in response to a change in the strike, which bears round from about west in Shanklin Down to south-south-west in St. Catherine's Hill. In the southward deflection of the strike from Appuldur-combe to St. Catherine's Hill we may detect (as at Calbourne) the waning strength of the Sandown anticline and the growing influence of the other principal fold of the same class, now to be described.

The *Brixton Anticline*, like that of Sandown, lies partly, but to a greater extent, outside the limits of the Island. The beds in the southern limb are hidden beneath the sea, and the course of the axis, skirting the south-western coast of the Island between Chale Bay and the Needles, can be only inferred from the trend of the strike on its northern side.

Near Chale and Kingston, the curved outcrops of the Lower Greensand divisions mark the rounding off of the anticlinal dome near its south-eastern end. The outward dips hereabouts are low or inappreciable, but quickly become marked as the strike bears round north-westward into parallelism with the trend of the axis between Chale and Compton Bays. The dip in the northern limb—which, like that of the Sandown anticline, attains its maximum inclination well to the north of the axial line—first becomes apparent in the Lower Greensand north-east of Kingston, and is plainly seen in the Chalk at the southern end of Chillerton Down.

North of Chillerton Down the dip decreases, and in a small area about Rowborough, Garstons, and Gatcombe the conflicting influences of the

---

[1]'Geology of the Isle of Wight,' *Mem. Geol. Surv.*, 2nd ed., 1889, p. 245.

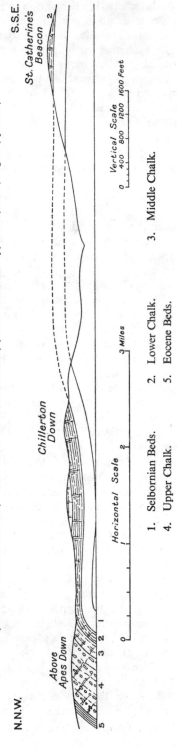

Fig. 32. *Section from Apes Down to St. Catherine's Hill*

(After A. J. Jukes-Browne, "Cretaceous Rocks of Britain", (*Mem. Geol. Survey*) vol. ii, 1903, Fig. 73, p. 409.)

1. Selbornian Beds.
4. Upper Chalk.

2. Lower Chalk.
5. Eocene Beds.

3. Middle Chalk.

Brixton and Sandown anticlines neutralise one another in a sort of tectonic no-man's land; the chalk-pits showing horizontal or but slightly-inclined bedding, while the relation of the boundaries of the Selbornian Beds to the contours of altitude point to the existence of a slight, flat-bottomed trough with an ill-defined northern boundary (Fig. 32, p. 140).

Continuing westward, we find the Brixton anticline increasing in strength as the Sandown fold weakens to the north of it, the dip produced by the former showing a progressive if wavering rise, to 80° or more in the Upper Chalk, and to 90° in the Eocene Beds, in the vicinity of Freshwater Gate. The overturning of the Chalk below the moat of the fort in Freshwater Bay occurs just near enough to the surface to raise the suspicion that it is due to superficial creep. The Oligocene Beds, as usual, are less disturbed. They show, however, a peculiarity in their outcrop that calls for passing comment, namely, an exceptionally broad dip-slope, which, in the case of the Bembridge Limestone, produces a kind of glacis near the foot of the Downs, in the neighbourhood of Shalcombe and Wellow. The flattening of the northward dip to which this feature is due, betokens the presence of a subsidiary east-and-west undulation, which seems to be the feeble westward continuation of the Sandown anticline.

The important fault in Compton Bay is described on page 12.

As far as tectonic structure is concerned, the cliff-section in Alum Bay (Fig. 33) is almost a replica of that in Whitecliff Bay, at the opposite end of the Island. There is a similar increase in the dip, from the highly inclined Chalk to the vertical and slightly overturned middle members of the Eocene system, and subsequent decrease through the Upper Eocene and Lower Oligocene. The induration of the upper beds of the Chalk, which becomes noticeable as one approaches the Needles (*see* p. 78), is due to molecular changes probably induced by pressure during the development of the Brixton fold.

FIG. 33. *Section from Totland Bay to High Down*

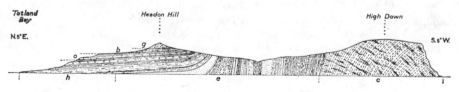

g. Plateau Gravel.   *b, o, h*. Oligocene (Bembridge, Osborne, and Headon) Beds.
e. Eocene Beds.   *c*. Chalk.

Near Freshwater Bay the Brixton axis alters its trend from north-west to west, and eventually to west-south-west near the Needles. Its subsequent course beneath the sea probably brings it into close syntactical relationship with the submarine extension of the Purbeck anticline, which crosses the opposite coast about eighteen miles distant. The two folds may be in actual continuity, but, having regard to their relative positions and axial curvature on shore, they are more likely to off-set and replace each other on parallel lines.

Turning now to the broad tectonic trough which underlies the northern half of the Island, and whose composite character is fairly evident from the map, we find that the line of maximum depression runs from Brading Harbour, by Rickett's Hill, Dorehill, the southern part of Parkhurst Forest, and Shalfleet, to Bouldnor Cliff.

This line marks the axis of what may be termed the *Bouldnor Syncline*, a persistent fold, which begins somewhere off-shore to the east-north-east of the Island, and is traceable for about twenty miles on the Hampshire mainland to the west-north-west. In its passage through the Isle of Wight, on a curved course which brings it into close complementary association with the Sandown anticline for a distance of about thirteen miles, this fold acquires, in a marked degree, the trough-like or cymboidal form characterising its fellows in the same fold-system; and it is largely to this circumstance that we owe the local preservation of Oligocene deposits elsewhere unrepresented in the South of England. The deepening of this fold from the east is proved by the decline of the base of the Hamstead Beds, on the axial line, from about 50 feet above sea-level at Rickett's Hill, to sea-level near Dorehill; while its more rapid shelving westwards is inferred from the fact that whereas the base of the Hamstead Beds is still below sea-level at Bouldnor Cliff, the Hamstead Beds themselves, together with at least 200 feet of subjacent Oligocene strata, are missing where the fold reappears on the opposite shore of the Solent, only four miles distant.

In the Sconce and Norton Green area, south of the Bouldnor syncline, the bedding as a rule is but slightly disturbed, but near Linstone Chine the Headon Beds are sharply folded (Fig. 23), and about half a mile to the south the How Ledge limestone is broken by small thrust-faults.

The northern limb of the Bouldnor syncline is of low inclination, probably nowhere exceeding 5°, and its boundary is not clearly defined, except in the neighbourhood of Newtown. Here the wellmarked *Porchfield Anticline* brings up the Bembridge Limestone at Hamstead Ledge, and the Osborne Beds north of Newtown River, on an axis running east-south-east through Elmsworth Saltern and Whitehouse Farm. This fold also has its counterpart on the Mainland, in the low anticline of Walhampton and Durn's Town, near Lymington,[1] but lacks persistence in the opposite direction, and soon dies out under Parkhurst Forest. It is succeeded, on its north-eastern side, by the parallel shallow syncline of Thorness Bay and Pallance Gate, which ceases to be discernible in the neighbourhood of Northwood.

About Gurnard and West Cowes the bedding is nearly level, with a slight dip, if any, to the south-east. The emergence of the Headon Beds at Norris and Osborne indicates a flexure running parallel with the coast between Osborne and Ryde; probably a monoclinal accentuation of the dip which brings up the Bracklesham Beds on the northern shore of Spithead.

Between Ryde and St. Helen's small, ill-defined undulations affect the Osborne and Bembridge Beds, and at Horestone Point the Nettlestone Grit is brought up by a fault, noticed on page 114. On the shore south of the Foreland the thin blue limestone near the base of the Bembridge Marls exhibits a number of little thrust-faults of diverse throw.

DEVELOPMENT OF THE EXISTING TOPOGRAPHY

The history of the Isle of Wight from late Miocene to early Holocene or Recent times is essentially a record of destructive changes wrought by denudation in the physiography which was created by the earth-movements above

[1] See 'Geology of the Country near Lymington, &c.' *Mem. Geol. Surv.*, 1915, p. 4.

described. Though the general purport of the record is clear enough, and recent advances in the study of land-forms have helped to elucidate some obscurities in the text, the early passages, especially, are so faint, and so over-written by the later, that their meaning can, at present, be only conjectured.

Initial and Early Phases. The larger of the folds described in the preceding pages probably acquired direct topographic expression at an early stage of their growth, and we may picture the joint anticlines of Sandown and Brixton (apparently formed simultaneously) as gradually giving rise to an upland ridge, which came by degrees to dominate the neighbouring areas of synclinal and feebly anticlinal structure, and which in turn gave birth to a number of consequent water-courses running northward and southward from a divide on the line of maximum elevation. It is unlikely that the local relief at any time possessed the strength which the observed curvature of the strata involved in the folding would seem to imply, for plication was almost certain less pronounced near the original surface of the ground than in the comparatively deep-seated regions now exposed to view; and contemporary erosion cannot have been without effect in tending to reduce the altitude of the ridge while the latter was yet in course of development.

Most of the primitive anticlinal upland has now disappeared. The surviving fragment, comprising two broken rings of monoclinal ridges and cuestas bordering as many interior vales, retains little of its original character; and of the southern dip-slope drainage, the only relics are a few small combes on the seaward face of the Southern Downs; yet, by comparing the topographic features of the Southern part of the Isle of Wight with those of a number of other, stratigraphically and tectonically similar, tracts of country in different stages of dissection, one can gain a fair idea both of the early character of the upland and of the sequence of changes whereby it reached its present condition.

In the beginning, the outward parts of the upland ridge consisted of Older Tertiary strata whose total thickness may well have exceeded that of the existing Eocene and Oligocene formations of the Island, none of which gives indication of thinning southward. The removal of these soft beds from the higher parts of the ridge was probably accomplished mainly through the medium of numerous, somewhat evenly spaced water-courses, which trenched the dip-slopes, and expanded more or less rapidly with the washing out of the sands and the foundering of the clays and marls exposed in their sides. Competition between these early consequent channels doubtless led to a reduction in their number, and on the southern slope the initial system of drainage is likely to have been much modified in the direction of greater integration before the exposure of the Chalk. It is to be inferred that the Chalk was first reached in the upper parts of the principal ravines, a little below their heads, and that the Tertiary Beds were thereafter rather quickly stripped from the crest of the upland and adjacent parts of the northern slope, but long remained in tongue-shaped sheets in the inter-stream areas of the gentler slope to the south.

In the mild climate of Miocene times the valleys eroded in the Chalk probably differed in their contours from their present-day representatives, which were largely moulded, or re-moulded, in the later subarctic phases of the Pleistocene. There is no reason, however, to think that they differed in their general development, and we may assume that here, in distant ages, as elsewhere, in times nearer our own, the valleys and combes of the streams which had cut their channels below the Tertiary Beds on the slopes of the upland, individually preserved throughout an approximately uniform rate of enlargement while confined to the Upper Chalk, but showed a marked tendency to lateral expansion when, and at the points where, they cut into the Middle Chalk, and broadened out into amphitheatral embayments comparatively quickly when they entered the Lower Chalk.

The destruction of the arch of Chalk in the higher parts of the upland would naturally follow upon the growth and intersection of a number of such embayments, whose development would also involve a further integration of the drainage; and the local physiographic conditions would then approximate to those now obtaining in the vicinity of Kingsclere, where the expanded and coalescent heads of several dip-slope valleys in the Chalk surround a dome of Upper Greensand, far below the original crest of an anticlinal upland similar to the one with which we are dealing (Fig. 34). The truncation of the corresponding, but more complex, Upper Greensand feature of the Isle of Wight, and the exposure of some of the weak strata below it, marked the initial stage in the opening of the inner vales of Sandown and Brixton, in the Lower Cretaceous rocks.

This stage not improbably was reached in the early part of the Pliocene period, by which time, it is believed, much of the constructive Miocene relief had been obliterated by erosion during an epoch when crustal movements of an elevatory character were locally in abeyance. The grounds on which this peneplanation has been inferred cannot be fully stated in the present work, but it may be remarked that the chief evidence in its favour is afforded by the relations of the Older Pliocene Beds to the underlying strata. On the North Downs of Kent and Surrey marine ironsands of Diestian (Lower Pliocene or Mio-Pliocene) age[1] rest upon a roughly planed surface, which is traceable beneath the Older Pliocene Beds far into France and Belgium to the east, and is inferred to have extended over much of the South of England, to the west.

Although the Diestian transgression was not necessarily, nor probably, co-extensive with the low-worn, faintly-undulating surface upon which the sands of Diest and Lenham were laid down, and the uplands of Hampshire and other Southern Counties have been searched in vain for traces of contemporary marine deposits, the possibility of a Pliocene submergence has to be borne in mind when discussing the topographical evolution of any part of the region. As will be shown in the next chapter, there are indications of an obscure marine episode in the Later Tertiary history of the Isle of Wight, at or rather before the time when the arch of the Sandown anticline had been reduced to the general summit-level of the Central Chalk Downs.

Later Phases. From this stage onwards the general succession of events becomes easier to follow, for the sedimentary record re-opens, and a substantial datum for reference is furnished by the summits of the Downs. By an elevatory movement, oft interrupted by periods of rest, or even of slight subsidence, erosion was stimulated to renewed activity, and the harder rocks, wasting more slowly than the others, were brought into increasing relief at their outcrops, and so by degrees gave rise to the series of secondary ridges which are now so marked a feature of the southern landscapes of the Wight.

By far the greater part of the immense mass of detritus formed during the excavation of the valleys and the reduction of the ridges below the general level of the Chalk Downs, was carried out of the district, to form new fluvial

---

[1]Upper Miocene, according to R. B. Newton, *Geol. Mag.*, 1917, pp. 259–269, 320–326.

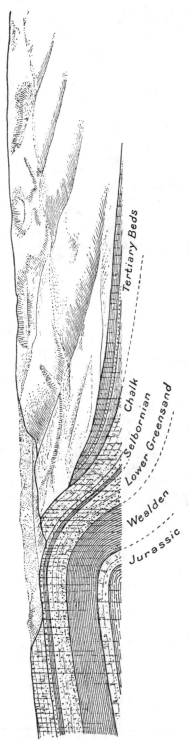

FIG. 34. *Representation of an Upland of the Sandown Anticlinal type, showing different stages in the truncation of the arch of Chalk, by the lateral expansion of dip-slope valleys*

Tertiary Beds

Chalk

Selbornian

Lower Greensand

Wealden

Jurassic

Near the right-hand (western) end of the figure, the Chalk crest of the upland, though stripped of its cover of Older Tertiary strata, is still almost intact. Near the middle, the crest is broken by the heads of dip-slope valleys, which are expanding into amphitheatres on the weak lower members of the Chalk formation, and have exposed small tracts of the more resistant Upper Greensand beneath. On the left, the Chalk arch has been demolished, and in its place a vale, encircled by escarpments, has been opened out. Wind-gaps in the farther side of the vale mark the upper ends of beheaded valleys following the gentle dip-slope on the southern limb of the anticline.

and marine deposits elsewhere. The relatively scanty but still impressive residue is seen in the sheets of Plateau Gravel, Valley Gravel, and other superficial accumulations, which, having been formed at various stages in the work of excavation, afford indications of the conditions under which that work was accomplished.

During the later dissection of the old anticlinal upland, there were yet further important modifications of the initial drainage. Within the present limits of the Island, the northern dip-slope streams, gaining ground at the expense of their southern neighbours, pushed the heads of the latter well to the south of the original water-parting, and appropriated all the interior drainage-area defined by the rim of Chalk—a not uncommon occurrence. The northern streams, while thus gaining ground as a whole, were reduced in numbers by mutual competition. A few of those which failed to retain a holding within the vales in the Lower Cretaceous rocks persisted long enough to cut definite notches in the Central Downs, such as the wind-gaps north of Brook and Shorwell; but it is long since the number of functional northern outlets of internal drainage, between the Needles and Culver Cliff, exceeded five, and one of the five has been put out of action comparatively recently by the arrival of the sea at Freshwater Gate.

We come now to the consideration of certain—

Features of the Existing River-systems. The five northern streams which effectively breach the Central Chalk Downs are the Western Yar; the Medina and its Carisbrook branch, the Lukeley Brook; and the Eastern Yar and its Yaverland branch; the last a mere wet-weather brook, which carries the run-off of a small tract of Lower Greensand to Brading Harbour, north-east of Yaverland.

The later history of the Western Yar affords a typical instance of the disintegration of a river-system by inroads of the sea. Once possessing a well-developed system of tributaries, which collected the drainage of a considerable portion of the Vale of Brixton through maturely-graded channels of open form, this river has by degrees been robbed of all its catchment south of the Chalk Ridge by the recession of the cliffs along the coast, and reduced from its former status as one of the chief rivers of the Island, to a brook of third-rate importance, with a disproportionately large estuary. Part of the floor or bottom-land of the old river-basin survives in the gently-undulating, gravel-strewn plain of Brook and Atherfield, forming the surface of a kind of terrace between the Chalk Downs and the sea; and all that remains of the ruined river-system are the small, now independent brooks which traverse the plain in valleys whose upper reaches retain their open character, but whose seaward ends are deepened into precipitous ravines.

Sheltered by the natural groyne of the Southern Downs, the River Medina has so far suffered little loss of territory by marine encroachment. But, on the other hand, its location with reference to the tectonic structure has for a long time held it at a disadvantage in its competition with its neighbours on the south-west and east. Owing to this drawback, the Medina has been late in reaching the erodible Lower Cretaceous rocks, and the expansion of its basin westward has been hindered by the resistant mass of slightly-inclined Upper Greensand and Chalk around Gatcombe and Rowborough. It is losing ground slowly to the Shepherd's Chine basin near Kingston and Chale Green on the south-west, and on the east it has comparatively lately been deprived of the greater part of its Blackwater branch, by the diversion of the Niton stream to the Eastern Yar near Little Kennerley, south-west of Merston. At the "elbow of capture" the old valley continues across the existing watershed, which is there barely 25 feet above the Recent alluvium of the Yar.

The Lukeley Brook system is even more unfavourably placed than that of the Medina. Situated on relatively low, sub-terminal portions of the Sandown and Brixton anticlines, it reaches no older stratigraphical division than the Upper Greensand, and is being slowly undercut along the Gault outcrop on the east by short subsequent branches of the Upper Medina. Two old dip-slope channels appear to be represented in the upper and lower ends of the main valley of the Lukeley Brook, while the middle section of the same valley, following the outcrop of the Middle and Lower Chalk in its curved path across the westward-pitching axis of the Sandown anticline, is the best example of a water-course of the "subsequent" type to be seen in the Chalk of the Island.[1]

The Eastern Yar, like the Western, has lost much ground through coast-erosion. Though the trunk, below Yarbridge, still retains part of its former drainage area south of the Central Downs, its hold on that is precarious, and would have been lost ere now, but for human intervention; the erection of the sea-wall across Sandown Level alone preventing the conversion of Brading gap into a second Freshwater Gate. When at its maximum development, the Eastern Yar system probably drained about as large an area to the east of the existing coast-line of Sandown Bay, as it still drains to the west of that line. The rivulets which cascade through Shanklin and Luccomb Chines are remnants of two of its branches, and the readjustment of their gradients now in progress appears to be a response to the change of conditions resulting from their detachment from the main stream by the recession of the cliffs.

The shape of the gaps in the Southern Downs between St. Boniface and St. Catherine's suggest that the valleys of the Wroxall and Niton branches of the Eastern Yar have lost a mile or two of their former length through the recurrence of landslips, such as have produced the Undercliff.

On passing for the first time from the Vale of Sandown into that of Brixton and Atherfield, few persons with an eye for country can fail to remark the higher topographic maturity, or, in other words, the comparative tameness, of the latter area. A probable explanation of this discrepancy is to be found in minor differences in the tectonics of the two tracts of country, and especially in the rather greater elevation of the Brixton fold; for this circumstance, in so far as it insured the relatively early exposure of the soft "core" of Lower Cretaceous strata to the agents of erosion along the structural axis, must have greatly facilitated the elaboration of subsequent drainage-channels, and concurrent reduction of inter-stream relief, in the old inner basin of the Western Yar. It is in keeping with the relatively backward state of this type of drainage in the area of the Sandown anticline, that the important readjustment of the boundary between the basins of the Medina and Eastern Yar near Merston, noticed above, should have occurred at a geologically recent date; and that the little Yaverland system should still survive, despite its close proximity to the main water-way of its larger competitor.

In the northern part of the Island, the bulk of the drainage of the Tertiary Beds is carried northward to the Solent and Spithead by streams which show

---

[1] Cf. the valley of the River Wey, above Alton, Hants.

so little regard for the attitude of the strata as to suggest that their courses have been superimposed on the latter from an unconformable cover of Plateau Gravel. Probably these soft beds have more than once been planed down to a gentle slope. Instances of local adjustment to differences in structure and hardness are, however, not wanting, as witness the westward deflection of the Clamerkin Lake stream along the southern flank of the Porchfield anticline, and the definitely subsequent course, along the outcrop of the Bembridge Marls, assumed by the Thorley Brook below Wellow.

The Solent River. In the foregoing description of the structure and physiographical development of the Island, attention has been concentrated, as far as possible, on local phenomena. Before passing to the consideration of the Superficial Deposits it is desirable to glance for a moment at certain cognate features of the surrounding region.

Prior to the latter part of the Pleistocene period, the northward drainage of the Isle of Wight and of its erstwhile extensions to the east and west, for long ages contributed to the maintenance of a considerable trunk stream, which has been termed the Solent River. A former continuation of the Dorset Frome, this river followed an east-ward course roughly indicated by a line drawn from Poole Harbour, through Bournemouth Bay, the Solent, and Spithead; and relics of its alluvia cap the cliffs on the Hampshire coast, and possibly also those on the north coast of the Isle of Wight. In the same district, signs of a large river flowing in from the west are met with in deposits of various ages as far back in time as the early Eocene, but however tempting it may be to look upon that ancient water-way as the lineal ancestor of the fluvial Solent, consideration of the probable extinguishing effects of the Miocene revolution on the pre-existing drainage must prevent, in this case, a too confident assumption of genealogical continuity.

The Solent River seems indeed to have owed its inception to the rise of the stronger Miocene anticlines athwart the dominant and pre-existing south-eastward inclination of the Secondary and early Tertiary strata, for the northern and southern limits of the remaining portion of its catchment area closely approximate to those of a structural depression (namely, the Hampshire Tertiary Basin), which is defined by the dissected anticlinal uplands of Purbeck and the Isle of Wight, on the one side, and of Pewsey, Kingsclere, and the Weald on the other.

When more complete, the Solent drainage-system bore a remarkably close resemblance to that of the Thames, but the sea has almost completely dismembered it by breaking into the main channel between Purbeck and the Isle of Wight, and by destroying that part of the southern side of its basin which lay to the south-east of Spithead.

So little remains of the former southward drainage of the Isle of Wight, that any discussion of its possible systematic relations might appear no better than idle speculation. Nevertheless, we may not unreasonably infer that, just as the Hampshire Avon and Test flow from the Pewsey-Kingsclere uplands towards their former confluence in the Solent River, so the streams on the southern slopes of the Purbeck and Isle of Wight range once ran down to, and were merged in, the main artery of another synclinal river-basin, that has all but disappeared beneath the waters of the English Channel.[1]

[1] On the subject of the Solent River, see, especially, T. Codrington, 'On the Superficial Deposits of the South of Hampshire, &c.', *Quart. Journ. Geol. Soc.*, vol. xxvi, 1870, pp. 528–551; A. Strahan, 'Origin of the River System of South Wales', *ibid.* vol. lviii, 1903, pp. 219–221; and C. Reid, '*Rep. British Assoc. for 1911*', 1912, p. 385.

Chapter IX

SUPERFICIAL DEPOSITS

"The classification of the superficial deposits presents considerable difficulty, for though the gravels of different areas indicate a similar sequence of events, yet the events in any two areas may not have been contemporaneous. The period, moreover, during which the gravels have been forming, though undoubtedly prolonged, does not seem to have been broken up by any marked changes of physical conditions, so that no classification can be proposed in which the deposits of one group shall not overlap in time those of another. Yet the position and character of the oldest gravel bring before us a picture of physical conditions so entirely different to those of the present day, that some classification by age becomes necessary.

"In the first place, an important series of gravels occurs near and often on the watersheds by which the existing valleys of the Island are divided, and forms well-marked plateaus. Though we have no guide as to the relative age of the separate patches of these gravels, except the doubtful test of height above the sea, yet the similarity in their mode of occurrence justifies their being grouped together under the title of Plateau Gravels. These gravels were obviously laid down before the valleys in their present form had been excavated. Yet their distribution and the direction of the slopes on which they rest point to a drainage system bearing some relation to that which now exists.

"A second group of gravels is arranged as terraces along the sides and lower parts of the valleys, and though, like the Plateau Gravels, now undergoing removal by the modern streams, yet showing an obvious connection with their valleys.

"Lastly, come the alluvial and peaty deposits still in process of formation along the courses of the streams, or such as might have been formed by the existing streams.

"Three principal groups may thus be established in the Superficial Deposits, capable of being arranged in chronological order. But other deposits of importance occur which cannot be placed in any one of these groups. Such is the angular flint-gravel of the Downs, which has probably been in process of formation from the time when the Chalk was first exposed to sub-aerial denudation up to the present day, and therefore runs through all three groups."[1]

The following table gives the sequence of the groups in descending order, the numbers indicating the order in which they are described in the following pages:

4. Recent Deposits, including some of those now in course of formation (Alluvium, Peat, Blown Sand, &c.).
3. Valley Gravel (the "Gravel Terraces" of the 1-inch Map) and associated Brickearth.
2. Plateau Gravel (including Raised Beach) and associated Brickearth.
1. Angular Flint Gravel of the Downs.

[1]'Geology of the Isle of Wight,' *Mem. Geol. Surv.*, 2nd ed., 1889, pp. 208, 209.

1. ANGULAR FLINT GRAVEL OF THE DOWNS

This is a subaerial formation of indefinite age, occurring on the summits and upper slopes of the Chalk Downs near the middle and in the southern part of the Island, where the low dips allow of a comparatively wide development of outcrop-surface. It consists of bleached, unworn flints and fragments of flints, mostly of greyish hue internally. The ground-mass or matrix of the stones is in some cases a mortar-like chalk-rubble; in others, a white gritty powder, composed of comminuted flint, siliceous meal (like that in the cavities of flint-nodules), and fine, dusty quartz-sand (probably of aeolian origin); and, in yet other instances, a red-brown clay—the gravel then approximating to the stony type of Clay-with-Flints. Rounded flint-pebbles, like those of the Eocene Beds, are among the accessory constituents, but they are seldom common, and in places hardly to be found.

The gravel, which is structureless—save for an occasional banding, attributable to settlement and creep—evidently represents the insoluble residue of a great thickness of Chalk, with some slight admixture of material derived from other formations. Every zone of the flintbearing Chalk seems to be represented; the large, flattish, *Inoceramus*-studded nodules of the Coranguinum Beds, and the thick, subcylindrical nodules of the Quadratus and Mucronata Beds, being often conspicuous. When underlain by decaying flinty chalk, as in the Central Downs, this gravel is doubtless still in process of formation, but the bulk of it, both there and in the Southern Downs, where little, if any, flint-bearing chalk remains, must be of high antiquity.

The most important accumulation of Angular Flint Gravel occurs on St. Boniface Down, capping the summit and spreading far down the western slope, where it is dug in numerous pits, to 10 feet in depth, opened at various levels. The maximum vertical thickness is not known, but may well exceed 30 feet.

Sections in other deposits, less extensively worked, can be seen on Shanklin, Rew, and Stenbury Downs, and on St. Catherine's Hill. The small patch on the last-named hill is noteworthy on account of its position, far away from and below the flinty chalk.

The thinner and more clayey deposits between Carisbrook and Westover Down mostly rest on the Upper Chalk, the boundary of which they overlap on the south. There are many shallow pits along the top of the Chalk scarp between Westover Down and Shorwell. Others can be seen at the northern end of the patch on the Middle Chalk outlier of Newbarn Down, above Gatcombe.

2. PLATEAU GRAVEL

With few exceptions, the gravels assigned to this class are high-level deposits, and form cappings to flat-topped hills, from 100 to 400 feet above sea-level. They occur in patches, with irregular boundaries indented by spring-combes, and in most cases are evidently but remnants of larger spreads.

Unlike the Angular Flint Gravel described above, the Plateau Gravels consist mainly of water-worn material, and, where thick, are usually stratified. The majority of them appear to be old stream-gravels, and of these the thick deposit of St. George's Down, south-east of Newport, may be taken as the type. The rest include raised beach, best exemplified at the Foreland, near

Bembridge; some sandy beds about Ryde, which look like mixtures or alternations of fluvial and marine deposits; and a few small gravelly accumulations
of doubtful origin, but probably the result of wash or creep.

The Plateau Gravels of the Island have so far yielded no contemporary
fossils, besides Palaeolithic implements, but there is no reason to doubt that
most of them are of Pleistocene age. The entire group is assigned to that period
in the last Geological Survey Memoir on the Isle of Wight, and attention is
there drawn to their similarity, in mode of occurrence and in the amount of
denudation they have undergone, to the gravels which occur on the north side
of the Thames Valley, and which, in places, are closely associated with the
Pleistocene Boulder Clay. It should, however, be remarked that the "Plateau"
group of that memoir does not include the few little patches on the Central
Chalk Downs, at and above 400 feet O.D., which form the highest deposits
coloured as Plateau Gravel in the current edition (1903) of the Geological
Survey Map on the one-inch scale. These, if not themselves of Pliocene age,
at least include remains of an ancient deposit which the present writer is
inclined to refer to that period.

The Plateau Gravels were laid down during an epoch which, for the Isle
of Wight and the South of England generally, was one of recurrent elevation,
and the larger spreads, resting upon gently inclined surfaces cut in the solid
strata, are believed to mark pauses in the upward movement, and consequent
accumulation of flood-plain and littoral deposits. The thickness, extent, and
prevailingly coarse texture of the sediments of this epoch point to climatic
conditions quite unlike those now obtaining in the region, but the only phenomenon strongly suggestive of ice-action is the contortion occasionally noticeable
in the gravels and in the solid rocks beneath them. Erratic boulders, such as
occur on the adjacent parts of the Sussex Levels, have not been observed.
Presumably the old strand upon which the transporting ice-floes grounded
lay entirely outside the present limits of the Island. In any case, their presence
in the local Plateau Gravel is hardly to be expected, in view of the low levels
to which the boulder-bed is restricted on the Sussex coast. The raised beach
at the Foreland alone falls low enough to form a likely hunting-ground for
ice-borne erratics, and it has been searched for them in vain.

The distribution of the Plateau Gravels in the Isle of Wight makes it difficult
to group them in a manner suitable for concise description without disguising
the mutual relations of certain parts. We shall notice first the abnormally-
constituted deposits of Brading-Mersley Downs and Headon Hill, which have
little in common beside their altitude and complete dissociation from the
other gravels; next, the suite of gravel-flats extending from St. George's Down
towards the Solent; then the remaining gravels north of the Central Downs
(in two groups); and, lastly, the deposits of the upper basins of the Medina,
Eastern Yar, and (old) Western Yar, south of those Downs.

a.   Brading and Mersley Downs

The three little patches of gravel resting on the edges of the upturned Chalk,
at 400 to 415 feet O.D., partly consist of large, incompletely-rounded beach-
pebbles or cobbles of flint and Selbornian chert and cherty sandstone (frequently
fossiliferous), having thick bleached crusts, covered with mastoid markings.
The ground-mass of the gravel varies from reddish-brown sandy clay to light
yellow and greyish loamy sand. Associated with these materials there are

little-worn and angular flints, well-rounded small flint-pebbles of the common Eocene type, a few pieces of iron-sandstone, and small pebbles of white quartz.

Except for their weather-worn condition, the cobbles of flint and chert closely resemble those of the raised beach at the Foreland (at a lower level by more than 300 feet), described on a later page, and evidently have at some time formed part of a coarse littoral deposit.

The gravel has been dug in a number of shallow pits on both Brading and Mersley Downs, but the only working still open is situated about midway along the northern side of the more western of the two patches mapped on Brading Down. Here the gravel contains much brown clay and angular flint, and is unstratified. The pebbles of flint and chert range up to about 10 inches in diameter. A better idea of the character of the deposit can be gained by examination of the thick washes which mantle the slopes of the Down in the vicinity, and which are exposed in the ploughed soil around the pit, and in an old chalk-quarry and some entrenchments to the south-east of it.

The gravels of Brading and Mersley Downs merit closer consideration than they have hitherto received, for although apparently referable, as a whole, to the widely-represented class of subaerial deposits which result from the fortuitous accumulation of slope-wash, they acquire a peculiar interest when their location is taken in conjunction with the distinctive elements in their composition. In the slight account of them given in the last Geological Survey Memoir on the Island (p. 210), where they are classed with the Angular Flint Gravel, it is remarked that, "the abundance of beach-pebbles is striking", but the subject is immediately dismissed with the suggestion that this material has "probably been derived from some Tertiary Bed". It appears practicable, however, to fix the age of the parent bed of the pebbles within narrower time-limits.

As far as is known, the existing Eocene and Oligocene formations of the Island are incapable of furnishing such coarse, imperfectly-rounded shingle, or, indeed, any débris of Cretaceous rocks older than the Upper Chalk. It would seem, therefore, that the bed whence this shingle was derived must have been of post-Oligocene, or, at any rate, of post-Hamstead age. Further-more, it would appear that the bed in question post-dated the local Miocene folding, for the presence of Selbornian cherts and cherty sandstones implies that the pebbles were formed at a time when the erosion of the Miocene folds had proceeded sufficiently far to expose the Upper Greensand within the present limits of the Island; the rapid reduction in size which the blocks of cherty sandstone undergo on the modern beaches making it improbable that the large cobbles of this material in the Brading Down gravel had been transported many miles from their source.

On the other hand, the deeply weathered state of the pebbles, and the altitude of the gravels in which they occur, jointly argue for them an antiquity considerably higher than that of any marine or other aqueous deposit in the Island which can be positively assigned to the Pleistocene period. Hence it seems probable that the Brading and Mersley Down gravels contain, along with much other material, the relics of a Pliocene beach.

The characteristic cobbles are common in the soil about Brading, but are absent from the Southern Downs, and appear not to occur westward of the Medina; so that it would seem that the bed from which they came was confined to, or had its chief development in, the north-eastern part of the Island, like the acknowledged raised-beach shingle of later date.

b.   *Headon Hill*

The gravel forming the highest part of this hill reaches an altitude of 396 feet near its southern edge, and attains a thickness of about 30 feet. It is separated from the Chalk Downs by a valley 200 feet or more in depth, and is cut off on the west and north by sea-cliffs.

The deposit is made up of unworn flints and pieces of ironstone, with a small proportion of Tertiary flint-pebbles and little pebbles of quartz. Chert and other foreign materials seem wanting. Much of the ironstone, especially the tabular sort, has been formed *in situ*. The ground-mass of the stones is in places a fine Barton-like sand (which also occurs alone in bands), but more often a ferruginous loam and loamy sand, full of small chips of flint, and resembling decalcified chalk-rubble. Stratification is exceedingly irregular and impersistent, as is also an oblique lamination, noticeable in the sands and loams. In addition to these features, the sides of the pits opened in the hill-top show frequent indications of the cutting and filling of small water-courses (Fig. 35); yet the gravel does not give one the impression of being a ·normal stream-deposit.

FIG. 35.   *Section of Gravel-filled Channel in the Plateau Gravel, Headon Hill*

Scale: About 1 inch = 5 feet.

The writer agrees with Mr. Hazzeldine Warren[1] in regarding the Headon Hill gravel as part of an old fan of rock-waste, derived from the higher ground of the Chalk and Eocene strata formerly existing to the south (Fig. 36, p. 154). Mr. Warren thinks that there is a close genetic connection between the gravel and a broad depression in the Chalk ridge half-a-mile distant; but, whether the gravel be a strictly local accumulation, or the relic of a larger apron of wash once extending along the northern side of the Central Downs, its formation implies the existence of meteorological conditions similar to those which, at a later date, gave rise to the Combe Rock and Rubbledrift. The amount of erosion indicated by the present isolated position of the Headon Hill gravel is so much greater than that which has elsewhere taken place since the formation of the Combe Rock, there there is hardly room for doubt as to the relative antiquity of the two deposits.

c.   *St. George's Down to East Cowes and Osborne*

"The sinuous outlier of gravel which spreads over the edges of the highly inclined Chalk and Greensands in this Down is one of the most remarkable in the Island, partly on account of its height above the sea and above the neighbouring valleys, and partly on account of the bold feature it presents

---

[1] 'Palaeolithic Flint Implements from the Isle of Wight,' *Geol. Mag.*, 1900, p. 409.

FIG. 36. *Section through High Down and Headon Hill, to illustrate the inferred relation of the Plateau Gravel to the Chalk Downs*

Scale: Horizontal, 1 in. = ⅛ mile; Vertical, 1 in. = 800 ft.

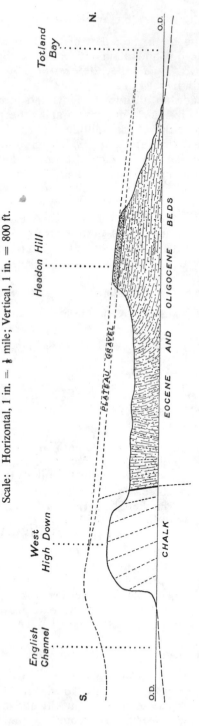

The wash-like gravel forming the higher parts of Headon Hill is here represented as the remnant of a larger deposit, once extending from the Chalk Ridge towards the low-lying tract now occupied by the Solent and Christchurch Bay.

to the south. The gravel, being thick and coarse, and having been partly cemented into a hard rock by iron oxide, forms an escarpment rivalling that of one. of the older sandstones, while its even surface, slanting gently away to the north, resembles a dip-slope. On the north side, the central part of the outlier has been deeply notched by a number of springs, each forming a combe, and producing scenery of remarkable beauty. The gravel stretches away far to the north, both on the east and west sides, along the nearly level tops of ridges composed of all the rocks up to the Chalk-with-flints."[1]

The St. George's Down plateau, which projects southward into the Vale of Sandown with the feature well described in the foregoing passage, extends northward into a gap in the Central Chalk Downs, about three miles in width. Here its original eastern limit is indicated by the rise of Arreton Down, and the gravel-flat, for a short space, assumes the character of a dissected terrace, occupying nearly half the width of the gap, and standing about 300 feet above the level of the River Medina.

When viewing the gap and terrace from the east (Fig. 37), little exercise of imagination is needed to discern in them the remains of an open valley whose floor once rose high into the openings of the Southern Chalk Downs a few miles to the south, and fell away gently towards the low area near the Solent, in the opposite direction.

Descending to the plateau, one notes, in a road-cutting near its south-eastern end, a massive cornice of iron-cemented gravel, which serves as a roof to a presumably modern rock-shelter.[2] Farther on, at short intervals along the southern and western edges of the plateau, several large excavations are to be seen, some of them 25 feet or more in depth, whose sides afford clear sections of iron-stained gravel, varying in texture, and consisting of flints, Selbornian cherts and cherty sandstones, quartz-pebbles, and Lower Greensand grits, in different stages of attrition, in a ground-mass to which the Ferruginous Sands of the last-named formation have largely contributed.

The upper 8 feet or so of the gravel is structureless, or but confusedly banded: the lower parts are well stratified and current-bedded, and show frequent lenses and seams of grey loam full of small bleached stones. The deposit becomes more ferruginous downward, and the cementation into iron pudding-stone, mentioned above, is usually confined to the basal layers, which crop out on the boundary of the gravel, and are not reached in the majority of the pits. Neither implements nor bones are known to occur in this deposit, but the latter may yet be found in the ferruginous pudding-stone, unless decalcification had been completed prior to the formation of the iron "pan".

The gravel above described is of fluvial origin: it is clearly an abandoned portion of the waste-load of a stream which flowed in the same direction, and through the higher part of the same gap, as the Medina, and which is therefore, on the principle of continuity, to be identified with that river. But the Medina of the St. George's stage must have differed greatly in habit from the modern stream, and at times have attained a vastly greater volume. It was no orderly, half-canalized brook that distributed the gravels of this stage with something of the grand manner of a river possessing a few thousand square miles of catchment to draw upon; and, realizing this, one asks oneself,

---

[1] 'Geology of the Isle of Wight,' *Mem. Geol. Surv.*, 2nd ed., 1889, p. 212.
[2] Lately fallen in.

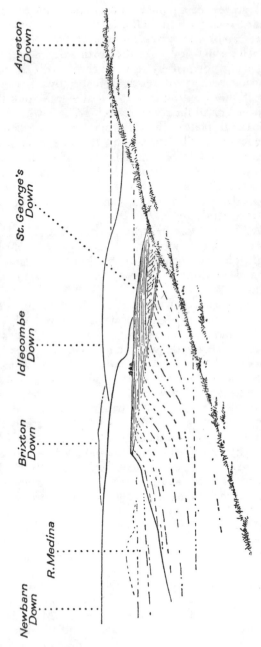

FIG. 37. *Sketch of St. George's Down, from the north-east*

The foreground is part of Arreton Down on the Chalk Ridge. The shaded area in the middle-distance represents the gravel-flat on St. George's Down, with the cottage and firs above the Dropping Well (p. 187) on its farther edge. The hills beyond are part of the small upland into which the Chalk Ridge broadens west of the Medina. In the background, to the right, the low country on the Oligocene Beds is indicated.

whence the necessary supply of water was derived. The Medina basin, as has been shown, was formerly larger than at present, but, even so, it would seem to have required a rainfall of Diluvial dimensions to enable it to support, or occasionally to afford, an effluent capable of producing the phenomena under consideration; and one turns to the hypothesis of rapid spring thaws of deep snow-fields, during a sub-arctic phase of the Pleistocene period, as affording a more probable explanation of the anomalous occurrence of a series of deposits, appropriate to a considerable river, in a drainage-area normally capable of nourishing only a little brook.

The gravel-flat at the golf-course, on the summit of Shide Hill, lies on a plane about 50 feet below that of the main mass of the St. George's plateau, and probably belongs to a later stage, when the Medina had shifted nearer to its present course.

On the soft Tertiary Beds north of the Chalk ridge, the terrace-feature, apparent at the western end of Arreton Down, is lost; the gravel-flats of Stapler's, Downend, Dorehill, Whippingham, and Wootton, forming the tops of plateaux on minor water-partings. The decline of the gravels from St. George's Down northward, to Osborne, is at the rate of about 1 in 136, in a distance of 3¾ miles. When engaged in distributing these and other Plateau gravels, the responsible streams were almost certainly in the "braided" condition, *i.e.*, split up into a net-work of shallow, shifting distributaries; a condition to which a comparatively steep gradient is appropriate. Still, the particular gradient mentioned above is so high as to engender doubt concerning the contemporaneity of the St. George's Down and Wootton-Whippingham gravels.

The deposits between St. George's Down and the Solent do not call for particular description, and we merely note the occurrence of Brickearth with chips of flint, &c., above the gravel at Downend (340 feet O.D.), and the existence of pits in which sections can be seen at Stapler's Heath (290 feet), Little Lynn Common (230 feet), west of Wootton Lodge (170 feet), Whippingham (130 feet), and north-east of New Barn near East Cowes (134 feet). Near the coast the gravel is more water-worn and better stratified than in most inland localities.

d. *Parkhurst Forest to West Cowes*

"West of the Medina, the gravels have the same general northerly fall, combined with a slight inclination towards the Medina. At the same distance from the Downs and from the Medina we find gravels like those [north of] Downend, and at about the same height. The outlier in Parkhurst Forest, at the Signal House, is 260 feet above the sea; the southern end of the Northwood outlier is 213 feet and the northern end at 120 feet, giving a fall of 140 feet in three miles, or 1 in 113."[1]

Most of the Parkhurst deposits have been dug, and in the Northwood spread there are sections near Northwood Church, at Place Brickyard, and at the eastern end of Tinker's Lane. These are all in gravel of ordinary, fluvial type, but a pit on the northern side of Ruffin's Copse is partly in sand of marine aspect, and will be described later, with other deposits of similar facies.

---

[1]'Geology of the Isle of Wight,' 2nd ed., 1889, p. 214.

e. *Thorness, Hamstead, Calbourne, High Down, &c.*

"The outlier east of Great Thorness shows no section. Its height is about 130 feet. The larger outlier west of Great Thorness is worked to a depth of 15 feet, and slopes markedly to the eastward, not to the west, where the larger valley lies.

"The sheet of Plateau Gravel at Hamstead appears to have no connexion with the present system of drainage. At the highest point, close to Hamstead Farm, it reaches 200 feet, but in every direction except the north-west, where it is cut off by the cliff, it quickly sinks to the 100-feet contour, or even lower. This sheet is composed of partly-worn flint gravel, with many quartz pebbles and occasional blocks of greywether sandstone. Greensand chert was not observed in it."[1] The deposit looks like a degraded river gravel. Its constituents seem to have come from the south.

The small spreads of flint gravel (230–160 feet) about Calbourne are old out-washes, of various ages, from the Chalk-combes south-east of the village.

Mr. S. Hazzledine Warren has called attention[2] to three little unmapped deposits, in the neighbourhood of Freshwater, which yield flint implements. From two of these, consisting of gravel which seems to be the remains of a terrace, about 80 to 100 feet O.D., on the eastern side of the Yar Valley between Freshwater Gate and Freshwater Church, he obtained worked flints of Eolithic types. The third and most interesting of the three deposits is a stony loam, passing down into yellow stony clay, overlying chalk-rubble on the bottom of the depression between East and West High Downs, south of Headon Hill. The main mass of it is described as occurring from 75 to 100 yards west of, and four or five feet above, the lowest point of the col, which is about 360 feet O.D. Trial-pits, sunk to a maximum depth of $3\frac{1}{2}$ feet, showed one or two layers of ironstained flints and other stones, together with a number of Palaeolithic tools, flakes, and cores.

The majority of the implements found are of the rudely ovate form, known as "Plateau palaeoliths", and classed as St. Acheul I.[3] Many of them are "corroded", and, "like the earlier Palaeolithic implements from Stoke Newington and elsewhere, nearly always bear evidence of having been twice abraded: once before, and again after, they received their ochreous patina; showing them to have been derived from an earlier drift". An ovate implement, which "came from the upper layer of stones", is of a more advanced type, and referable to the St. Acheul II class: a type abundantly represented in the lower Plateau Gravels of the Solent basin.

f. *Fluvio-marine Deposits: Thorness to Foreland*

The gravels and associated sands now to be noticed are placed under one heading for convenience of description, and are not to be regarded as a naturally distinct group. In several cases they are either laterally replaced, or overlain, by purely fluvial and subaerial deposits. We follow Nature, however, in dividing them into two stages, of which the higher comprises the series of gravel plateaux, between 170 and 120 feet O.D., ranging along the northern coast of the Island from Thorness Bay to Node's Point. It will be observed that the

---

[1]*Ibid.*, p. 215.
[2]*Op. cit., Geol. Mag.*, 1900, pp. 406–412.
[3]S. H. Warren, *in. lit.*, Nov. 1919.

gravel-flats of Northwood, Osborne, and Wootton, already briefly noticed, are impliedly included in this higher stage: we have here an instance of the lateral replacement of marine by fluvial deposits, referred to above. The Plateau Gravels of this stage seem to be parts of a once-continuous sheet that was spread out on low-lying ground forming the southern shore of the Solent River estuary.

The lower stage, 50 to 0 feet O.D., comprises only one well-defined deposit, namely, the raised beach at the Foreland.

These two stages have their correlatives in the neighbouring parts of the Mainland; the upper stage corresponding to the higher, Portsdown-Goodwood range of raised beaches; the lower to the Brighton-Worthing raised beaches, and the topographic feature by which they are represented near Havant and Titchfield.[1]

The sands regarded as marine are first seen in the Rew Street outlier, where they have been dug to a depth of 12 feet, at the south-eastern corner of the spread. Farther east, a pit on the north side of Ruffin's Copse formerly exposed:

	ft
"Gravel and mottled clay, mixed	5
Fine white sand with black specks, about	10
Gravel (now hidden), said to be	2
	17"[2]

A trial-boring a few hundred yards farther east is said to have proved 20 feet of the sand, under 11 feet of gravel.

"The sand crops out in Ruffin's Copse, and there yields a considerable supply of water.

"The resemblance of this sand to that found in Goodwood Park, near Chichester, is so great, and the height (130 feet) coincides so exactly, that careful search was made here for marine shells. Nothing, however, could be found, the bed appearing to have been thoroughly decalcified; it has no impervious covering like that which has preserved the deposit with its shells at Goodwood."[3]

We pass over the river deposits about Cowes and Osborne to the Quarr Hill outlier, pausing on the way to take note of the low and apparently slipped mass of Plateau Gravel on the side of Wootton Creek, near Ashlake. In the Quarr Hill deposit the sand seems wanting, but two pits south-west of Binstead Lodge are in gravel which resembles the modern beach-material of the Solent in containing a notable proportion of incompletely-rounded flint-pebbles; and the Ryde gravel, as far as can be seen, is mostly of a similar character. Relics of a higher gravel-spread survive in the blocks of ferruginous pudding-stone on Shrine Hill (about 200 feet O.D.), between Haven Street and Newnham.

---

[1]See Geol. Survey Memoirs on the 'Country near Fareham' (1913, pp. 72, 80) and "Lymington" (1915, pp. 50, 51).

The common practice of treating these two ranges of raised beaches as if they were identical is to be deprecated, as the cause of no little confusion.

[2]'Geology of the Isle of Wight,' 2nd ed., 1889, p. 214.

[3]*Ibid.*, p. 215.

The sand reappears in the larger spread of Oakfield, and has been worked in the brickyard at Preston, where a pit (now degraded) showed:

	ft
"Shingle and mottled clay, contorted together	2 to 6
Fine sand with seams of loam and scattered flints	9

"Several other pits between this brickyard and Oakfield [showed] similar beds, the sand always lying below the gravel. Search was made for fossils, but none could be found."[1]

The St. Helen's gravel is mostly subangular, with some patches of shingle. It is covered by loam and has been little dug except on its eastern border, above Priory Bay. In the pit by the Fort at Node's Point, about 120 feet O.D., it is well stratified, contains bands of gravelly clay, and is overlain by loam; the total thickness exposed being about 12 feet. Priory Bay is the chief locality for Palaeolithic implements in the Island. They were first observed on the beach by Professor E. B. Poulton in 1886, and were traced to the gravel at the top of the degraded cliff some 16 years later by Miss Moseley, of Sea View. Specimens obtained from the gravel are mostly unworn. Perch-backed, ovate-lanceolate, and irregular forms are met with; also notched triangular flakes; but the predominant type of implement is the common Acheulian ovate.[2]

The easternmost patch of gravel belonging to this stage is that near Knowles Windmill, south of Bembridge. It lies about 50 to 60 feet above the Foreland raised beach, now to be described.

Few raised beaches in the South of England are so clearly displayed in cliff-section as the example which forms the coastal terrace between Bembridge Point and Howgate Farm. Its coarse, shingly gravel, composed mainly of flints and Selbornian chert and sandstone, with a small admixture of ironstone, quartz, and other material from the Tertiary Beds and Lower Greensand, is seen to rest on an evenly-planed surfaced of Bembridge Marls, which rises gently south-westward, from near high-water mark at Ethel Point, to about 50 feet above that datum at its abrupt termination near Howgate. The surface of the ground above rises in the same direction, but at a slightly higher angle, so that the gravel, which is only a few feet thick near Ethel Point, expands to about 35 feet south-west of the inn at Foreland. As the deposit thickens, it coarsens; flints and sandstones over a foot in diameter become abundant, and, standing out on the face of the cliff, give the gravel the appearance which geologists of an earlier generation were wont to describe as "torrential".

All along the section there is a pronounced oblique bedding, with a persistent north-eastward dip of 2° to 5°, indicating lateral accretion by longshore drift. Close to its south-western limit, the gravel suffers a rather rapid thinning, due to a decline in the height of its upper surface, and, *pari passu* with this change, an overlying brick-earth, elsewhere thin, swells out to about 35 feet. At the critical point, where the gravel is in the act of thinning out, the section is much obscured by one of the usual junction-slips, but, from the fact that nearly the whole depth of the cliff section a few yards to the south is occupied by Bembridge Marls, it is evident that the gravel, and most of the brickearth above it, abut against a buried bluff or cliff trending at approximately a right-angle to the existing coastline at that point (Fig. 38).

---

[1]*Ibid.*, pp. 216, 217.

[2]R. W. Poulton in F. Morey's 'Guide to the Natural History of the Isle of Wight' (Newport: 1909), pp. 37–41, and 2 plates.

Inland, the position of the buried cliff is marked by a slight feature, which dies out in the direction of Bembridge.

An ovate palaeolith, the first recorded from the Isle of Wight, was found about 1870 by Mr. T. Codrington, in the brickearth above the old cliff near Howgate Farm. It is figured in Sir John Evans's "Early Stone Implements".[1]

FIG. 38. *Section of the Raised Beach at the Foreland, near Bembridge*

Distance, about ⅛ mile.   Vertical scale, 1 inch = 210 feet.

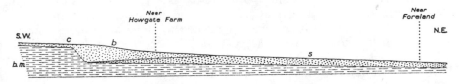

c. Buried cliff.   b. Brickearth.   s. Shingle of Raised Beach.

b.m. Bembridge Marls, in which the raised-beach platform is cut.

g.   *Basins of the Upper Medina and Eastern Yar*

Here the Plateau Gravels are all of non-marine types, and occur in less extensive sheets than those in the northern part of the Island. Not a few of them lie on pronounced slopes and are probably or certainly subaerial reconstructions.

Blake Down, on the divide between the Medina and the Eastern Yar, is capped by stratified gravel similar to, though not so thick as, that on St. George's Down, which clearly belongs to another and older stage. The Blake Down gravel is dug in several pits, to a depth of about 8 feet. At present, the best exposure is at the cross-roads a quarter of a mile west of Upper Yard.

"The series of outliers extending northwards from Blake Down are clearly portions of a once continuous sheet. A line drawn along their western margins forms a regular curve, and probably corresponds approximately with the original boundary of this area of gravel. But on the eastern side the sheet has been deeply eroded by the streams draining into the Blackwater. Two small patches of gravel occur on the west side of the Medina, but they lie at a lower level, contain more chert than those last described, and are probably of later date.

"Excluding these two patches, we find the level of the upper margin of the series of gravel outliers falling northwards from 278 feet at Blake Down to 200 feet near Blackwater, and with such regularity as to convey the impression that the gravel must have been deposited along one continuous valley."[2]

Near Rookley Green, the Yar-Medina water-parting turns abruptly eastward, across this line of gravels, into the low ground between the head of the Blackwater and the sharp bend of the Yar near Little Kennerly, where it is only 25 feet above the Yar alluvium. The capture of the Upper Blackwater at this spot by the Yar was noticed in the last chapter (p. 146). The diversion was effected after the deposition of the Blake Down series of Plateau Gravels,

---

[1] 2nd Ed., 1897, p. 687, Fig. 467. The Foreland section is described by T. Codrington, *Quart. Journ. Geol. Soc.*, vol. xxvi, 1870, pp. 541, 542.

[2] 'Geology of the Isle of Wight,' 2nd Ed., 1889, p. 218.

which follow the original valley northward and parallel with the existing (Lower) Blackwater; and it did not long precede the deposition of the local Valley Gravels, which follow the new course of the river, but stand only a few feet lower than the water-parting at the point where the capture occurred.

"In some parts of the broad tract of Lower Greensand which runs eastwards to Sandown, the remains of an old gravel-covered plain are very striking. They occur at a fairly constant level, but there are scattered patches also at a variable height on the sides of the hills [*e.g.* to the south-west of Arreton]. . . .

"Near Newchurch good examples of gravel-covered plateaus may be observed. One extends through the village and along the steep bank overhanging the alluvial flat, showing in its course a tendency to slope downwards towards the north, that is towards the valley of the Yar. Another, cut by denudation into a sinuous outline, is well exposed at Skinner's Hill, on the road from Newchurch to Borthwood, and is worked in many places for gravel. . . .

"The hill near Sandford is capped with a conspicuous outlier of these gravels at a height of 200 feet above the sea; and similar but very thin patches occur near Apse and Apse Heath. At Alverstone the gravel caps the top of the steep bank which bounds the modern alluvial flat, as at Newchurch."[1] These terraces are about 80 to 90 feet above the Yar, and are probably much older than the raised beach at the Foreland.

Two patches of gravel, sand, and loam are seen in section at the top of the cliff between Shanklin and Sandown. Some of the flints derived from them on the beach below seem to have been artificially flaked. A few other patches, sloping towards the Yar, occur on the northern side of that river between Alverstone and Yarbridge.

It is to be inferred from the disposition of the Plateau Gravels in this area that the lowest part of the old valley in which they were laid down followed nearly the same line as the bottom of the existing valley.

h.   *Old Basin of the Western Yar*

"The greater part of the series of gravels and brickearth, which caps the cliff at Brook and Brixton belongs to a later group, and will be described under the head of Valley Gravels, but four small patches may be referred with more probability to the Plateau Gravels.

"The Valley Gravels, it will be noticed, follow an old line of valley, which runs nearly parallel with the coast. The encroachments of the sea have removed the south side of this valley, except for a distance of about a mile between Brook and Chilton Chines, where the slight convexity of the coast leaves room for just the lower slopes of some hills which formed the south side of the old valley. The cliff section shows that the valley deposits thin away against these slopes, leaving the Wealden Beds bare, but on mounting the slopes we find another series of gravels of a different character coming on at a higher level. . . . The difference between the two gravels at Brook consists in the comparative absence of brickearth and stratification in the higher and older set, and especially in the peculiar contortions which appear both in the older gravel and in the Wealden Clays on which it rests. The clays have been bent and puckered, and the gravel forced into the puckers so as to occur in pockets,

---

[1] *Ibid.*, p. 219.

while the beds of loam or sand in the gravel are doubled up and bent, or dragged over towards the west. There are four places only where the cliff rises high enough to reach these older gravels, and their thickness barely reaches 8 feet. The contortions are best seen in the patches at the east and west ends respectively. As mentioned before, these contortions are regarded as probable evidence of the action of ice during the deposition of the gravels, perhaps in the form of frozen soil, or of masses imbedded in the gravels."[1]

3. Valley Gravel, Brickearth, and Head

"We have already mentioned that [the Valley Gravels] differ from the Plateau Gravels in having been distributed along the lower parts of the existing valleys. They were no doubt made up principally of the materials of the older gravels, redistributed after the excavation of the valleys to nearly their present depth.

"They occur as terraces, often nearly level, bordering the modern Alluvium, but at a variable height, up to 50 feet, above it, and often separated from it by a steep bank. The streams having lowered their beds below the base of the gravel, the greater part of this bank is formed by rock in place, usually the Lower Greensand. This is particularly the case along the upper part of the eastern Yar, where, as may be seen on the map, a narrow strip of Greensand nearly always intervenes between the gravel and the Alluvium. The greater age which this difference in level indicates, together with the difference in character, justifies the placing of the gravels and the Alluvium in separate groups. It will be seen also that great changes in the physical geography of the Island have taken place since the gravels were deposited.

"The Valley Gravels are most fully developed in the valleys of the two Yars at the eastern and western ends of the Island respectively. Those of the Medina are comparatively unimportant."[2]

a.   *Valley of the Eastern Yar*

"The longest feeders of this river descend from Whitwell and Niton, and from Wroxall. From near Whitwell northwards an almost continuous terrace of gravel borders the Alluvium on one side or the other. The gravel ranges in thickness up to 10 feet, and is generally loose and stony, but occasionally consists in the upper part of loam. Small pits for road metal may be seen almost everywhere, and a good section occurs at Beacon Alley in a road-cutting.

"The gravel of this part of the valley has doubtless been derived from the Blake Down plateau, and from the continuation of it, which is indicated by the small patches north of Whitwell. The terraces cease at Budbridge, and the streams which descend from Godshill, where there are no Plateau Gravels, are entirely devoid of gravel terraces.

"The Wroxall feeder, on the other hand, draining a country in which out-liers of Plateau Gravel form a marked feature, is bordered by the most extensive gravel terrace in the Island. The terraces near Sandford are narrow, but the gravel is well seen in several pits. A little further north the valley widens out into a nearly level space a mile broad, and about 1½ miles long, uniformly overspread with gravel, except in the sides of the channels which the river and

[1]*Ibid.*, p. 220.
[2]*Ibid.*, pp. 220, 221.

its tributaries have cut in it. This gravel has been extensively dug at Horringford in a siding from the railway, where the cuttings show well the irregular surface of Lower Greensand on which it rests.

"From Horringford eastwards the terraces occur on the north side of the river only. The gravel appears repeatedly on the top of the bank of Lower Greensand, at a height of only about 6 feet above the Alluvium.

"In the lower part of the Yar there are no terraces, but the tributary which descends from Apse has formed a large gravel-flat near Black Pan. The gravel, dug near Ninham, and near the high road to Sandown, contains much chert and greensand, but has no doubt been principally formed from the old Plateau Gravel of which patches still remain on the neighbouring hill-tops, as previously described.

"North of the Downs patches of stony brickearth at Bembridge, near Howgate Farm, and in the valley south-east of Sea View, may be referred to this series, or may be considered as thick deposits of rainwash. Such local deposits of loam are common over the Tertiary area, but can seldom be mapped, as without sections they are indistinguishable from the older Tertiary clays."[1]

b. *Wootton Creek*

Though too small to be shown on the one-inch map, the deposits of Brickearth here are said to attain a thickness of 20 to 30 feet on the lower slopes of the western side of the valley.

c. *Medina Valley*

The upper parts of this valley, above Shide, are remarkably deficient in deposits of the class under consideration.

At and north-west of Shide, brickearth has been much worked in the spread which extends to New Village. Associated bones and a tooth of elephant were found in it, in the early part of last century.[2]

Half-a-mile north of Shide, gravel occurs on both sides of the Medina, and is well exposed in pits opened in a low terrace on the right bank. The high proportion of Upper Greensand material implies that the solid rocks, not the Plateau Gravels, have been the principal source of the stones in these deposits.

d. *The Western Yar*

"The most remarkable fact in connection with the valley gravels of this tract is the entire disappearance of the river by which they were deposited. For nearly the whole of the southern side of the valley of the Yar, as well as a large part of its drainage basin, has been removed by the encroachment of the sea, so that the old river gravels have come to occupy the position of a terrace of gravel capping the sea cliff, while the small streams, which drain what is left of the basin of the old Yar, now find their way direct to the sea by deep notches or chines cut in this cliff. The evidence on which this gravel

---

[1]*Ibid.*, pp. 221–223.

[2]A drawing of these remains existed for many years in Newport Museum, now closed. It may be mentioned here that the Geological Collection of that institution has been transferred to the Free Library at Sandown. The relics of Wealden and Oligocene vertebrates are noteworthy features.

terrace is attributed to such a river was first recognised by Mr. Codrington in 1870,[1] and is singularly impressive.

"The breach in the Chalk range at Freshwater is out of all proportion large in comparison with the stream which now occupies it. Moreover, the river gravels conclusively prove the valley to have once formed the channel of a river comparable in size to the Medina, or eastern Yar. The distribution of these gravels further shows that this river, like the others, flowed from south to north, draining lands which, lying to the south of the Chalk range, have since been washed away. We may further assume that some of the sources of the river lay in the direction of St. Catherine's Down, in the area which has formed the principal watershed of the Island from a very early period.

"The gravels at Brook occur in the line which the old river might have been expected to take, and at such a height above those of Freshwater Gate, as would be required to allow a gradient for the stream. When we add to this that the gravels and brickearths bear every appearance in themselves of being old river deposits, there is left no room for doubt that they mark the course of the old Yar. . .

"The continuous section afforded by the cliff gives unusual opportunities for examining these gravels. In describing the section, we will commence in the upper part of the valley and proceed westwards to Freshwater.

"Gravel first makes its appearance on the top of the cliff between Blackgang and Atherfield. It is seen as a band 2 to 4 feet thick underlying a considerable depth of alluvial deposits and blown sand (see p. 177), and is composed principally of chert."[2] It is probably contemporaneous with the thicker deposits which come in farther west.

These are mainly loams or brickearths, usually underlain by stratified flint gravels and sand. They are first encountered near Brixton Mill, and are clearly exposed in the sides of (Brixton) Grange Chine, where it is evident that they are the work of the stream which now runs in the bottom of the ravine, many feet below them. Near Brixton Grange, a little to the south of which the chine-stream probably joined the old Yar, the brickearth and gravel spread westward along the top of the cliff, and attain in places an aggregate thickness of 25 feet. Remains of mammoth (*Elephas primigenius* Blumenb.) have been observed at a point 100 yards east of Grange Chine, at 60 or 70 feet above the sea,[3] and about 600 yards west of that chine a bluish silty clay with pieces of wood is intercalated in the gravel exposed in the cliff.

"Four hundred yards to the west of Chilton Chine the cliff rises a little in height, and is bare of gravel for a distance of 300 yards. This slight rise, like those referred to in the description of the Plateau Gravels (p. 163), evidently formed the foot of the slopes which enclosed the Yar valley on the south. In observing the thinning away of the river deposits against the slope it will be noticed that the brickearth passes beyond the limits of the gravel, so as to rest directly on the Wealden Beds, before it also thins out.

"There are likewise variations in the thickness of brickearth due to erosion, for the small stream which now follows the old valley has cut out a smaller valley in the old deposits of the larger one. The sand and gravel beneath are fairly constant in thickness. . .

---

[1] *Quart. Journ. Geol. Soc.*, vol. xxvi, p. 528.
[2] *Ibid.*, pp. 222, 223.
[3] Codrington, *op. cit.*, p. 539.

"We now reach the parts of the cliff which were described on p. 163, as being capped with Plateau Gravel. The Valley Gravel, it will be noticed, runs to the edge of the cliff between the low hills on which the Plateau Gravels rest, so that the relations of the two can be conveniently studied. Remains of *Elephas primigenius* have been recorded from a point half a mile east of Brook Chine, about 96 feet above the sea.[1] Apparently they must have occurred in what has been described as Plateau Gravel, but the point is uncertain.

"On the east side of Brook Chine gravelly loam, 6 to 8 feet thick, rests on 4 feet of well-bedded sand and gravel; but at the chine, and for a few yards west of it, the gravel has been re-arranged and will be described among the more recent deposits (p. 171 Hazel-nut Gravels).

"At Hanover Point the Valley Gravels thin away against a slope of Weald Clay rising to the south, as near Chilton."[2] On the eastern side the brickearth is underlain by sand with gravelly bands.

FIG. 39.   *Section in Valley Gravel, Compton Bay*
From "Geology of the Isle of Wight", (*Mem. Geol. Survey*), 2nd Ed., Fig. 79, p. 226.

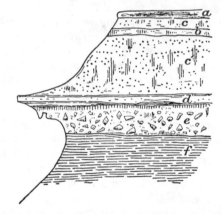

a. Soil, 2 feet.

b. Iron-band.

c, c. Sand, 7 feet.

d. Sand cemented into a rock by iron, 9 inches.

e. Coarse angular flint-gravel, containing iron, clay, and quartz-pebbles.

f. Wealden Shales.

At Compton Grange (or Shippard's) Chine the Hazel-nut Gravels reappear, but farther on are again succeeded by the older gravel and brickearth. Finally, in a small chine 350 yards north-west of Compton Grange Chine, we have the section illustrated in Fig. 39. This is the last section in the Valley Gravels, for at about 50 yards farther to the north-west they thin away on rising ground, and they are cut off to the west by the coast, which here completely intersects the old river-course.

At Freshwater Gate, the cliff gives a good cross-section of the Yar Valley where it breaches the Chalk ridge of the Central Downs. At this point the valley is narrower and more sharply defined than in the soft Wealden Beds near Brook. Much of the superficial material mapped as Valley Gravel on the sides of Freshwater Gap is of a different character from any of the deposits in that class described in the preceding pages. Valley gravel, consisting of partly-worn flints with chert and ironstone, in places cemented by iron oxide, is seen low down on the sides of the gap; the bulk of it is probably derived from older gravels in the country, that once existed to the south; but the

---

[1]Codrington, *loc. cit.*

[2]'Geology of the Isle of Wight,' *Mem. Geol. Surv.*, 1889, pp. 224, 225.

superficial deposit most in evidence in the cliff-section (Fig. 40) is a banded chalky wash, or rubble-drift, which overlies parts of the gravel, and was formed under different conditions (*see below*).

North of the Chalk ridge, the Valley Gravel is exposed in a pit opened in a terrace about 60 feet above the Yar at Easton. "On the opposite side of the Yar the gravel occupies a plateau 30 to 50 feet above the sea, and a pit shows 25 feet of coarse gravel resting on Bagshot Sands. In Afton Park a large pit was opened to supply ballast during the construction of the railway. It showed about 6 feet of gravel, resting in one place on shelly clay—probably Barton Clay—but the gravel itself yielded no fossils. The sheets further north show no sections, and are only interesting as fringing the present estuary."[1]

FIG. 40. *Sketch of the Eastern side of Freshwater Bay, showing Chalky 'Head' or 'Rubble-drift'*

c. 'Head,' composed of irregularly-bedded chalk-rubble and loam covering inclined Upper Chalk in the cliff and the Stag Rock.
v. Valley Gravel, underlying the 'head' at extreme left,
The old coast-road is intersected by the cliff near the middle of the figure.

Head. This appears to be the proper point at which to notice certain old, overgrown screes and washes of chalky and other material, met with on hill-sides in various parts of the Island. These accumulations are, in most cases, of late Pleistocene date, and were formed under meteorological conditions, which, if they ever obtain at the present day, are too transitory to produce comparable results. The washes of a calcareous nature are evidently mouldering down into stony loams, through the solvent action of percolating soil-water.

On the eastern side of Freshwater Bay, a sheet of the chalky gravel and loam, mentioned in connection with the Valley Gravel, occurs on the top of the cliff (Fig. 40), and a little outlier of it, which has long seemed in imminent danger of destruction, clings with remarkable tenacity to the apex of the Stag Rock. The deposit thickens as it descends into the valley at Freshwater Gate, and is well seen in the cliff near the protective fascines. A tooth of *Elephas primigenius* has been obtained from it on each side of the valley, and Godwin Austen, by whom these finds were recorded, observed numerous shells of the land molluscs, "*Pupa muscorum*" and "*Succinea oblonga*", in the wash on the eastern slope.[2] The deposit belongs to the widely-represented class of late Pleistocene "heads", of which the well-known Elephant Bed, overlying the Brighton raised beach at Kemp Town, is a type.

In Compton Bay, the highest 20 feet of the cliff in which the Upper Green-sand is exposed, is made of chalky rubble and wash from the slope of Afton

[1]*Ibid.*, p. 228.
[2]See Geological Survey Memoir on the Tertiary Fluvio-Marine Formation of the Isle of Wight, p. 2 (1852).

Down (Fig. 14, p. 59). Another deposit of the kind is to be seen in the road-cutting between Brixton and Calbourne, near Rock, where the stratified talus has spread over the Upper Greensand, and become hardened. A similar hardening, by tufaceous cement, is noticeable in the talus cut through by the road west of Apesdown. Other sections occur to the west of Gatcombe, and in many chalk-quarries elsewhere. At Alum Bay, Nunwell, and other places, a chalky wash extends over the Reading Beds, but there seem to be no definite fans of "combe rock" in the Island. Taluses at the foot of Lower Greensand scarps are common, but less noticeable. A good example is seen in the road-cutting west of Arreton: but for the occasional seams of flints, much of the material might be mistaken for Lower Greensand in position.

Dr. Mantell described and figured part of a skull of a reindeer (*Rangifer tarandus* (Linn.)) found by him in a fissure in the Bembridge Limestone at Binstead; and mentions the similar occurrence of bones of horse and ox in the neighbourhood.[1]

4. RECENT DEPOSITS

The last of the long succession of elevatory movements, of which we have evidence in the raised beaches and gravel-capped terraces and plateaux, seems to have ceased just before the end of the Pleistocene period. By that date the river valleys have been cut to their maximum depth, and the local relief was stronger both than it is now and than it had been at any time since the early Pliocene peneplanation mentioned in the last chapter.

To judge from the records of dock-yard and other excavations on the South Coast, the sea-level at that time was at least 50 feet, and possibly as much as 80 feet, lower than at present.[2] Little information is available concerning the depth to which the river valleys of the Isle of Wight descend below the surface of the alluvial deposits covering their floors. A trial boring on the west bank of the Medina at Cowes ended in a clay, tersely described as "alluvial", at a depth of 47 feet below Ordnance Datum.[3] Out in Spithead, drift-wood and a band of "vegetable matter" were found about 50 feet below high-water mark at Horse Sand Fort, and a jaw-bone of red deer about 80 or 90 feet below the same datum at Noman's Fort.[4] These remains, however, were associated with marine shingle and sand forming parts of shoals which may have been accumulated by currents in Recent times.

About the beginning of the Recent period there set in a comparatively rapid, though not uninterrupted, movement of depression (or rise in the sea-level), which continued through the Neolithic age, and is inferred to have ceased somewhere about 2,000 years before the Christian era.[5] Results of this displacement are seen in the drowned and aggraded condition of the lower reaches of the rivers that open on the north coast of the Island, and in the occurrence of peat-beds and rooted tree-stumps below high watermark.

The same movement probably was responsible, in a large measure, for the final separation of the Isle of Wight from the Mainland, for the character of the flora and fauna of the Island seem to imply the existence of a land-connection within the Recent period. In an earlier chapter of this work it was

[1]'Geological Excursions round the Isle of Wight, &c.' 1847, pp. 103, 104, lign. 4.
[2]C. Reid, 'Submerged Forests', 1913, p. 106.
[3]'Water Supply of Hampshire,' *Mem. Geol. Surv.*, 1910, p. 177.
[4]*Ibid.*, pp. 169, 170, and T. Harris and W. Dennis, *Geol. Mag.*, 1865, p. 46.
[5]C. Reid, *op. cit.*, p. 115.

stated (p. 148) that the Solent-Spithead strait lies in the course of an ancient trunk-stream, named the Solent River, whose system has been dismembered by encroachments of the sea east and west of the Isle of Wight. The dimensions of the gap between the western end of the Solent and the mouth of the Frome at Poole Harbour, on the Dorset Coast, are such as to convince one that the Solent River had been cut in two by the sea, to the west of the Isle of Wight, before the beginning of the Recent period; while, on the other hand, the form of the ground and the character and distribution of the gravels in what remains of the Solent River Valley, strongly suggest that this event did not occur till rather late in Pleistocene times.

Now if, at the point (presumably in the Bournemouth Bay area) where the sea first cut into the Solent River, the bed of that stream were appreciably above the sea-level of the time, the incursion would not have involved the severance from the Mainland of the eastern or Vectian portion of the southern versant of the Solent River basin: to the east of that point there would have remained an isthmus which, though retreating eastward before the attack of the sea, might well have endured into Recent times. But it may be contended that the Solent River, admittedly a stream of considerable volume, is likely to have been tidal at least as far up its course as the point where the sea broke into its channel, in which case the detachment of the Vectian land-mass, and the initiation of the Solent-Spithead strait, must date from the moment at which that irruption occurred.

Admitting, however, that the strait, in its inception, is of Pleistocene date, its continuous existence from then to the present day does not follow as a matter of course. The probable effect on the early strait of the late Pleistocene elevatory movements has to be borne in mind; for those movements, as we have seen, not only brought the land to a higher level than had been attained in long preceding ages, but also left it 50 feet or more higher than it is now. Hence it would appear that any opening of the strait occurring at a date decidely anterior to the Recent period, is likely to have been of a temporary nature, and not to have been confirmed until the setting-in of the Recent subsidence, noticed above.

After much discussion, in its archaeological as well as its geological aspects, the problem of the last tie between the Island and the Mainland remains unsolved. The final break is commonly assumed to have occurred in the neighbourhood of Yarmouth, but a good case can be made out for the Egypt-Stone Points line, and the possibilities of the area of shallow water and quickly-wasting cliffs beyond the western end of the Solent, are not to be ignored. Little reliance is to be placed in the legends of low-tide causeways existing in the Historic period, whether they have reference to the carriage of building-stone to the Mainland in the Middle Ages, or of tin to the Island in late pre-Roman times.[1]

---

[1] On the subject of the detachment of the Isle of Wight from the Mainland, see, *inter alia*, W. Fox, 'When and How was the Isle of Wight severed from the Mainland', *Geologist*, vol. v, 1862, p. 452. A. Strahan, 'On the Physical Geology of Purbeck', *Proc. Geol. Assoc.*, vol. xiv, 1896, p. 407. W. Boyd-Dawkins, 'Early Man' in *Victoria History of Hampshire* (London, 1900), vol. i, pp. 253–263. C. Reid, 'The Island of Ictis', *Archaeologia*, vol. lix, 1905, pp. 1–8. *Id.* 'On the Former Connexion of the Isle of Wight with the Mainland', *Rep. Brit. Assoc. for 1911*, 1912, p. 384. *Id.* 'Submerged Forests' (London 1913), pp. 76, 106. T. Rice Homes, 'Ancient Britain and the Invasions of Julius Cæsar' (Oxford, 1907), pp. 501–507.

The Recent deposits described in the following pages are, Alluvium (mostly freshwater flood-loam), Peat, Tufa, Rain-wash (a few fossiliferous deposits), and Blown Sand. Remarks on the landslips are appended.

ALLUVIUM AND PEAT

Chronological arrangement being impracticable among such beds, the alluvial and peat deposits will be taken in the geographical order of the streams with which they are associated.

"a. *The Western Yar, and the Coast from Freshwater to Yarmouth*

"The small stream which now follows the old valley of the Yar takes its rise at Freshwater Gate in a spring known as the Rise of Yar, situated on the eastern edge of the Alluvium at a distance of 200 yards from the high-water mark. Though fresh, this spring ebbs and flows coincidently with the tide. In dry weather it ceases to flow soon after the tide begins to fall.

"The Alluvium, consisting of peat, silt, and marsh clay, extends continuously southwards to the foreshore, where, however, it is almost always covered with sand and shingle. In digging a foundation for the sea-wall, this peaty deposit was excavated to a depth of 10 feet without the bottom being reached, and was found to be abundantly charged with fresh water. The ponding back of this water by the rising tide is probably the cause of the spring alluded to above.

"The tide flows up the Yar as far as Freshwater, where it is stopped by a dam. Formerly the whole of the marsh must have been part of the estuary, for shells of the common cockle occur abundantly just below the peat opposite Afton House."[1]

"b. *The Coast from Freshwater to Blackgang*

"It has been previously explained that the streams which now empty themselves into the sea between Freshwater and Blackgang have once been tributaries of the old river Yar. In consequence of the encroachment of the sea by which the river was intercepted, some curious anomalies have been brought about in the position of the alluvial deposits.

"It will be noticed that a long strip of Alluvium which commences near Chilton Chine, only 50 yards from the edge of the cliff, winds away westwards parallel to the coast, catching a little land drainage in its course. At Brook it passes out to the edge of the cliff, and the water from it, cutting through the Alluvium and deep into the Wealden Beds, escapes by the chine so formed to the sea. But a few yards west of Brook Chine another strip of Alluvium appears on the top of the cliff, and, winding round Hanover Point, passes out to the cliff again at Shippard's Chine. This latter isolated strip is, without much doubt, the continuation of the other which runs westward from near Chilton Chine. The separation of the two strips has resulted from a comparatively recent encroachment of the sea in Brook Bay. The alluvial tract follows the centre of the Valley Deposits of the old Yar, coinciding in position with what must have been the course of that river."[2]

---

[1] 'Geology of the Isle of Wight,' *Mem. Geol. Surv.*, 2nd Ed., 1889, p. 228.
[2] *Ibid.*, p. 230.

The section of this Alluvium at Shippard's Chine has long been noted for the occurrence in it of timber and the shells of nuts. These were first noticed by Thomas Webster, who described them as follows:[1]

"It was near to this place, that I had been informed, fossil fruits had been found in great abundance, and which were regularly called in the island, Noah's nuts. . . . Near the top of this cliff lie numerous trunks of trees, which, however, were not lodged in the undisturbed strata, but buried eight or ten feet deep under sand and gravel. Many of them were a foot or two in diameter, and ten or twelve feet in length. Their substance was very soft, but their forms and the ligneous fibre were quite distinct: round them were considerable quantities of small nuts, that appeared similar to those of the ,hazel. None of the wood nor fruits were at all mineralised. . . ."

FIG. 41.   *Sketch of Gravels with Hazel Nuts in Shippard's*
(Compton Grange) Chine

From "Geology of the Isle of Wight" (*Mem. Geol. Survey*), 2nd Ed., Fig. 82, p. 231.

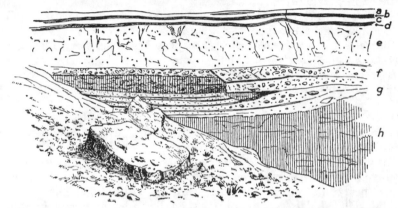

		in.		
a.	Ferruginous loam	6	*f.*	Angular flint gravel, hardening into conglomerate.
b.	Black clay	6	*g.*	Coarse sand, with fragments of fine sandstone, nuts, twigs, branches, &c.
c.	Pale ferruginous clay	6		
d.	Black carbonaceous clay	6	*h.*	Red mottled clay of the Wealden."

"The sketch forming Fig. 41 was made in the southern side of Shippard's Chine in June, 1856. The upper two feet consisted of black peaty clay and ferruginous pale clay, overlying ferruginous loam, which rested on angular flint gravel, sometimes hardening into conglomerate, beneath which was a coarse sand enclosing fragments of fine sandstone. This sand, based upon red mottled Wealden clay, contained numerous shells of nuts, and the remains of beetles mixed with matted fragments of the twigs and branches of trees. The latter, which were sometimes coated with phosphate of iron, retained their original shapes and general appearance, and were saturated with water, which on evaporation left a light shrivelled substance behind. The largest fragments did not exceed two or three inches in diameter.

"In more recent years a causeway has been made on the north side of the chine, and in the approach to it the following beds have been cut through:

[1] In Sir H. Englefield's 'Isle of Wight', p. 152.

	ft	in.
"Brick earth, a reddish loam	6	0
Grey silt, with much soft and blackened wood and bark, and black, brittle nut-shells	0	6
Hard cemented gravel	2	6
Dark earth, with much wood, as above	0	6
Gravel	1	0
Vegetable layer, not continuous	0	2
Gravel	2	0
Wealden Clay	—	
	12	8

"On the opposite side of the cutting a still more recent alluvial peat and rootlet bed, about 18 inches thick, lies above the brickearth of this section, probably the black peaty clay seen in 1856.

"On the west side of Brook Chine also there occurs a peaty layer in gravels of the same age as those at Shippard's Chine, and probably once continuous with them, as previously mentioned. . . .

"The stream which has cut out the great ravine known as [Brixton] Grange Chine, is fed by the two powerful springs of Bottlehole Well and Shorwell. The alluvial flat of the former consists of peat where the stream runs over the Lower Greensand, that of Shorwell of silt, sand, and fine gravel. The chine begins where the two streams join at Brixton, and has been of course cut through the Alluvial Deposits deep into the variegated beds of the Wealden series.

"The water which enters the sea by way of Shepherd's Chine (Cowleaze Chine on the former edition of the one-inch map), is principally derived from springs issuing at the foot of the escarpment which we described on p. 39 as running past Pyle and Kingston. The springs being highly charged with iron, the alluvial flat at Atherfield contains much ochre; the broad flat west of Corve is peaty. The stream meanders through Little Atherfield bordered by a narrow alluvial flat, which, however, in the area underlain by clay (the Atherfield Clay and Wealden Beds) widens out, and becomes indefinitely bounded.

"The chine commences at Combtonfield as a small notch, but slants down towards the sea so as to gain a depth of 90 feet at the sea-cliff."[1] Excavated along the middle of the alluvial flat, the chine gives a section of the alluvial deposits along both of its sides. On the north side, near the cottage named Chine on the 1-inch map, the section is:

	ft	in.
"Sandy loam	2	0
Flint gravel	2	6
Grey loam and grit, with many small fragments of stems and nutshells ..	1	6
Flint gravel, with many fragments of Wealden Shales, and with fragments of wood	4	0
	10	0"[2]

The deposit is doubtless of about the same age as the alluvium with nut-shells at Shippard's (Compton Grange) Chine. About the year 1810, the

[1]'Geology of the Isle of Wight,' 2nd Ed., 1889, pp. 231–233.
[2]*Ibid.*, p. 233.

mouth of Shepherd's Chine stream was situated 350 yards farther north than it is at present. Before Dr. Fitton visited the spot, some 15 years later, a change had taken place, which he thus describes. The streamlet "was very tortuous near the shore, and formerly came close to the edge of the cliff near its present outlet, but made its way to the beach at Cowleaze; till the soft and narrow barrier at top having been cut through, the water soon deepened the chasm, and formed a new chine, leaving its previous bed, with Cowleaze Chine itself, deserted and dry."[1]

"The change is reported to have been hastened at the last by a shepherd having dug through the narrow barrier of shale, whence the name of Shepherd's Chine for the new mouth. The old ravine of the stream remains much as it was, except that the sides are overgrown. It runs near, and roughly parallel to the sea-cliff, and is separated from it by a long and narrow flat-topped ridge, capped with two small outliers of alluvium; a remarkable position in which to find remains of such a deposit. The stream has greatly deepened the new chine since it gained an exit by a shorter route—a result which followed naturally from the temporary steepening of the gradient, and the consequent temporary increase in the rate of erosion. The case is precisely analogous to those of Brook Chine and Shippard's Chine described on p. 170-1.[2]

"Whale Chine forms the outlet for a small stream taking its rise in the western slopes of St. Catherine's Down. The sides of this extremely precipitous ravine are capped, like those of Shepherd's Chine, with an alluvial deposit, consisting of loamy beds above, and gravelly beds below, the majority of the stones in the latter being chert and ferruginous sandstone. The subjoined section may be seen at the top of the cliff, on the north side of the chine:

	ft	in.
"Loam	9	0
Black peaty seam	0	3–4
Grey silt, with bands of chert gravel below	4	0
Chert gravel	4	0
	17	4

"On the north-east side of the Military Road, the chert gravel comes to the surface, and has been dug for road metal. On the south side of the chine it is overspread by Blown Sand, which will be described subsequently, but the gravel can be traced beneath this covering in the face of the cliff for about three-quarters of a mile, rising, south-eastwards from about 145 feet above the sea at Whale Chine to about 200 feet at Walpen Chine."[3]

The Whale Chine stream, which enters the head of that chine with a right-angle turn, seems formerly to have flowed north-westward, by Atherfield Green to Cowleaze Chine; a coarse in harmony with the prevailing surface-slopes. Appearances suggest the diversion of the stream along a joint-fissure, subsequently enlarged to form Whale Chine.

---

[1]"On the Strata below the Chalk.' *Trans. Geol. Soc.*, Ser. 2, vol. iv, p. 197; 1836 (read 1827). The deserted channel had been breached by the recession of the sea-cliff, but was still almost entire in November, 1920.

[2]"Geology of the Isle of Wight,' *Mem. Geol. Surv.*, 2nd Ed., 1887, p. 223.

[3]*Ibid.*, p. 234.

"c.   *The Medina*

"The Alluvium of the River Medina commences at Chale Green, and forms a long strip of marsh land, gradually widening to about 200 yards in the part known as the Wilderness and near Gatcombe, but narrowing down as it passes the projecting spur of Upper Cretaceous Rocks of Gossard Hill [or Sibdown], and [the gap in] the central range of the Island. The alluvial deposits are generally marsh clay and silt, with a black peaty soil on top.

"On the other hand the Alluvium of the tributary which joins the Medina at Blackwater is principally peat, as perhaps the name indicates; its boundaries on the low watershed near Meston are extremely indefinite . . . Below Newport the Alluvium consists of estuarine clay and silt.

"d.   *The Eastern Yar*

"The Alluvium of the two longest feeders of this river, namely, those which descend from Whitwell and Wroxall, consists superficially of a narrow strip of marsh-clay spread over the bottom of a shallow trough cut through the Valley Gravels into the Lower Greensand. The alluvial flat is bounded for some miles by a low bank of Greensand with a thin covering of gravel. But the streams which rise on the north side of Godshill, and join the river above Horringford, drain some extensive peaty flats and are bordered by peaty land, until they join the Yar. The development of peat has resulted from the form of the ground and the issue of the springs which mark the outcrop of a clayey bed in the Lower Greensand, as described on p. 40.

"Below Newchurch the alluvial flat is bounded by steep banks of ferruginous sand (Lower Greensand), and is extremely irregular in its boundaries, the river in its wanderings having undermined first one bank then the other. The soil is of the usual dark character, but there is no great thickness of peat.

"At Sandown the river must have been formerly joined by an important tributary, for the alluvial flat, known as Sandown Level, which branches off to the south, is at least as broad as that of the main river. This tributary Alluvium runs only half a mile before it is cut off abruptly by the sea, so that nearly the whole of the basin of the river which formed it has disappeared. The streams of Shanklin and Luccomb Chines were probably some of the head waters of the river, and a little patch of gravel on the south side of Shanklin Chine may have formed part of its valley deposits. The tract of land on which Yaverland and Bembridge are situated is isolated from the rest of the Island by this alluvial flat and that of the Yar, and would be literally an island at high tide in certain winds, but for the artificial bank along the seaward margin of Sandown Level. It corresponds curiously to the "Isle of Freshwater" at the opposite extremity of the Isle of Wight.

"Brading Harbour was continually inundated at high water until the end of February 1880, when the sea was finally shut out by the present permanent embankment, which encloses an area of 600 acres. . . .

"Near Lane End, Bembridge, a hollow in the older gravel contains a newer peat and gravel. It was impossible to separate the two gravels on the map and no determinable fossils were observed in the peat, but these deposits seem to be merely the Alluvium of the small stream which now flows through Lane End.

"The alluvial deposits of the smaller streams that flow into the Solent consist of marsh-clays with trunks of trees, but in the absence of clear sections there is little to be said about them. It may be pointed out, however, that the Alluvium of all the streams descends far below their present beds."[1]

TUFA

A deposit of Recent tufa and tufaceous marl, containing land and fresh-water shells, occurs on the top of the cliff in Totland Bay, between the north-eastern end of Headon Hill and Widdick Chine. It rests on an uneven surface of Upper Headon sands, at a height of about 60 feet above the sea. Small exposures are still to be seen, but the clear sections that were visible about the middle of last century, and first described by J. Trimmer, have disappeared.[2]

FIG. 42.   *Tufaceous deposit of Totland Bay*

From "Geology of the Isle of Wight" (*Mem. Geol. Surv.*), 2nd Ed., Fig. 81, p. 229.

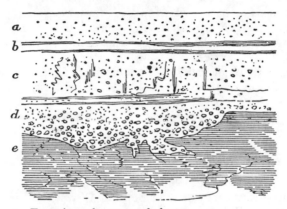

a. Ferruginous brown sandy loam.
b. Brown clay and perished shells.
c. Fine tufa.
d. Coarser tufa.
e. Potamomya sands of the Upper Headon Beds.

About the year 1856, the deposit could be seen to occupy the upper part of the cliff for a distance of nearly 350 yards. "On the top lay an unequal thickness of brown loam (a. Fig. 42), containing a few scattered angular flints, beneath which was a layer of brown clay and decayed shells, resting on four or five feet of calcareous tufa (with a few black lines derived from decomposed vegetable matter), sometimes equalling [Oligocene] limnaean limestone in hardness. This tufa was the finest in the upper part, and became gradually coarser towards the bottom, where it was full of round calcareous concretions of various sizes, and of what seemed to be the twigs and stems of plants, which having fallen into water highly charged with carbonate of lime became incrusted

---

[1]*Ibid.*, pp. 235–236.

[2]J. Trimmer 'On the Superficial Deposits of the Isle of Wight', *Quart. Journ. Geol. Soc.*, vol. x, 1854, p. 53. See also E. Forbes 'On the Tertiary Fluvio-marine Formation of the Isle of of Wight' (with notes by H. W. Bristow), *Mem. Geol. Survey*, 1856, pp. 105, 106; and A. S. Kennard and S. H. Warren 'On the Recent Tufaceous Deposit of Totland Bay, Isle of Wight', *Geol. Mag.* 1904, pp. 19–22.

with it. The concentric concretions were largest at the base of the deposit. . . . Occasionally a layer of small angular flints intervened between the tufa and the sands."[1]

The majority of the shells recorded are of land molluscs, *Helix nemoralis* (Linn.) unbanded, *Pyramidula rotundata* (Müll.), and *Pomatias reflexus* (Linn.), with less frequent *Cochlicopa lubrica* (Müll.) and *Jaminia muscorum* (Linn.), occurring throughout. Other species included are *Vertigo substriata* (Jeff.) and *V. pusilla* (Müll.), which are unrecorded as living in the Island at the present day; *Succinea oblonga* Drap., and *Limnaea truncatula* (Müll.). Fragments of *Unio*, or, more probably, *Anodonta*, have been observed in the lower part of the loam.

The tufa and associated loam and sand were formerly thought to be lacustrine, but Messrs. Kennard and Warren point out[2] that "both the molluscan fauna and the nature and position of the deposit itself clearly indicate a damp land-surface, over which oozed the water, highly charged with carbonate of lime, which was thrown out of the Headon Hill limestones by springs." Owing probably to the recession of the cliff having opened other outlets for the ground-water, the springs ceased to flow, and the tufa became covered by a thick wash of loam from the slopes above.

Another smaller patch of shelly tufa occurs immediately below the outcrop of the Headon limestone a quarter of a mile farther east, and is seen in the road-cutting east of York's Farm.

Hard tufa has been met with in excavations at Ventor. Shingle cemented by it, and known as "bean-rock", occurs under the Pier.[3]

RAIN-WASH

Fossiliferous chalky rain-wash of Recent age has been observed in several places on the sea-ward slopes of the Southern Downs, and in the Undercliff below it.

The best known deposit of the kind is that on the summit of Gore Cliff (east of South View House, near Blackgang Chine), which consists of small bits of chalk and chalky mud with a few pieces of chert, and attains a thickness of about 9 feet. "It is clearly a rainwash from the slopes of a hill of Chalk, which must have once existed to the south, but of which the small outlier is the only surviving fragment. The remainder of the hill has slipped down to various positions in the Undercliff, one of the most striking features of which is the great slices of Chalk and Upper Greensand, still retaining their relative positions."[4]

The numerous land-shells included are all referable to species now living in the Island. The deposit is being wasted rather quickly by the wind, and presents a vertical or overhung face to the south-west.

Similar accumulations are exposed in the path-cutting at Orchard Cove, in the cutting of the new road at Steephill, and in the quarry east of Steephill Castle, Ventnor. In the last of these localities the wash is overlain by a pre-Roman and probably Neolithic kitchen-midden. From the rain-washes of

[1]'Geology of the Isle of Wight,' 2nd Ed., 1889, pp. 229, 230.
[2]*Op. cit.*, p. 21.
[3]M. W. Norman's 'Guide' (Ventor: 1887), p. 171.
[4]'Geology of the Isle of Wight,' 2nd Ed., 1889, p. 238.

this part of the Island 29 species of Recent land mollusca have been recorded, mostly on the basis of a collection made by Mr. A. Loydell.[1] Among the most abundant forms are *Helicella virgata* (Da Costa), *Helix nemoralis* Linn., *H. hortensis* Müll., and *Pomatias reflexus* (Linn.).

BLOWN SAND

"The largest area of Blown Sand in the Isle of Wight is to be found on the top of the vertical cliff between Atherfield and Chale, at a height of 150 to 250 feet above the sea. The sand is blown up from the face of the cliff, not from the beach below, and consists merely of disintegrated Lower Greensand. . . . The greatest thickness of it seen was about 20 feet, but it probably exceeds this in parts of the line of dunes which it forms along the edge of the cliff. It extends also for some hundreds of yards inland in the form of a thin covering of dusty sand. The most westerly patch of this sand lies on the outcrop of a bed of iron-sand, and contains vast quantities of spherical grains of iron-oxide derived from it.

"On either side of Ladder Chine the sand is piled up in small hummocks or dunes, and, if we descend into the chine, the source of the sand becomes sufficiently obvious. The chine appears to have commenced its existence as a small notch cut by the surface-drainage from the adjoining fields. The wind, especially that from the south-west, entering the notch has gradually widened it out into a beautifully symmetrical amphitheatre, leaving the harder beds and concretions standing out in tiers of benches, but whirling every loose particle of sand up over the top of the cliff. The chine thus provides an interesting illustration of wind-erosion, comparable on a small scale to the scenery of parts of the desert region of Western America.

"Very small spits, consisting partly of blown sand, extend half way across the alluvial flats of the Western Yar and of the Newtown estuary. At the mouth of the Eastern Yar a more extensive tract of Blown Sand rises here and there into small dunes, used for the Golf Links, and serves to protect Bembridge Harbour on the north-east side. The sand travels in all cases from west to east."[2]

LANDSLIPS AND SOIL-CREEP

The sapping of the cliffs by the waves, aided by the loosening and lubricating effects of land-springs, causes repeated slipping in all the more clayey strata of the Island where they meet the coast. The cliffs in the Wealden Beds are bordered by almost continuous belts of sub-tabular founders, diversified by sludge-streams; those in the Atherfield Clay, by welters of mud; the Lower Eocene clays, the Upper Eocene loams, and the Oligocene Marls, all have their more or less characteristic slips; but the formation whose innate qualities conspire with local physiographic, stratigraphic, and tectonic conditions to make it the medium of the most impressive débâcles, is the Gault.[3]

"The beautiful and romantic scenery of the Undercliff or 'Back' of the Island has been mainly caused by the sliding of the Chalk and Upper Greensand

---

[1] See A. S. Kennard and B. B. Woodward, 'The Post-Pliocene Non-Marine Mollusca of the South of England', *Proc. Geol. Assoc.*, vol. xvii, 1908, pp. 229, 230.

[2] 'Geology of the Isle of Wight,' 2nd Ed., 1889, p. 237.

[3] Known as "blue slipper" in the Island, where the term "slipper" is applied to any unctuous clay. "Platnore," another local name for firm dark clays, is almost obsolete.

over the unctuous surface of the Gault clay, the tendency to slide being principally due to a rather pronounced seaward southerly dip, and to the outburst of springs at the junction of the porous Upper Greensand and impervious Gault.

"Through the greater part of the Undercliff the slipped materials assumed a position of rest before the commencement of the Historic period. It seems likely that in the belt of ground occupied by the slip, the southerly dip was steeper than it is in the existing cliff, and that the strata now forming this cliff will never be in a position to slide so readily as those portions that have already gone. Still, as the sea, in the course of centuries, removes the fallen *débris* which forms the coast, the movements will doubtless be renewed from time to time. Indeed, at Blackgang and Bonchurch, the west and east ends respectively of the Undercliff, there have been great slips within the [last 120 years]."[1]

At the western end of the Undercliff, below Gore Cliff, a great founder occurred in 1799, and the movement has been renewed at intervals ever since. A description of the East End landslip, which took place in Bonchurch and Luccomb in 1810, will be found in Sir Henry Englefield's "Isle of Wight".[2]

"The most striking feature in the central parts of the Undercliff is the succession of short escarpments produced by the fall of slices of the Upper Greensand cliff. These portions range in size from mere blocks up to slices of half a mile in length. They have broken off along the vertical joints by which the sandstone is traversed, and as their bases slid forward over the Gault, have slowly acquired a steep landward (northerly) dip. The process has been repeated several times, thus producing at different levels in the Undercliff a series of Upper Greensand escarpments, separated by deep hollows, which have been not uncommonly occupied by natural lakes. The distance to which they have descended varies indefinitely. Above Bonchurch a very long but narrow slice has moved a few feet only, and still forms the principal face of the cliff. But many others, with a portion of Chalk above them, have descended to the beach some 300 feet below, and from a quarter to half a mile distant.

"Such wholesale slipping is, generally speaking, confined to the coast, but some large masses of Greensand have slid down on all sides of St. Catherine's Down, and from the shoulder which separates Shanklin and Luccomb."[3]

"In some places the clay has flowed down in the form of mud-rivers, keeping usually to the lines of hollow in its descent, but overspreading also many of the higher parts of the Carstone feature. The course and limits of these mud-rivers or gutters may be distinguished, for many years after they have ceased to move, by the large sods of turf which have been torn off and heaped in a little irregular bank along their edges, and by the lines which still serve to indicate where the mass of moving clay was traversed by long curving cracks, convex in the direction of movement. The mud-rivers extend sometimes to a distance of a quarter of a mile or more beyond the base of the Gault."[4]

"At Winstone, a fine example of a mud-slide is crossed by the railway cutting,

---

[1]'Geology of the Isle of Wight,' 2nd Ed., 1889, pp. 60, 61.

[2]Page 131. See also Norman's 'Guide to the . . . Isle of Wight' (Ventor, 1887), pp. 181–189 and other guide-books to the Island.

[3]'Geology of the Isle of Wight,' 2nd Ed., 1889, p. 62.

[4]*Ibid.*, p. 58.

now grassed over. Another a little to the east has travelled down a hollow in the hill-side, and is now being dug for bricks."[1]

In the Central Downs, where the dip is steeper, and usually into the hill-side, slips in the Gault are comparatively rare, and of small extent. Falls of conspicuous pinnacles of the Needles occurred in 1764 and 1772.[2]

FIG. 43. Deflection of Bedding in weathered Chalk, by Soil-creep

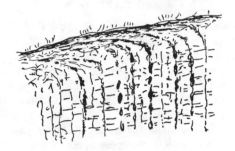

The series of black spots represent courses of nodular flints in highly inclined Chalk.

Indications of solifluction or soil-creep are observable all over the Island, either in the conformation of the surface on the slopes, or in the deflection and drawing-out of the edges of the solid strata, in the direction of the prevailing inclination of the ground, along the brows of quarries and cliffs. Good examples of the latter phenomenon can be seen in the chalk-pits about Shide and Brading (Fig. 43). At Alum Bay, the accentuation of the overturning of the London Clay, noticeable at the top of the cliff, is most probably due to creep.

---

[1] Ibid., p. 59.

[2] C. Lyell, 'Principles of Geology', 4th Ed., 1835, p. 100; and A. Strahan in 'Geology of the Isle of Wight', Mem. Geol. Surv., 1889, p. 73.

Chapter X

ECONOMIC GEOLOGY

SOILS AND LAND-DRESSING

Soils. The Wealden Beds, as might be expected from their lithological character, weather into clayey soil. Often cold, wet, and tufted with coarse grass and rush in the low grounds, which are mostly given up to rough pasture, it forms fairly good heavy arable land on the slopes, where its stiffness is mitigated by washes of sandy material from the Lower Greensand or the Plateau Gravels. A comparatively light soil occurs on and about the outcrop of the thick Wealden sandstone of Barnes High (p. 13).

The Lower Greensand generally forms light friable soils, of warm brown to reddish tints, and affords some of the best arable land in the southern part of the Island. This is especially true of the Ferruginous Sands, which make up the bulk of the formation. The purely sedentary soil of the Sandrock is poor and hungry. Carstoneland, with a thin natural or artificial dressing of marl, is excellent, but is met with only in small patches, for the position in which the Carstone crops out renders it liable to be smothered by hillwash and gutterings of the Gault.

Around the Southern Downs, the Gault is marked by a belt of rough, hummocky ground, wet and heavy in winter and during rainy seasons; hard, cloddy, and seamed with gaping cracks in dry weather. It is partly copsed with oak and ash, but is mostly under coarse grass. Its narrower outcrop-surface along the southern foot of the Central Downs is commonly masked by a wash of stony loam and marl from the Upper Greensand and the Chalk.

The Upper Greensand normally appears at the surface in scarped ledges and hog-backed ridges with slopes often so steep as to discourage attempts to cultivate them. Hence, like the Gault, it is for the most part under grass and timber (oak and beech). The soil however, is light, and although inferior to the rich hop and wheat land of the true malm-rock of West Surrey and East Hants, it works into good friable loam, and where—as at Yaverland and Rookley—the copse has been grubbed and the grass broken up, it has proved profitably cultivable, despite the difficulties of the ground.

As in other parts of the country, the high Chalk Downs are mainly used as sheep-walks. The slopes, where not too steep, are usually cultivated, and tracts of arable land are not wanting on the summits. The areas occupied by the thicker accumulations of Angular Flint Gravel are moors of heather and furze. The humified superficial parts of this gravel afford the nearest approach to purely sedentary soil to be found on the Chalk. The loams which form the usual covering of the Chalk—a covering in places so scanty that the rock shows white between patches of turf—all contain much material derived from other formations. Their variability, both in composition and thickness, was well exhibited in the entrenchments that were dug athwart the upper slopes of the Downs in 1914. Much of the downland in the Island, now covered only by short turf with occasional stunted thorns and furze, has been under

180

cultivation at some former period. Besides the few definite lynchets, such as those above Lynch, near Calbourne, faint ridges and furrows, and levelled flats, hardly discernible under normal conditions, become clearly apparent in many places after a light fall of snow.

In the country underlain by the Tertiary strata, the thick Eocene sands, tilted on end, crop out in the foot-slopes of the Central Downs, leaving the greater part of the area to the predominantly clayey Hamstead Series. In consequence, most of the land here is under grass, interspersed with extensive copses of oak, ash, and hazel. The arable ground is generally of heavy type, and has to be liberally under-drained. On the Gravels the soil is freer-working, but, even there, heavy ground is not uncommon. Some good soil occurs on the broad dip-slope of the Bembridge Limestone near Wellow. The firmer parts of the Alluvium are occupied by grass-meadow and pasture.

Land Dressing. The Upper Chalk was formerly much dug for marling land on the Tertiary Beds, to which it could easily be carted down from the northern side of the Chalk Ridge. The Lower Chalk, nearly as accessible from the southern side of the Ridge, and also obtainable from the upper slopes of the Southern Downs, was similarly utilised on the light soils of the Lower Greensand, for which, by reason of its argillaceous character, it is better suited than the more purely calcareous beds of the Upper Chalk. The beneficial effects—both chemical and physical—of calcium carbonate on heavy clay soils are becoming more widely known, and with the rise of a new generation of practical agriculturists there will probably be a marked revival of the ancient practice of marling.

In the winter of 1913–14, some heavy ground on the Eocene Beds north of Yaverland was treated to a thorough dressing of Chalk from a neighbouring pit in the Marsupites Zone, with appreciable benefit to the crops in the succeeding years. In the past, chalk for dressing has not always been so well chosen. One occasionally sees evidences of former marling with hard, nodular chalks from the *Holaster planus* and *Micraster cortestudinarium* Zones, whose defects as cumberers of the soil almost outweigh their virtues as alterative manure.

Lime has been used for dressing, and was in favour during the latter part of the 18th and the early years of the 19th century. Where hard limestones, such as those of the Headon and Bembridge Beds, only are available, a calcareous dressing is more cheaply obtained by burning the rock than by the alternative method of grinding it to powder. In the case of chalk, the softer part of the raw rock, ploughed in after disintegration by exposure to frost, is preferable to lime, for, though slower in its action, its effects are more enduring.

The shelly marls of the Headon Beds have been dug for dressing, but the writer has heard of no recent instance of their use.

BUILDING MATERIALS

Stone. The Wealden Shales contain bands of durable flaggy limestone, and the Lower Greensand some firm shelly ferruginous sandstone, but not in sufficient quantity to be worth quarrying; and it is probable that the blocks of these stones often to be seen in old buildings in the southern part of the Island were obtained from the beaches and landslips on the coast. The conglomeratic bands of the Wealden Marls have been much used about Brook and Mottistone, and tuberous ironstone concretions from the Ferruginous Sands are frequently employed in the rococo ornamentation of gate-pillars and garden walls near Sandown Bay.

The Upper Greensand furnishes by far the best building stone, and has been quarried from time to time in many places, though principally in the neighbourhood of Ventor and Shanklin. The most important bed commercially is a band of freestone, from three to five feet thick, which occurs close below the Chert Beds (p. 49). It is almost confined to the Southern Downs, and is especially noticeable in the cliff between Bonchurch and Blackgang. Between it and the Chert Beds lie one or two softer bands of "firestone" and "rubstone". The freestone is durable, and can be used for ornamental as well as structural work. Most of the houses in Ventnor, Bonchurch, St. Lawrence, and Niton are built of it. The walls of Carisbrook Church include this stone, together with specimens of most of the other building-stones of the Island. Quarrying has declined during the last 40 years, owing partly to the lessened demand for new buildings, partly to the use of brick in place of stone; but there are now signs of its revival.

Many old dwellings, farm-houses, and enclosure-walls are constructed of chalk, obtained, as a rule, from the Upper division of the Chalk formation. Large flint-nodules are commonly utilised for dry-walling, and nodules of medium size, both in the rough and dressed, as building-stone in conjunction with brick or other material.

Of the harder Tertiary rocks, the Bembridge Limestone has had the greatest vogue, and for centuries ranked among the chief natural products of the Island. The principal quarries were at Binstead and Quarr. Most of the firm rock there obtained was carried over to the Mainland, and used in the construction of several churches in Sussex, and of Lewes Priory, Beauleiu Abbey, Winchester Cathedral (interior), and other monastic and ecclesiastical buildings. Yarmouth Castle is one of the many buildings in the Island of which it forms the main constituent.

The sea-walls on the north coast of the Island are mostly built of the same stone, which is now seldom used architecturally, save for repairs. Small quantities of stone have been got from the Osborne Beds near Sea View and at Headon Hill; the Nettlestone Grits being worked in the former locality, and the siliceous concretions in the lower part of the formation in the latter.

Lime and Cement. For grey- or stone-lime, the massive, homogeneous, slightly marly chalk of the *Holaster subglobosus* Zone is preferred, and is quarried and burned for the purpose at Yarbridge and Mersley. The white blocky chalks of the higher zones are suitable for white-lime, used for lime-wash and plaster. Old lime-kilns are to be seen in many of the larger quarries in the Upper Chalk, chiefly those excavated in the Quadratus and Mucronata Zones, the outcrops of which are easy of access on the northern slope of the Central Downs. Chalk of the two zones just named is extensively quarried at Shide, for use in the manufacture of cement at the Medina Cement Works, the excavations being partly open, partly below-ground. The same zones were formerly quarried by both methods at West Ashey. At Brading, cement is made from the Bembridge Limestone, excavated on the spot. The factory, which had been disused for some time, was re-opened in 1920.

Bricks and Tiles. The clays and loams of the Hamstead Beds, which occur at or within a few feet of the surface over the greater part of the northern half of the Island, have long formed the principal source of raw material for the local brick-industry. They are worked, among other places, at Skinner's Grove and Werror in West Medina, and at Alverstone (near Whippingham), Staplers, and Ashlake in East Medina.

Brickearths as good as any in the Hamstead Beds, but less worked by reason of their slighter development, are furnished by the coarse Pleistocene loams, the larger patches of which are distinguished as "Brickearth" on the Geological Survey maps. Deposits belonging to this class are, or have been, worked at New Village and Gunville near Carisbrook, Downend near Arreton, Howgate near Bembridge, and on Wootton Creek, to the north of the Central Downs; and at Borthwood near Newchurch, and Brixton, to the south of that range. The Gunville and Wootton deposits are not shown on the one-inch geological Map. At Gunville and Downend the Brickearth is worked in conjunction with clays and loams of Eocene age. The Brixton deposit, which is the largest, has so far received little attention: bricks for the viaduct of the Military Road over Grange Chine were manufactured from it.

Argillaceous beds of nearly all the other formations represented in the Island have been laid under contribution for brick or tile making at various times. Weathered Wealden Shales are worked in a small yard close to Sandown Station; the dark, sandy clay which forms the highest member of the Ferruginous Sands has been dug for bricks at Sandford and Lower Hide, and a gritty clay, in the Sandrock Series, west of Gatten.

Brickyards have been opened in the Gault at Rookley, and at Bierley near Niton; also in foundered masses of this clay by the railway west of Shanklin.

The plastic mottled clays of the Reading Beds make good tiles. There was formerly a pottery in these beds at Newport. Overgrown pits are not uncommon on their outcrop. The London Clay has been but little worked. Vestiges of an old brickyard in it are to be seen near Longlands sand-pit, at the foot of Bembridge Down. Loams of the Bracklesham and Barton Beds have been dug at Gunville; those of the Headon Beds, near Totland Bay; and those of the Osborne Beds, east of Newtown River, and in Little Apley Wood, near Ryde. Lastly, the Bembridge Marls supply yards near Carpenter's (on the northern side of Brading Harbour), at Ashlake, Werror, and Ningwood.

Pipe-clay in the Bagshot Sands used to be excavated in the cliff at Alum Bay, and in a pit half-a-mile east-south-east of East Afton.

FUEL AND MINERALS

The brown-coal seams of the Bracklesham Beds have been worked at Alum and Whitecliff Bays, but are of small value. The coal crumbles into dice in drying, and burns with difficulty, emitting sulphurous fumes. Remains of the timbering of the open trench in which the thick seam at Whitecliff Bay was dug, nearly 50 years ago, can be seen at times on the shore. The coal is still used by fishermen, salvage-parties, and other sojourners in the bay.

Upland peat has been dug in the small tract of moor on the summit of Wroxall Down. The alluvial peat-deposits have been little exploited, in spite of the high prices that have long ruled for imported fuels.

Alum was formerly manufactured in the Island from the pyritous clays of Alum Bay. An alum-works existed in Parkhurst Forest as early as 1579.

During the 18th century iron pyrites was collected on the shore about Shanklin for shipment to London, while clay-ironstone nodules, derived from the Hamstead cliffs, were sent to Swansea.

Phosphatic concretions and phosphatised bones and wood are of common occurrence in the Wealden Beds, but nowhere form deposits of workable thickness. The nodules of the "coprolite beds" in the upper part of the Ferruginous Sands at Redcliff are probably the richest in phosphoric acid. Phosphatic nodules in the Chloritic Marl at Gore Cliff were exploited for a short time about the middle of the last century. The percentage of phosphoric acid in the nodules was ascertained to range from about 8 to 24, while in their sandy matrix it was less than 2.[1]

ROAD METAL

Most of the hard rocks have been employed for road-mending. The Selbornian cherts, which have been dug in the western side of St. Catherine's Down, and on Hoad Down, make fairly good roads when broken small enough, and for so long as they are kept wet by rain, but break up into sharp chips and dust during drought. The surface lasts better when the cherts are mixed with the tough, calcareous ragstones of the same division.

When properly sized and laid, the tough angular flints of the Chalk Down gravels afford as good a surface as can be obtained with any kind of flint metalling, and are preferred to the worn flint gravel of the Plateau and Valley series. The Angular Flint Gravels are dug in many places on the Southern Chalk Downs, the principal workings being on the western slope of St. Boniface Down, above Ventor. The chief source of metalling, however, is the thick deposit of ochreous Plateau Gravel on St. George's Down, the material of which is widely distributed by rail and road, and can be recognised by its orange colouring. Valley Gravel has been extensively worked at Horringford. Much of the gravel in the north-eastern parts of the Island is too pebbly for satisfactory metalling, and for the same reason the use of beach-shingle is still more to be deprecated.

Chert and cherty sandstone is much used for kerbs and paving setts. Cobbles from the beaches, both ancient and modern, serve as pitching for courtyards and garden paths.

WATER

With an average annual rainfall grading from about 29 inches on the coast up to more than 33 inches inland, and with a comparatively large exposure of permeable strata, the Isle of Wight is well provided with underground water, to which access is facilitated by the structure and conformation of the country.

Stratigraphical divisions like the Wealden Beds, Gault, and Reading Beds, which consist mainly of clay or marl, necessarily rank low among the water-bearing formations, such sandy beds as they include yielding only enough to meet the small requirements of isolated cottages. These formations, however, perform an important function in controlling the direction of flow of the water in the intervening permeable strata, and in determining the location of spring-lines.

---

[1] L. L. B. Ibbetson, 'Notes on the Geology and Chemical Composition of the various Strata in the Isle of Wight', (London, 1849), p. 36.

Around the Southern Downs, much of the rain absorbed by the sands of the Lower Greensand is thrown out, after a short descent, by one or other of the intercalated bands of sandy clay. The principal line of springs here follows the outcrop of the clay at the top of the Ferruginous Sands, the water being derived from the Carstone and Sandrock. The Ferruginous Sands as a whole are less permeable than the overlying divisions, and provide few well-defined springs; their water, usually strongly ferruginous, exudes along the clayey seams at various levels in the cliffs and on the sides of the valleys. The spring named Shanklin Chalybeate Spa, first noticed by Dr. Fraser, physician to Charles II, flows from this division of the Lower Greensand, but the other well-known spa, near Chale, is in the upper part of the Sandrock Beds. When purged of their soluble iron salts by deep weathering, the Sandrock and Carstone yield soft water, of unexceptionable quality. Ryde is partly supplied from wells in these beds at Knighton. Spring-water from the Sandrock is collected by drains at Lord Alverstone's waterworks in Newchurch parish.

Hydrologically, the Upper Greensand and the Chalk constitute a single formation, and the most important in the Island. Ventnor is entirely supplied from it; Shanklin, Sandown, Ryde, Newport, Yarmouth, and Freshwater, largely so. In the Southern Downs, where the dip of the strata is low, the water absorbed by the Chalk percolates downward into the Upper Greensand, and is discharged, together with the Greensand water, along the outcrop of the Gault. A small but notable exception is the trickling spring known as St. Boniface's Well, which issues from a vertical fissure in the Middle Chalk, high on the precipitous slope above Ventnor, 350 yards north-north-west of Trinity Church.[1]

The most copious springs at the Gault outcrop in this part of the Island occur at Wydcomb, Niton, Bierley, Whitwell, south and east of Wroxall, Luccomb, and in Greatwood Copse—the last situated south-west of Shanklin, and tapped by headings for the supply of that town. Ventnor is supplied in part by a strong spring from the Upper Greensand, met with in driving the tunnel on the Isle of Wight Railway through St. Boniface Down. Other springs in the neighbourhood, once employed to drive a mill, form the cascade on Ventnor sea-front.

Along the narrow central range of Downs, where the strata are highly inclined, springs issue from the lower part of the Upper Greensand on the southern side, and from the top of the Chalk, at low points on the boundary of the Reading Beds, on the north; also from intermediate horizons in the river-gaps at Brading, Shide, and Freshwater Gate. The more noteworthy of the springs on the southern side of the ridge are those of Bottlehole or Buddlehole Well near Brixton, Shorwell, Chillerton Street, and Gatcombe. The

---

[1]At present, the 'Well' is a mere water-hole, kept open by the downland cattle. The local southward dip, the vicinity of the Plenus Marls, and the existence of a rather wide and slightly-troughed ledge (suggestive of landslip) about 50 feet above the Well, may be among the factors determining the site of the spring.

It is to be observed, that the steep face of the Down around and west of the Well is an old and somewhat degraded slip-scarp, formed by the detachment of a portion of the great mass of foundered rock upon which Ventor stands. With such a feature, abnormal outflows of ground-water are likely to be associated, owing to the rude dislocation and exposure of natural subterranean conduits which the slipping entails. The rubble by which a great part of the southern slope of St. Boniface Down is mantled, and into which the water running from the Well immediately disappears, not improbably hides other springs of the same kind.

most interesting spring on the northern side is that known as the Rise of Yar, which comes up from the Chalk beneath the Alluvium at Freshwater Gate, at a distance of 200 yards from high-water mark. Though fresh, it ebbs and flows with the tide, and in dry weather ceases to run soon after the tide begins to fall. The flow of the spring is attributable to the pondering back of the freshwater, with which the Alluvium is known to be abundantly charged, by the rising tide. With the fall of the tide, this water finds an easier outlet southward beneath the Alluvium and the beach. At the Waterworks well, close by, sea water has been drawn in by continuous pumping.

At the boundary of the Reading Beds small springs can be seen issuing from the Chalk both at Alum Bay (Mother Large's Spring) and at Whitecliff Bay. More important sources are situated at Shalcombe, Calbourne, and Carisbrook. At Frogland, south of the last-named village, a strong spring is thrown out at the base of the Chalk; an unusual position, which becomes intelligible when the relation of the topographic to the tectonic features of the neighbourhood is perceived.

Winterbournes or intermittent springs from the Chalk occur a little to the south of the normal sources at Shalcombe and Calbourne, and in the valley of the Lukeley Brook above Bowcombe.

The Chalk plunges northward so steeply along the greater part of the Central Downs as to be out of reach by ordinary wells sunk at a distance of more than a few yards from the outcrop, and, as far as the writer is aware, no boring out in the area of the Tertiary Beds has been carried deep enough to touch it. Probably water under artesian conditions could be obtained from it by deep boring in most parts of that area, but whether the yield would prove satisfactory is another matter, for experience has shown that the circulation of water in the Chalk beneath a thick cover of Tertiary Beds is apt to be sluggish.

But for its high inclination at the outcrop, and consequently restricted opportunity for collecting rain, the London Clay, with its thick beds of sand, would be a water-bearing formation of no little importance. Placed as it is, its feeble springs serve only to supply a few ponds.

The Bagshot-Bracklesham Beds and the Barton Sands give rise to a number of small springs throughout their extent, water flowing from them in all the valleys which cross their outcrops. No information it available concerning wells in the first two of these divisions in the Island. Horse Sand and Noman's Forts, which stand on shoals out in Spithead, north-east of Ryde, obtain water from the Bracklesham Beds by means of borings, respectively $569\frac{1}{2}$ and 579 feet deep. In the well at Noman's Fort the water rose to within a foot of high water-mark of ordinary spring tides. Good supplies are got from the Barton Sands by boring in several places, e.g., Bembridge Water Works (Home Farm), where water overflows at the surface; Newport Gas Works, West Cowes, and East Cowes Water Works (722 feet; apparently the deepest boring in the Island).

The Headon and Osborne Beds together form the chief source of supply in a number of bored wells distributed over the northern part of the Island. In at least one instance (the Railway Works, Newport) the water rises to the surface. Artesian water was obtained also from the top of the Bembridge Limestone at Longford House, Haven Street, but proved to be too ferruginous to be palatable.

In the Hamstead Beds there are many sunk and bored wells of moderate depth (20 to 80 feet). Fair supplies are obtained from sands about 60 feet above the base of this formation in East Medina (*see* p. 134).

The larger spreads of Plateau Gravel, where not immediately underlain by loose sand, and the low-level Valley Gravels, can usually be counted upon to afford supplies. In the Isle of Wight, superficial deposits of this sort are largely drawn upon, both for public and private use. East and West Cowes, and Osborne, were formerly entirely, and are still partly, supplied by water collected in drains trenched in neighbouring deposits of Plateau Gravel. Shallow cottage-wells in gravel and unmapped stony loam abound in the area of the Tertiary Beds. Their liability to fail in drought, and to suffer contamination by manure and by seepage from cess-pits, makes them undesirable as sources of supply. In the thick gravel of St. George's Down, which lies mostly on permeable strata, water is held up by sheets of iron pan, cementing the stones and sand of the lower part of the deposit. Near the cottage on the southern brow of the Down (Fig. 37, p. 156) a small perennial spring, known as the Dropping Well, issues from a layer of this concreted gravel.

Water is usually obtainable from beneath the Alluvium in the bottom of the valleys. Derived from masked springs in the solid strata beneath, its quality varies greatly from place to place. In the Lower Greensand country, the springs in the river-meadows are strongly chalybeate, and form a rusty deposit on the vegetation in the ditches.

Small spring- and surface-water ponds are common on the Tertiary Beds, and a few dew-ponds can be seen on the expanded part of the Chalk Ridge, as on Idlecombe and Cheverton Downs.[1]

Swallow-holes. While instances of the re-absorption of water issuing from small springs or seepages may be observed in many places, well-marked swallow-holes, causing the abrupt disappearance of the brooks in whose paths they lie, are of rare occurrence in the Isle of Wight. The only examples known to the writer are situated near the boundary of the Chalk in the combes on the northern slope of St. George's Down, about three furlongs east-north-east of Garrett's, and 100 yards north of Great East Standen. It is probable that some of the water taken in there reappears at the group of little springs on the boundary of the Eocene Beds about Burnt House.

[1]For further information concerning the water supply of the Island, see W. Whitaker, 'Water Supply of Hampshire', *Mem. Geol. Surv.*, 1910, also *Proc. Hampshire Field Club*, 1917, pp. 55, 56.

INDEX

Printed in England for Her Majesty's Stationery Office by Commercial Colour Press
Dd 289657 K16